PENGUIN BOOKS

CONSUMING PASSIONS

Philippa Pullar was born in London in 1935 and educated at Brondesbury-at-Stocks, Bartram Gables and Harcombe House Domestic College. She received a Cordon Bleu Certificate of Cookery and has been a restaurant manageress, a mother and grandmother, Sufi student, author, adventurous traveller, Fellow of the Royal Horticultural Society and animal lover. At her death in 1997 she was a student of Egyptology at the University of London and had just completed an MA in the study of Mysticism and Religious Experience at Canterbury University. Her books include *Frank Harris* (1975), also published as a Classic Penguin, *Gilded Butterflies* (1978), *The Shortest Journey* (1982) and *Spiritual and Lay Healing* (1988).

Paul Levy was born in Lexington, Kentucky. He writes on the arts for the *Wall Street Journal*, and on food and wine for *You* magazine in the *Mail on Sunday*. He is a Fellow of the Royal Society of Literature. His collection of writings, *Out to Lunch*, was published by Penguin in 1988 and he edited *The Penguin Book of Food and Drink* (1996). He lives in Oxfordshire with his wife and two daugh

Boiling the Christmas Pudding
By Seymour

CONSUMING PASSIONS

A History of English Food and Appetite

BY

PHILIPPA PULLAR

With an Afterword by Paul Levy

PENGUIN BOOKS

PENGUIN BOOKS

Published by the Penguin Group
Penguin Books Ltd, 27 Wrights Lane, London w8 5tz, England
Penguin Putnam Inc., 375 Hudson Street, New York, New York 10014, USA
Penguin Books Australia Ltd, Ringwood, Victoria, Australia
Penguin Books Canada Ltd, 10 Alcorn Avenue, Toronto, Ontario, Canada m4v 3b2
Penguin Books India (P) Ltd, 11, Community Centre, Panchsheel Park, New Delhi – 110 017, India
Penguin Books (NZ) Ltd, Private Bag 102902, NSMC, Auckland, New Zealand
Penguin Books (South Africa) (Pty) Ltd, 5 Watkins Street, Denver Ext 4, Johannesburg 2094, South Africa

Penguin Books Ltd, Registered Offices: Harmondsworth, Middlesex, England

First published by Hamish Hamilton 1970
Published with a new afterword as a Classic Penguin 2001

1

Here, then, are the English: a stream of Germans bottled up on a small island, with a few ingredients of native Celt, Roman and Norman French, a few currants and some yeast to make the cork pop: and the fine mixture not unnaturally spurts to the other end of the world and in time overflows one-fourth of the habitable globe.

'Climate and Character'—WILLIAM GERHARDIE

Contents

List of Illustrations

between pages 118 *and* 119

between pages 150 *and* 151

ENDPAPERS

Author's Note

Although I am critical of our modern conditions I would not like people who, during the course of my researches, have been kind and helpful, to think that any view in my book is a reflection or denigration of them personally. It was my aim to discover the pattern of our eating habits and set it down as truthfully as I could.

CHAPTER ONE

ROMAN SPRING

Epicurus affirms that our sensations and prenotions and our feelings are the criteria of truth.

DIOGENES LAERTIUS

Pleasure is a real good, in itself . . . wherefore, Pleasure seems to be not only a Good, but also the Essential *Reason*, or very *Root* of Good.

EPICURUS

I

Instruments of Pleasure

OUR ENGLISH tradition of cookery is a strange and hybrid affair. It emerges like some rare botanical experiment, with Rome the root and stock on which our modern flowers are grafted. The native sap twists and turns through foreign branches, blasted by winds and wars, stunted by moral fungus; trembles here with brilliant day-blossoms; hangs there with yellow fruit. A mongrel tradition. For what people eat and how they behave is a strange and complicated matter affected by knowledge, predators and superstition as well as finance and agriculture.

In the beginning, contrary to now, it was the East that was rich, possessing arts and luxury, gold and silver, silks and spices, precious stones, knowledge and politeness, while the West was inhabited by rude and rapacious barbarians. It was from the Mediterranean, as Samuel Johnson said, that almost all that is civilized, almost all that sets us above savages, came. It was Rome, through her efficient government, her predatory intentions, that transported civilization hither. From the Forum a giant web of

highroads, a chain of communications slung between each branch
of the Empire, radiated out to the darkness, penetrating mountains,
crossing rivers; east into the rising sun to Thrace, Greece and
Macedonia, south to Africa, west and northwards to the cool
green forests of Britain and Gaul. At the centre the parasite city
waited, a fat shining spider, to gather the spoils; enjoy and abuse
the advantages of wealth. In from the East the victorious armies
marched, carrying spices and silks, one-legged tables and ivories;
out again westwards to subdue and ransack, to tame and exploit
the savages, encage them within brick towns. It was not Rome's
primary intention to improve, educate and civilize, but to a
certain extent these measures were necessary in order to milk the
land of its maximum yield. Down the highroads into the dark
forests trailed the stalks of knowledge—knowledge of letters and
building, systems of agriculture and food preparation—establish-
ing themselves among the flora and fauna, winding together with
the wild convolvulus minds, blossoming with the native weeds;
systems which flourished, seeding, proliferating, in spite of the
Empire's collapse,[1] in spite of the plunder of barbarians.

The Roman fondness for food is a historical fact. Fortunes
were squandered by men who lived for their palates, at whose
behest the world was ransacked for delicacies. Professor Balsdon
writes in *Life and Leisure in Ancient Rome* that even under the
comparative austerity of the Republic such dainties as whole boar,
goose, foie gras, peacock and Trojan pig—stuffed with all kinds
of sausages, vegetables and surprises—were served at the most
lavish feasts. A disciple of good living was one who fed on
oysters, fattened birds and fish. These facts are undermined by the
general view today of the Roman kitchen, which pronounces it to
be pretentious and disgusting—overspiced with unspeakable zests
and extracts, putrid with abominable sauces. Moralists are often

---

[1] It has been suggested that the final collapse of the Empire was due to lead
poisoning. Water pipes, cosmetics, paint, cooking pots and storage jars all contained lead and it is reasonable to suppose that considerable quantities were consumed, leading perhaps to anaemia, toxicity, miscarriages, still-births and sterility.
Gibbon, however, suggests that the lack of virility and low birth-rate were due to the
crippling tax systems. Parents simply could not afford to raise children; they exposed
them instead.

explaining that excessive occupation with these malodorous concoctions, together with sexual deviations at the bath-houses,
were the major diversions of the Roman oligarchy before the
collapse of their Empire.

A melancholy picture springs up of this Empire, furnished as a
luxurious bath-house; warm jets of water rush perpetually out
from massive silver mouths; all is marble and magnificence; some
of the oligarchy can be seen, pink and plump, reclining before
mounds of food while eunuchs[1] stroke oil into their skin; others
vomit. Trimalchio is there behind a pillar, his wife lies in adultery
with Augustus, while Claudius bends over a steaming sausage,
stuffing handfuls into his mouth. In the middle distance porticoes
swing out to the hills revealing several hairy barbarians leering
in, while on the horizon with erected spears their hordes approach,
surging to take the Empire.

However successfully one banishes this rude vision, no doubt
remains that Rome, both under the Republic and the Empire,
was a world where it was only agreeable to live if one were
rich, and where the greater part of one's life would have been involved in the pursuit of pleasure—but a kind of pleasure that most
of us have never known. Entirely unclouded by guilt it was seen
as a good in itself. Its pursuit, the search for different means of
gratifying the appetite, not only became a way of life for many,
but provided a living for thousands, who were 'variously, but
incessantly employed, in the service of the rich. In their dress,
their table, their houses and their furniture,' Gibbon added, 'the
favourites of fortune united every refinement of convenience, of
elegance, and of splendour, whatever could soothe their pride or
gratify their sensuality.'

---

[1] For the most part attendants at the baths were eunuchs who, according to
Juvenal, were in demand to serve not only as slaves and bath attendants, but as
lovers. They were smooth to the touch, there was no worry about abortions and,
provided their operations were properly handled, they were capable of bestowing all
kinds of gratifications. Juvenal loses no opportunity of revealing the gory surgical
details. 'The biggest thrill,' he tells us with relish, 'is one who was fully-grown, a
lusty black-quilled male, before the surgeons went to work on his groin. Let the
testicles ripen and drop, fill out till they hang like two pound weights, then what the
surgeon chops will hurt nobody's trade but the barber's.'

It was, in the opinion of these 'favourites of fortune', an unwise, synthetic thing to deprive their appetites. 'Pleasure is a food that builds me up,' Ovid said, adding endearingly, 'I've never disappointed a girl.' These were literally men of sense who, like Polyarchus, were of the persuasion that

> when nature speaks in her own voice, she bids us follow our pleasures, and declares that is the right course for a man of sense; but to resist them, to subjugate the appetites, is the mark of one who is neither prudent nor happy nor comprehends the composite character of human nature. A strong proof of this is the fact that all men, whenever they attain to a power of sufficient magnitude, are borne along in the direction of their bodily pleasures, and regard this course as the end and aim of power . . .

Food and sex to these men were more than just utilitarian means of sustaining and reproducing mankind. They were instruments to procure the supreme felicity. Moreover they were closely bound together in religious celebration, of an orgiastic nature, symbolizing fertility and life; they were sensual experiences to be varied and expanded, sometimes, apparently, to be enjoyed simultaneously. It is significant that Apuleius in *The Golden Ass* uses the cooking image to provoke lust.

> Dear Fotis, how daintily, how charmingly you stir that casserole: I love watching you wriggle your hips [his hero, Lucius, says preparing to seduce his host's slave]. And what a wonderful cook you are! The man whom you allow to poke his finger into your little casserole is the luckiest fellow alive. That sort of stew would tickle the most jaded palate.
>
> Go away you scoundrel [Fotis replies nastily], keep clear of my little cooking stove! If you come too near even when the fire is low, a spark may fly out and set you on fire; and when that happens nobody but myself will be capable of putting the flames out. A wonderful cook, am I? Yes, I certainly know how to tickle a man's . . . well, his palate, if you dare call it that, and how to keep things nicely on the boil—between the sheets as well as on the kitchen-stove.

Soon they repaired to the bedroom and with 'flushed hands' snatched off their clothes. And then 'it was as though the apple-bough of love had bent down,' reported Lucius, 'and I was gorging myself with the fruit until I could gorge no more'. And they plunged and they gasped and they wriggled until their limbs dripped and they had to pause and refresh themselves from the bedside table, covered with little dishes of food and generous cups of wine, until 'we presently revived and continuously renewed our sleepless struggle, with intervals for refreshment, until day, break'. Shortly after this he massages himself with an ointment composed of crucified men's noses and fingers, and is converted into an ass.

Virility was of course vital to sexual pleasure and fecundity. Impotence was the ultimate dread. Not only were the genitals exalted instruments of pleasure but they were also worshipped as symbols of fertility and procreation, of returning spring and growth. This is rooted, Professor Allegro tells us, in antiquity, when primitive man lived in the hot parched lands of the Middle East, depending for his life almost entirely on rain. Somewhere above him in the sky, he believed, there was a divine phallus; rain was its semen that came down to fertilize the earth-womb. From there, it was logical to assume, he could stimulate rain in the same way as he stimulated his own sexual orgasms: by dancing, singing and orgiastic displays, and above all by the sex act, which was performed particularly in the fields, where the sacred semen was most needed. All over Italy statues of phallic temper were to be found. No difference was remarked in the reproductive powers of plants and animals; the human genitals symbolized all fertility and reproduction. In some cases the model was of the simplest construction: a head shouldered upon a plain pedestal from whence protruded an enormous penis; with others the composition was more physical, the penis could be manipulated, lowered, raised and detached at will. It was of course the erected instrument that was revered. Impotence was the end: a winter death. Against this flaccidity, aphrodisiacs were sought and applied. Often these were disgusting like Lucius's ointment, often of a supernatural nature—for the Romans were superstitious and well-versed in the interpretations of dreams and omens, astrology and divination. No business, whether military or civilian, was entertained without previously sacrificing to the gods and consulting them for favour, able signs. And when the lightning flashed across the sky and thunder rattled on the floor of the heavens, when statues roared with laughter and comets crossed one's gaze, these were signs from the gods, in warning. Night was a dangerous dark world where ghosts floated, necromancers inhabited bodies and witches mutilated corpses, then transformed themselves into owls to flap through the blue air casting spells of impotence. In *The Satyricon* Petronius shows us Encolopius who believes himself to be bewitched after an unelevated few hours with a seductive lady. He retires forlornly into a grove of plane trees, an old woman emerges, binds round his neck a string of coloured threads, then, to his disgust, marks his forehead with dust and spittle. But all was to be well.

> After completing this spell she instructed me to spit three times and drop down my chest, again three times, some pebbles which she had charmed and wrapped in purple. Then she began to test my virility with her hands. Faster than you could speak, the nerves obeyed the command, and the little woman's hands were filled with a mighty throbbing . . .

Other measures for building up ardour were to employ cosmetic brushes soaked in aphrodisiac, swallow decoctions of cantharides,[1] satyrion[1] or hippomane.[1] Some whipped their genitals with nettles, and for improved service, the luckier ones lubricated theirs with oil, ground pepper and nettle seed.

It was a promiscuous society, embracing and enjoying unions both homo- and heterosexual. 'Does it really matter so much where, or with whom you perform the sexual act?' Antony asked Augustus in a letter. Making love was a pastime that alleviated boredom. One suspects that such a life of leisure—every menial task was performed by slaves—hung heavy for many people and their lives were great plains of monotony punctuated with affairs and mealtimes. One feels a bloated ennui hanging constantly over the narrow uncomfortable streets; everyone faced the long dragging dog-days of summer, the mud and darkness of winter, borne down by a brown staleness. New orgies and pleasures, different foods and sex partners were always in demand.

Rich women were especially prone to boredom. They had few abilities and occupations apart from sewing and weaving. What was there for them to do but enjoy themselves, to sit about, loose their long hair to be combed, abuse their slaves when they pulled, and plan with whom they would next be going to bed? Hours

[1] See Appendix I, page 238-9.

passed in calculating who might be likely to give the nicest presents, for apparently most women were mercenary. Some of noble birth openly became prostitutes and prowled naked in the brothels. The birth rate was low, there were 'sure-fire drugs for producing sterility', pessaries, fumigations, douches and skilled abortionists, but in spite of these some managed to produce babies. Then the custom was to lay the child on the ground the moment he or she was born for the husband to acknowledge or disown; if it were disowned then the child was left exposed to die, unless someone took it in and cared for it.

For all their shortcomings women, to men like Ovid, gave life its spice. The sun rose from between their thighs; suddenly the sky was bluer, the trees greener. Love was a game; without it life was dull indeed; 'offered a sexless heaven I'd say *no thank you*, women are such sweet hell,' writes Ovid engagingly.

There were people, however, more inclined to make food the object of their desires. They went along with the Epicurean view that the satisfaction of the belly was the root of all good. Mealtimes were oases in long brown days. Yet these are the very meals that are now supposed to have been endless pageants of disgusting, almost uneatable dishes. In effect, this is saying that a people of great intelligence and vitality, of cultivated taste and wealth, patrons, in a sense, of all the arts pertaining to pleasure, who bequeathed to the West wonderful architecture and learning, these people were only able, after several hundred years, to produce a kitchen that was worthless and from which it is possible to retrieve nothing that is of historical or of practical use. Is this really reasonable? Surely not. Surely by unravelling the facts a different truth is revealed.

From a menial office Roman cooking grew to be a highly sophisticated art. Like many Scandinavian and Chinese dishes, it consisted of subtle combinations of sweet and sour tastes, smooth sauces, and piquant flavourings. The results were obtained by liaisons of especially prepared wines, vinegars, honey, brine, pepper, herbs and spices. It was an intelligent kitchen, calling for experience and talent, the results depending on the skill of the cook. There were, for example, several different combinations of sweet wine[1] that could be added to a dish, each bringing a different nuance to it. To present a meal plainly would have been considered vulgar. 'No meat is pleasant by itself,' writes Petronius, 'it's adulterated in some way and made acceptable to the reluctant stomach.' This was not because of the inferior quality of the meat —Roman agriculture achieved a high standard of competence and fresh meat came nightly into Rome—it was because Romans genuinely did not like the taste and the texture of plain meats. They liked variety at their meals, sometimes hot and peppery dishes, sometimes soft and voluptuous. There is also a cynical point to be raised; many of the richest Romans were *nouveaux riches*—emancipated slaves, freedmen like Petronius's Trimalchio —who could not bear to be outdone by anyone; to present plain meat would have given no indication of the quantity of expensive and skilled cooks that were employed in the kitchen. Experienced cooks[2] commanded a high price: over a thousand pounds, and more, was sometimes paid. Often to display the skill (and the price) of his cooks the host would serve trick food; there might be one course all composed of the same ingredient to set the guests guessing. Who could imagine what they were eating? Huge joints, tiny cakes, vegetables and birds all appeared, created from minced pork perhaps or almond paste. Or there might be mechanical devices, needing great skill for the making—almost an engineering talent. The Romans had a banana-skin type of humour. They loved to see a stream of saffron squirted from a cake into a neighbour's eye, or thrushes and blackbirds flying from under his nose out of a roast boar—to be caught with twigs and birdlime and cooked for the next course.

As the Republic passed into the Empire, cooking techniques, along with all facilities for luxury and sensuality, became more elaborate and more sophisticated. Rare foods were in demand. Traders were able to exploit the desires of the rich and prices rose

---

[1] *Defrutum, caroenum* and *sapa* were three kinds of differently reduced slightly sweet wine; *passum* was sweeter, and *mulsum* sweeter again, being mixed with honey.

[2] Roman cooks considered themselves so superior that they formed themselves into a hierarchy, some grandly labelling themselves with splendid titles like *vicarius supra coenas*. During the reign of Hadrian they established for themselves an élite academy, *collegium coquorum*, whose premises were on the Palatine Hill.

absurdly. Once, under Tiberius, three mullets were offered at one hundred gold pieces each. The waste of food, overflowing from the cook-shops, eating houses and dinner parties, must have been huge,. for Tiberius proposed that market values should be annually regulated by the Senate, and that the amount of food offered on sale should be restricted. He himself led the campaign by serving at his dinner half-eaten dishes left over from the day before. Apparently his proposals were not adopted, for we find about twenty years later Nero passing laws limiting private expenditure and restricting the food sold in wine shops—measures of which he himself seems to have taken no notice. 'True gentle-men,' he said, 'always throw their money around,' and he certainly made his friends throw theirs. One was forced to lavish 40,000 gold pieces on a turban party; another even more on a rose banquet, whatever that might be. Not that he was careful with his own money: he built an enormous palace of innumerable dining rooms whose ceilings could rain flowers and scents and rotate in time with the sky; money for this he expected lay in some African caves, a hoard of undiscovered treasure deposited there by Queen Dido. It remained undiscovered; he bankrupted him-self, involving the country in his ruin.

By the third century Athenaeus, who had lived first in Alex-andria and then in Rome, wrote: 'There has also been an increase in the refinements not only of cooks but also of perfumers, so that a body could not be satisfied even with diving into a tank full of ointment . . . All too flourishing, also, are the arts pertaining to the making of sweetmeats and the nice luxuries of sexual com-merce, resulting even in the invention of sponge suppositories in the belief that they conduce to more frequent intercourse.'

Athenaeus, the learned grammarian, was a contemporary of Heliogabalus: a degenerate whose languid appetites could be roused only by the unnatural and the nearly unobtainable. 'To confound the order of the seasons and climates, to sport with the passions and prejudices of his subjects, and to subject every law of nature and decency were in the number of his most delicious amusements,' Gibbon wrote. Rewards were offered for the in-vention of new sauces, but if the new concoction was not relished then the inventor was allowed to eat of nothing else till he had discovered another more agreeable to the Imperial palate. To tempt this elevated organ, pies were made of song-birds, or tongues from those birds able to imitate the human voice; sows' wombs[1] were served filled with stifled pigs, or red mullet brought gasping to the table, to be cooked inside a glass vessel, slowly, before their prospective consumers, who watched greedily and attentively as the fish passed through a succession of the most beautiful shades as they died. Another degenerate, Vitellius, on his entry into Rome was served a feast consisting of 2,000 fish and 7,000 game birds. One dish he dedicated to the goddess Minerva; the recipe comprising pike-livers, pheasant and peacock brains, flamingo tongues and lamprey milt, the ingredients having to be collected from every corner of the Empire.

Many of the historians' pages show that several Emperors were excellent illustrations of Polyarchus's dictum. No sooner had they attained a power of 'sufficient magnitude' than they were borne off on floods of pleasure. Even the revered Augustus was indiscreet enough to give a fancy-dress banquet at a time of food shortage—his guests arriving dressed as the deities. The next day voices were raised in the streets: 'the gods have gobbled all the grain.' His behaviour was often predatory at the table; he liked to remove his friends' wives between courses, returning flushed and in disarray, leaving no doubt as to what had been going on.

And his successors, what a crew they seem, these Imperial Caesars as they limp, stumble and strut out of Suetonius's chapters: dribbling, drunken, debauched; pustular, malodorous, cruel and incredibly greedy. They pass, small yellow fragments from 2,000 years ago. Tiberius among the grottoes of Capri, 'little nooks of lechery', interesting himself in a singular way with babies and little boys; Caligula with his hairless head and hirsute body ravishing his sisters, feeding prisoners to wild animals, promiscuously slaughtering friends, family and foes; Claudius, lame and frightened, his nostrils always ready to sniff out food and drink,

---

[1] Sows' wombs together with sows' udders were considered great delicacies. They were frowned upon by the more austere members of the community, such as Pliny, who considered such dishes to be extravagant depravities.

interrupting the law courts because of a delicious aroma of food, entering the dining room of the Leaping Priests—whence the smells issued—and taking his place at table, never leaving a dining-hall except gorged and sodden, exterminated by a sauce of mush-rooms; Nero, spotty and smelling nasty, marrying a eunuch,[1] feasting from noon till midnight in drained lakes, never floating down the Tiber to Ostia without causing a row of brothels to be temporarily erected, rushing from a den wrapped in the skins of wild animals and attacking the genitals of men and women bound to stakes; Vitellius ravenously snatching lumps of meat and cakes from altars and bolting them down.

One is left amazed that anybody was able to remain living in this seething tumult of assassinations, heaped dishes, steaming-black pies and daggers. All within the Empire, one feels, were plotting against one another, coveting one another's riches and position.

2

From Poetry Dinners to Wanton Junketings

A good kitchen relies on the plentiful supply of good-quality ingredients and the time, or the labour, to prepare them. The Romans had both: slaves provided plentiful cheap labour and the food came freshly every night into Rome from the country. In spite of being part of highly urbanized society the Romans had a real appreciation of their land. The origin of Roman greatness was deeply rooted in the cultivation of the soil: their wealth was based on crops and their flocks—the Latin word for money having the same derivation—*pecu*. It was at bottom an agricultural nation. Love of the land and of gardens, love of the country and nature lay inside every Roman. It was the inspiration of literature,

[1] Delighted by the abnormal, Nero tried to turn Sporus into a girl by castration, then, attended by the court, married him with full ceremony, bridal veil, dowry and all, afterwards treating him in every way like a wife, dressing him in the fine clothes of an Empress.

painting and religion. The deities themselves were primarily protectors of the crops and herds, and the controllers of the elements. Many of the richest villas contained frescoes of cool water and delicious gardens and orchards. The walls from a room in the villa of the Empress Livia, wife of Augustus, still exist. To go into the room is to enter an exquisite painted garden, filled with bird-song, the fragrance of flowers, the feel of the earth. An opening through a low wicker fence leads to a lawn hedged around by a curving ornamental brick wall on which are placed caged birds. Behind there is an orchard, white birds perch on yellow shrubs, fly up to alight on trees laden down with red apples. The green recedes into a cool darkness lying below the heat of the afternoon, and above the leaves, pierced on the horizon by spikes of cypress, is a continual ribbon of blue-painted sky.

It was out of such country that Rome's food, each night, came rumbling in on waggons through a fine cobweb of roads—fish caught from the gulfs and bays, abundant game from the forests, meat and milk from the flocks and herds in the open country. Cheeses, oils, vegetables of every sort: cabbages and lentils, beans and lettuces, radishes and turnips, gourds and pumpkins, thundered through the narrow labyrinth of streets. The shouts of the drivers, the rumbling of the wheels echoed up the dark well of the houses to bedrooms where the Romans lay twisting and turning, drunk still from the evening before when the tables had danced, each light showed double and the ceilings spun dizzily. The noise was appalling, especially a problem for the poor whose windows opened directly on to the street, while those of the rich faced the quiet of a courtyard.

The rich had country estates which produced their own food; that too came lumbering into the city together with the public supplies. Wool, lemons and pepper, vegetables and meat. Some sent out to different parts of the world for the rarest animals and plants for their farms—bees from Athens, mushroom spores from India. Many of the largest properties had their own quarries, brick works and mines. They were self-sufficient units.

Their farm management was no less profit-conscious than our own today. But Cato and Varro throughout their agricultural

manuals stress the *dignity* of the farmer, the dignity and the practicality. He must plant elm trees along the roads, and fence-rows,
that during winter his cattle and sheep might have leaves for fodder
and he timber. He must plant reeds along the streams that osiers
might grow to tie the vines. And he must make enclosures, very
similar to our modern broilerhouse systems, to fatten his stock.
Ironically the husbandry systems of the notoriously cruel Romans
are largely more agreeable than our own. Treatment and conditions
for the animals and birds were generally more comfortable; it was
only when their time came to fatten that their environment deteriorated. Varro shows a diagram for recommended enclosures. In
the centre there is a small island for the purpose of keeping snails;
when their time came they were moved into jars and either fed
with milk or a gruel of must and corn-meal. Round this are sea-
and fresh-water ponds in which to house fish. Close by are the
pigeon houses and aviaries, where quail, ortolan, thrushes and
blackbirds were fattened, either for the public market, or especially for a particular banquet. These, Varro advises, should
be lit only dimly, but generously supplied with perches and
a narrow stream of water running continuously through. The birds
were to be fed with small balls of figs and corn-meal. Often
hundreds of pigeons and turtle-doves were stored in the pigeon
houses. Here there must be plenty of water for the pigeons to
bathe in, for, Varro noted, pigeons are clean birds, and plenty
of millet, wheat, beans and vetch. Breeding pairs were able to
fly in and out. It was the poor squabs which were most highly
prized for their meat and which underwent some unfortunate
handling: they were left in the nests, but so that they should not
move their legs were broken. Dunghill, jungle, and guinea fowl
were stocked in houses, with open yards in which to dust themselves. For the shelter of a flock of two-hundred birds Varro
advises two houses ten by five feet and five feet in height. Cocks
were caponized by cauterizing their spurs. All poultry, when
their time came, were fattened in darkened coops, their feathers
were pulled from their wings and tails and they were crammed on
balls of barley paste. Ducks, teal and coot were sometimes favoured
with an epicure's diet; besides their wheat, barley and must they

were fed lobsters and prawns. Hares, until they must enter the hutches, enjoyed special enclosures with lairs of bushes and high grass and broad trees to guard against eagle attacks. Dormice and guinea pigs lived in shady nut plantations feasting on mast and chestnuts until they were removed indoors to be fattened in dar-kened jars. Further out there were great enclosures for wild boar and roe buck; and there, near the bee pastures, were the bee houses. Honey, depending on the district, differed in quality, the most prized being that of Sicily from the aromatic thyme pastures.

Often the rich had quite a number of estates. There were summer villas high in the mountains where a refreshing breeze blew up over the terraces and you could look down past the vegetable gardens and vineyards, the myrtles and the olives to meadows where white bluebells grew, rising slowly up the other side of the valley through woods to distant mountains. In spring there would be wild flowers and hot thyme; summer would make warm white dust and the rhythm of cicadas, the nights would be scented, there would be nightingales and the dark valley would dance with fireflies. The gardens were beautiful: green ivy trellises and topiary work; bright emerald lizards darting between the full-blown grasses from one white stone to another; cool paths winding between canals and cypresses, under great pines and shade trees, the hours heavy and still with resin; streams wander-ing and falling, refreshing and spraying the hot air; and there were roses.

When one reads of the younger Pliny's garden one senses a calm green peace, the feeling that emanates from someone who understands and loves his garden, who is nourished and rested by it, who uses it. He writes of great plane trees, and of a bent acacia, smooth with age, and by its side a marble alcove where water fell incessantly to a polished basin. 'When I sup here,' he wrote, 'this basin serves as a table, the larger sort of dishes being placed round the margin, while the smaller ones swim about in the form of vessels and waterfowl.'

Nearer to Rome there were winter villas, built on the hills that surrounded the city, or further away by the sea at Ostia, where Pliny had his, designed carefully for comfort and beauty. There were good-weather rooms, with views of the sea moving and sparkling and other villas scattered along the shore-line, where he could lie lazily and listen to the murmur and break of the waves. There were centrally-heated winter rooms, lined with books and sheltered from winds, placed to catch the warmth of the sun, whose windows were arranged to trap the fiery lights of its setting and rising. There were dining rooms, grand large ones for big parties, others for small affairs; there were anointing rooms and mosaic baths where he could swim in warm water and watch the sea. Outside the landscape showed the bones of winter to advantage. Woods stretching out like arms to hold the view, then releasing it to rush out to meadows whitened with hoar frost where sheep and cattle waited to fatten in the spring warmth. There were porticoes and colonnades built so the low winter sun could slant between the columns, throwing out long pale January shadows. There were avenues bordered with box and rosemary where he exercised, a little riding perhaps, or a little walking. There were tennis courts and violets and fig trees and mulberries; and for the summer, shady vine plantations with soft paths where he could wander bare-foot. And there were vegetable gardens for lettuces, artichokes and spring leeks.

In the country the day passed slowly, perhaps sometimes even peacefully. But in Rome it was different. In summer dawn came early, the moment all wheeled traffic must leave. Swallows swooped and whirled down over the slow-moving yellow Tiber, past the arches and columns, the sun-dried bricks and marbles of the forum, filling the thin air with the shrieks of unoiled wheels; inside the houses servants rose and banged and clattered. Light filtered through shutters, making a sylvan semi-darkness, a glimmering dusk, 'the half light shy girls need'. Pigeons bubbled and cooed on tiled roofs, water dripped from aqueducts, streets began to fill and ennui pressed. Soon litters moved through the brown stifling streets, musicians and slaves in tinselled livery accompanying the pretentious towards the law-courts and the amphitheatres. Moving rivers of noise and dust, tavern waiters weaving between scarlet cloaks, yellow robes and purple, elbows buffeting ribs, carrying pyramids of hot dishes on their heads: a coloured stream of humanity twisting and moving, flowing down between the tall houses.

Not only was it crowded as you walked and pushed your way, but it was also dangerous. There were often fires and the standards of building were shaky, whole houses could suddenly collapse. Any time a tile might fall and hit you on the head, a face might appear at an open window bordering your route and toss out a cracked or leaky pot. In fact the housewives seem to have used the streets below as dustbins and sanitary disposal units; you prayed and hoped as you went along that nothing worse than a pailful of slops would drop on your head.

Sooner or later, towards the seventh hour, most people arrived at the baths. These were in every part of the city, constructed with imperial magnificence for the indiscriminate service of all. The most splendid were those of Caracalla and Diocletian: lofty apartments covered with mosaic, Egyptian granite and precious green marbles. Eunuchs displayed themselves and women lingered long hours there together with their oil jars and unguents. Slaves circulated, selling refreshments: cakes, sausages, lettuce, eggs and lizard-fish. Men hung about hoping for invitations to dinner. Many a lady enjoyed herself so much that she dawdled, exercising the weights and dumb-bells, dallying with the masseur 'craftily slipping one hand along her thigh and tickling her until she comes', so that her guests, arriving for dinner, would have to wait half-dead with hunger until she eventually appeared.

The stifling summer days would pass, the evening would come, the timelessness of a Roman sunset, then as now, when the whole sky moves with swallows, rushing against the pink firmament. And the view looking down from the Palatine Hill would be filled with yearning: the Tiber pink from the sky, the heavy plane trees, the stones, new then, and marbles would be made of melancholy and a sudden chill would fall. People made their way through the darkening streets, lighted by torches, big brass lamps or just a guttering candle, to dinner, to taverns and brothels. Women rushed back from the baths past sounds coming from the open windows: everyone preparing dinner, everywhere the savoury smells of food. In the streets there was pushing and jostling and treading on people's heels; the night traffic beginning, cartloads of pine logs, creaking marble swaying down the streets, fir trees poking out behind into the crowd. And as the evening continued the brothels and taverns filled, the rich travelling with a bodyguard on account of the burglars and ruffians who lurked about waiting to start fights and brawls.

At dinner guests were not always well chosen, the meal could take on a dramatic turn if wife, husband and lover all attended the same table. To Ovid such an evening was an anguished occasion.

Your husband going to the same dinner as us?
I hope it chokes him.

You'll lie there snuggling up to him? He'll put his arm
round your neck whenever he wants?

Refuse all food he has tasted first—
it has touched his lips.

Don't lean your gentle head against his shoulder
and don't let him embrace you

or slide a hand inside your dress
or touch your breasts. Above all don't kiss him.

If you do I'll cause a public scandal,
grab you and claim possession.

I'm bound to see all this. It's what I shan't see
that worries me—the goings on under your cloak.

The preparation of dinner was a serious matter, requiring a huge amount of space. Mazois in the *Palais de Scaurus* describes the enormous one-hundred-and-forty-eight-foot arched kitchen, the great fireplace holding spits, skillets and gridirons, the wall paintings depicting sacrifices to the Goddess Fortunax as well as all the foods necessary for the feast—fish, hams, venison ready for the spit, birds and hares—and a wonderfully ingenious porous floor comprising layers of brick and charcoal, cemented with hot cinders, lime and sand, polished with pumice stone so that it was always dry and warm. Such space was essential when one realizes the number of slaves required to prepare the meal.

Each had his own job allotted him. Besides the cellarer, the butler, the water carrier and the wine pourer there was the *coquus*, the head cook, the *focarius*, the fire stoker, the *coctor*, who superintended special sauces and dishes, the *pistor*, who prepared stuffings and ground corn to make bread and cakes, and the *nomenclator*, who arranged the entertainments and order of guests at the dinner-table.

The national diet was originally a farinaceous one, the poor existing largely on *pulmentos*, a gruel prepared from barley and *spelt*—very similar to polenta. From this *potus* a great many liquid concoctions derived, all potées, pots au feu and pottages. The only manuscript of Roman cookery which survives is a highly sophisticated one compiled by the famous epicure Apicius. But one can see through its fat to the bones constructing the Roman kitchen. One can see the *pultes*—the barley and puréed pulse broths—have sprung from the basic *pulmentos*. One can see that many of the dishes are not unlike Creole cookery in their combinations of sweet and sour, fish, meat and spices; using for liaisons either eggs, breadcrumbs or ground nuts, or a fine ground flour, similar in texture and effect to cornflour. But it is not until the relationship with Eastern dishes is realized, with the peppery spiced dishes that we now call curries, that the real light dawns.[1]

The meal was divided into three courses: *gustatio*, *mensae primae* and *mensae secundae*. But first, to refresh the brain, slaves arranged flowers and sweet-smelling herbs upon the head; to prevent ill consequences of drink it was bound with a wool rib-bon. *Gustatio*, then, was the hors d'oeuvre, consisting of vegetables and herbs, radishes and purple asparagus. Then *mensae primae* which followed embraced all kinds of dishes, Apicius's *minutalae*, *isiciae*, *patinae* and *salacattabiae*. These are savoury stews and spiced meat puddings, forcemeats and every kind of sausage—tiny ones made from chopped scallops and herbs, or larger com-posed of liver, or pheasant, wrapped in bayleaves and smoked. Other dishes included lobster and crab croquettes, oysters, pheasant dumplings and kromeskies of hare, stuffed marrows, cabbages, hams cooked with figs, pork stuffed with mussels, marinaded chops and steaks, sardine omelettes, milk-fed

---

[1] See Appendix II, pages 245, 246.

lambs, kid, pig and snails, roast meats glazed with honey, or basted with crushed spices, dates and raisins, and all kinds of spiced piquant sauces to be served with root vegetables, meat or fish. Finally come the *mensae secundae*, the dessert, the *dulciae*, sweet-meats of stuffed dates and sweet egg custards, apples, preserved pears and grapes. Often guests were graded in order of importance so that the most important might receive the most expensive dish, tableware and wine; thus a client might have to make do with eel while his host and his superiors enjoyed lamprey, or rare and choice fishes—delicacies which were particularly relished. All bones, fruit pips, vegetable husks and other waste matter the diners dropped to the floor; debris which inspired many a mosaic pavement.

The Romans loved soft voluptuous food, sauces with a seductive feel that caressed the mouth. There is no doubt some of the dishes—like many subtle curries and Eastern dishes—had a sensual, faintly sexy air.[1] The idea these days of anything smelling sexy is not acceptable to us. We are ashamed of smells, particularly of those exuding from the human body. We have been conditioned, according to Lorus and Margery Milne,[2] by the propaganda of the 'manufacturers of toiletries'. Our olfactory sensitivity has been persuaded into thinking natural odours are unpleasant, unde-sirable and dirty; by using the nice manufactured products they can be supplanted by desirable factory-produced aromas. This the Milnes consider to be overstatement and generalization. Nothing, they point out in their chapter. 'The Importance of Odours', is nicer than a skin fragrance issuing from those we love, made by no soap or lotion; nothing is more comforting on the departure of our husbands, wives or lovers than 'nosing into a clothes closet in which the absent one's worn garments are hanging'.

The inhabitants of Rome were not in the least ashamed of smells. Dinner was a lengthy meal. Often at the more elaborate banquets scents would rain down from the ceiling between courses

[1] See Appendix I, page 237 and Appendix II, pages 241, 242.
[2] A husband and wife team of naturalists, experts on animal senses and be-haviour, and authors of many books and papers including *The Senses of Animals and Men*.

and slaves would massage into the feasters extravagant unguents:
the rooms would be redolent with heavy Eastern aromas—myrrh,
incense and frankincense, musk, civet and ambergris. The digestion it was believed was soothed by leisurely dinners and it was
thought advantageous to punctuate the courses with suitable
varieties of entertainment. The digestive system was held, at least
in theory, in great respect. There was the notorious vomitorium to
which many a man resorted for the purposes of swallowing an
emetic.[1] 'Men eat to vomit and vomit to eat,' grumbled Seneca
liverishly, 'their dishes are fetched from every corner of the earth,
and then they do not even deign to digest them.' There were of
course milder carminatives. Spiced wine and snow were supposed
to be excellent. Pliny believed in the soothing powers of rhetoric
and recitation, but unfortunately he read appallingly. His friends,
able no longer to endure the excruciating torture of his poetry-
dinners, begged him to desist. Pliny was undaunted, he hired a
reader, then was himself tormented. What was the proper posture
for a poet during the reading of his poems? It was a vexing
question. One however which was not raised by his friend
Ligurinius who, to Pliny's indignation, inflicted on him his own
poetry-dinners. 'There is one reason, and one reason only why you
give a dinner party, Ligurinius,' he wrote crustily. 'You want an
opportunity of reading your dreadful poems. I have taken off my
slipper, the lettuce and fish sauce is served, and here comes Book 1.
The main course is held up so that we can hear Book 2, and before
the dessert Book 3, Book 4, Book 5.'

Pliny was adamant in his likes and dislikes. When all is said and
done he was rather a fuddy-duddy. Together with his friend
Genitor, he believed it was vulgar to have anything more extravagant in the way of dinner entertainment than music or poetry-
reading. 'I have received your letter,' he wrote to Genitor, 'in which
you complain of having been highly disgusted lately at a very
splendid entertainment by a set of buffoons, mummers and wanton
prostitutes, who were dancing about round the table.'

---

[1] A habit said to have come from Egypt, where such was the number of diseases
supposed to have proceeded from luxurious living and the abuse of food that three
consecutive days each month were set aside for aperients and vomiting.

It was true, these persons were often introduced to tables of the affluent for purposes of mirth and gaiety. They constituted an essential part in polite entertainment. Acrobats were suspended from ropes, dangling above the table by one foot, or the neck; jugglers vomited flames; girls and men performed such lascivious dances that, according to Juvenal, they caused orgasms and urination among the ladies. Heliogabalus was a master at mirth and gaiety. He ordered special leather couches and filled them with air instead of wool. How hilarious to inflate them while the guests were drinking and see them rolling on the floor! Imagine eight gouty, eight bald and eight greyheaded old men all pressed together so they could not move their hands; imagine their contortions. Everyone—like all good bananaskin humorists—loved to laugh at another's misfortunes. They liked physically afflicted people about their houses to make them laugh; they split their sides watching various dwarfs, hunchbacks and deformed children perform singular tricks, preferably of an undignified sexual nature. Imagine a dwarf enjoying intercourse with a massive slave from Colchester perhaps—it was exhilarating.

It is significant that violent sensation, particularly anything to do with killing and blood, seems to have been termed especially gay and beneficial to the appetite. Caligula, said to have been maddened by decoctions of hippomane administered by his promiscuous wife, was one of the cruellest of emperors. He delighted in beholding pain and torture. 'Make him feel that he is dying' was his familiar order to executioners. He invented new kinds of baths and the 'most unnatural dishes and drinks', swallowing valuable pearls dissolved in vinegar and providing his guests with golden bread and golden meat. He loved as he dined to watch trials by torture and gladiators fight duels, round and even on top of the dining tables; once one was slain there, everyone's clothes getting drenched with blood and pools of gore flowing away among the fruit, the bowls and drinking cups.

But, however much Pliny and his crew might disapprove of extravagant junketings, these entertainments, combined with loaded tables of good things, were apparently, for at least one of their acquaintances, more attractive propositions than their own more sedate and intellectual evenings. There is a small suspicion that Pliny's simplicity was not born purely out of dislike of vulgarity and pretension. When it came to entertaining he was a little mean, and when Septitus Clarus stood him up in favour of another more exciting occasion Pliny wrote at once crossly informing him of the expenses he had incurred. 'Justice shall be exacted;—you shall reimburse me to the very last penny the expense I went to on your account; no small sum, let me tell you. I had prepared, you must know, a lettuce a piece, three snails, two eggs, and a barley cake, with some sweet wine and snow. Olives, beet root, gourds, onions and a thousand other dainties equally sumptuous. You should likewise have been entertained either with an interlude, the rehearsal of a poem, or a piece of music, whichever you preferred, or (such was my liberality) with all three. But the oysters, sows' bellies, sea urchins and dancers from Cadiz of a certain ... I know not who, were, it seems, more to your taste.'

One of the most famous and amusing illustrations of a pretentious dinner party is Petronius's scene from Trimalchio's evening. It began—as all good evenings did—at the baths, with Trimalchio exercising himself with green balls and relieving himself simultaneously into a silver chamber pot. After his bath, during which the masseurs quarrel and spill the wine, everyone proceeds to his house to dinner. Singing shrilly, Alexandrian boys pour snow over the guests' hands, execute pedicures and remove hangnails while an elegant hors d'oeuvre is served in adorned dishes. Panniers suspended from a bronze ass contain white and black olives; silver dishes are inscribed with their own weight and Trimalchio's name; there are dormice, seasoned with honey and poppyseed, supported on bridges, and smoking sausages on a silver grill with plums and pomegranate seeds below to imitate coals. Everyone is in the middle of this when Trimalchio is carried in to the sound of music and set down on a pile of stuffed cushions. He looks astonishing—a bald head poking out from a scarlet coat, his neck well muffled up, and over all this he has laid a purple striped napkin dangling with tassels.

IA. Stucco ceiling from the Roman building of the Farnesina—in which some say Cleopatra lived. This, the National Museum of Rome tells us, shows an initiation scene of the Dionysiac cult, a boy being led to an old Silenus and young Satyrs enjoying a Bacchic orgy. Note the three phallic statues—the two on the right being of the pedestal kind, the one on the left representational

IB. Relief from a Roman tomb showing a butcher marketing his joints. Note the sows' udders suspended three from the left

2A. An erotic fresco from Pompeii showing a religious act of copulation, performed to the accompaniment of singing, dancing and piping, to stimulate rain and encourage fertility of crops

2B. Pompeiian fresco of a country villa with its winding porticoes

He picks his teeth, plays a game of draughts and swears like a trooper.

A basket is brought in containing a wooden hen and as the orchestra plays two slaves discover some pea-hens' eggs under it. 'My God!' Trimalchio declares, 'I am very much afraid they are half hatched.' At which everyone takes up his spoon (weighing half a pound at least) and cracks the eggs which are made of pastry. Poor Encolpius—he of the witch's grove—imagines he can detect an embryo inside his and nearly throws it away; however, encouraged by a friend, he searches the pastry shell with his fingers and finds a figpecker swimming in yolk of egg, flavoured with pepper.

Suddenly there is a crash from the orchestra and the waiters, still singing, snatch away the hors d'oeuvre, pour wine over everyone's hands and bring in bottles of Falernian, a hundred years old. Everyone is drinking it down when, as a cabaret turn, an agile silver skeleton enters propelled by slaves. But the applause is interrupted by an unpromising-looking second course: a deep circular tray with the twelve signs of the zodiac arranged round it, food being suitably placed over each—above the Heavenly Twins for example there are fried testicles and kidneys, Virgo, a sow's udder, Sagittarius, a bull's eye; inexplicably in the centre there is some grass and a honeycomb. Everyone rather sourly starts to eat, four dancers hurtle forward (in time to the music) and remove half the dish. Underneath are stuffed capons, sows' udders, and a hare with wings fitted to look like Pegasus; at each corner four figures pour a peppery sauce from wine skins over some fish swimming round in the stream of the dish. At this everyone cheers up and claps, and the carver posturing in time to the music cuts up the joints.

After Trimalchio has delivered a short lecture on the theories of astrology—which spell-binds the guests by its erudition—the slaves lay embroidered pictures of hunting over the couches and a pack of hounds career in followed by a huge dish with a wild boar wearing a cap on its head; baskets filled with dates are suspended from its tusks and it is surrounded by piglets, made of dumplings, as if at suck. The carver—a new one—sporting a beard, a damask hunting coat and leggings makes a furious lunge at it and a flock of thrushes fly out to be caught by the birdcatchers, with lime-covered twigs, and distributed to the guests.

A pretty boy appears wreathed in vine and ivy leaves, carrying grapes and pretending to be various versions of Bacchus, and, in a high-pitched voice, renders a recital of compositions by Trimalchio, who at this stage goes to the lavatory. After some time he returns to discuss the condition of his urinary tract and to hope that no one at the table is holding himself in, too embarrassed to relieve himself—*he* has no wish to hinder anyone. With a flourish of music the tables are cleared and three white pigs are brought, decked with muzzles and bells. The oldest is selected for the next course, the cook is summoned and duly led away to the kitchen by the meat. Very soon a server carries in the boar, at which Trimalchio peers and announces it is not gutted. The cook says he has forgotten, and is stripped immediately, ready for a good whipping. Everyone pleads and instead he opens the pig and out come sausages and blood puddings.

At this point in the festivities an accountant reads an inventory of the host's properties, slaves who have been crucified on his estates, notices of divorces, details of adultery, but is interrupted by the acrobats. One is a tiresome dull fellow who holds a ladder up which a boy climbs, dances about on top and jumps through blazing hoops, a wine jar in his mouth. Trimalchio is just saying how lovely it all is when the boy falls down on top of him and everyone screams. All is disorder. Trimalchio groans terribly, doctors race to the scene and the boy grovels abjectly begging for mercy. But this is only a ruse, organized to display Trimalchio's humanity. With gestures and applause the boy is granted his freedom. Then there is a frightful lottery with witty prizes based on puns; for example if some guest drew a ticket saying 'head and foot' he won a hare and a slipper—'lights and letter' got a lamprey and some peas. Unfortunately this, together with all the wine, causes people to start quarrelling and abusing one another, until a troupe of actors appear with erected spears, banging their shields and reciting Homer. A boiled calf, dressed with a helmet, is brought in (on a plate weighing two hundred pounds); Ajax

rushes like a madman, slashes it to pieces and distributes the
flesh to the astonished guests on the point of a sword. The ceiling
starts to rattle and the whole dining room shakes, which makes
everybody think more acrobats are descending through the roof;
the ceiling splits and not acrobats are lowered on string but jars
of unguents and money.

Meanwhile, on the table, Priapus is in position, rising in
pastry from a tray of cakes and buns, supporting on his generous
parts apples and grapes. Greedily everybody grabs them but as
soon as each bun is touched saffron spurts into their faces,
drenching them. Everyone produces a variety of obscene whistles
and squawks which are, they say, imitations of musical instruments. Trimalchio blows a fanfare of trumpets and looks round for
his little lamb—Croesus—who turns out to be an unappetizing lad,
sore-eyed, with filthy teeth, cramming down the throat of a fat
black puppy loaves of bread which are instantly vomited back.
There is a dog fight between the fat black puppy and an enormous
watch dog that is admitted, during which a chandelier is upset
spilling hot oil over some of the guests. Trimalchio, unconcerned,
kisses his little lamb and gives him a piggy-back. Fortunata, the
wife, appears and giggling drunkenly compares her jewellery with
that of a friend until someone creeps up, flings her legs into the air
and tips her over. The floor is scattered with gold and scarlet
sawdust, a slave imitates a nightingale, another imitates some
trumpet players. Pastry thrushes stuffed with nuts and raisins, and
quinces stuck with thorns, enter, together with an astonishing
dish looking like a fat goose surrounded by fish and all kinds of
game: everything on the dish is made from pork. Two slaves
come in from the well, quarrelling and breaking each other's
water pots with their sticks, alarming the guests until they see
oysters and scallops sliding out; the chef, singing in a high
grating voice, serves snails on a silver gridiron.

And then everyone is massaged with unguents; legs and ankles
are wrapped in flowers, everyone reeks of scent, oils pour down
their foreheads, they become maudlin. Trimalchio reads his last
will and testament, some people burst into tears and all adjourn
to the bathroom to play games like running round the bath

hand in hand, or bending backwards, trying to kiss the points of their toes.

The evening is not finished yet. There is another dining room spread with still more things. 'Let us,' Trimalchio shouts, 'whet our throttles and not stop eating till daylight,' when unfortunately a cock crows—dreadful omen—and must be caught and cooked. Everyone lurches and shouts about, Trimalchio examines the shroud in which he is to be buried, and the embalming fluid; the cornet players strike up a dead march and blow so loud that the fire brigade rush in with water and axes thinking the house is on fire, the party scatters and comes to an end. Everyone waddles home.

Of course Rome was not entirely populated with Trimalchios and Heliogabali; they serve to illustrate the distorted summits a perverted gastronomic appetite can achieve. But there was no doubt that much of the system swung on a circle of jealous competitiveness. A Roman could not bear for another to do something better, or be more popular than him. He was very touchy about this. To lose face, particularly for the *nouveau riche*, was a dreadful thing. He lived by the equations: money = success = energy = virility. To illustrate his success and virility, therefore, it was necessary for a Roman to display as many possessions as possible: polished tables inlaid with ivory, the softest, richest couches, course after course at dinner. Thus, rather like today, a great many people had possessions for the wrong reasons. They did not make a room beautiful, a dinner delicious, except as a means of impressing the neighbours. It was partly to promote their envy and admiration that one ate from plates as elaborately adorned as possible, drank from curious vessels, sometimes encrusted with precious stones, or hewn from beech and olive woods, sometimes chiselled from dead men's skulls, or blown from glass dilated into large phalluses.

The popular notion that all Roman food was revolting seems to have sprung from the eighteenth century. It was closely related to the puritan notion that 'dishes simple in themselves, and easily prepared, mark the manners and morality of a nation'.[1]

[1] This was voiced by the good Doctor Hunter of York.

'Nothing,' complained the Reverend Mr. Warner, in his *Antiquitates Culinariae*, 'nothing can be conceived more disgusting than many of the dishes, since a variety of ingredients from which a modern would shrink with abhorrence were cast into them by the cooks of Rome with the most lavish hand. We meet repeatedly with the extraordinary mixtures of oil and wine, honey and pepper . . .' And in the nineteenth century Doctor Hunter of York (a scholar whose thesis was *De cantharidibus*), disguised under the name Ignotus, declared the Roman sauces and dishes 'according to our notion of good eating' to be 'no better than what may be seen in the kitchen of a Hottentot'.

This, as the three English translators of Apicius's famous recipe book have pointed out, is really not true. Many of the dishes were delicious and may be still prepared today. The two most recent translators, Barbara Flower and Elizabeth Rosenbaum, essayed many of the recipes themselves—as I myself have done—and pronounced them excellent. Scholars, as all three pointed out, are generally not cooks. It is true Doctor Hunter of York besides being an expert on Spanish Flies considered himself one with food. He compiled a cookery book; his receipts being transmitted to him 'from persons of established reputation of Culinary Art'. But although he faults a Hottentot's kitchen his own does not appear reliable. In 1805 he entertained to dinner Mr. Alexander Gibson Hunter who announced it 'a very poor performance on the whole'.[1]

The truth is that deciphering and translating page after page of recipes—foreign recipes—is an unappetizing, exhausting task. The mind boggles at so much unshaped food and, unless it belongs to an experienced cook, is unable to imagine anything delicious. The book on which the scholars base their conclusions was compiled

---

[1] 'Next our DINNER—two course, of course. Now for it technically: in the centre a bad thin soup, poisoned with celery; at top a dish of threaded skate, bedevilled with carrots and turnips—this supposed in York to be both a Phoenix and a chef d'oeuvre; at bottom, roast beef, *so-so*; at side, ill-boiled beetroot, stewed with a greasy sauce, without vinegar; potatoes, veal cutlets, cold and not well-dressed; anchovy toast and tartlets. Second course: two partridges, ill-trussed and worse roasted; at bottom, an old hare, newly killed and poorly stuffed; at sides, celery and some other trash; in short, a very poor performance on the whole.'

by Apicius, a gourmet whose kitchen was likely to have been less disappointing than his critic's; he spent approximately £1,000,000 on food, then poisoned himself rather than subsist on the remaining 100,000 gold pieces: a sum, in his view, inadequate for an epicure. He was an educated man, as indeed were all recipe compilers. These books were not written for the majority of people with little or no cooking experience—many of whom would in any case have been illiterate. The ingredients were meant only as a rough guide, for the rest one used one's experience, intelligence and flair. Most of Apicius's recipes are vaguely and hastily jotted down, carelessly edited. The author generally does not state quantities but merely lists the ingredients. This accounts for the faulty reasoning that all dishes were over-spiced. There is no reason to suppose one was meant to add shovelfuls of spices any more than nowadays one is meant to add shovelfuls of salt and pepper, or shovelfuls of parsley when garnishing. It goes without saying that a little of each is used to bring out the flavour; and so it is with spices; with sympathetic handling they bring delicacy and depth, subtle rhythms to a dish. It is with the application of spices and herbs a cook may measure with an artist, working with his palate to bring nuances to each dish: mixing the freshness of ginger, the green-searing of cloves, the brown-warmth of cinnamon with the paleness of liquorice, the gold of honey, the purple of grape-juice, making combinations, now slightly hot, now deliciously sweet.

One can picture them, those scholars, peering shortsightedly at the manuscripts, their crabbed hands jabbing disgustedly at the pages; as for *trying* any of the recipes the idea was inconceivable; they swallowed down their nausea, scribbled out the ingredients together with their remarks on the indigestibility and nastiness of it all; and that was that. The main target for their invective was *liquamen* or *garum*.[1] 'An *abominable* sauce,' one called it, a 'putrid distillation from stinking fish.' It was manufactured commercially and was a basic ingredient to most recipes. There are two translations in *The Roman Cook Book* for making *garum*; my experiment turned out remarkably like a delicate cousin of Worcester Sauce— a mixture which if analysed by a hostile stranger could rouse equal

[1] See Appendix II, page 245.

mistrust. It contains soy sauce prepared by fermenting the beans until mouldy, and fish. But we are all familiar with Worcester Sauce, we all know it, and how delicious it can be. We all know too how successful a marriage of fish and meat can be: oysters with steak pie, veal with tunny fish, cockles with mutton, mussel and oyster sauce with turkey, smoked haddock with bacon, anchovy sauce with chops, shrimps and prawns with chicken. Combinations such as these appear in world-famous recipes, not the least of which being the delicious Creole dishes, the spicy concoctions known as gumbos, liaisons of fish, meat and vegetables.

CHAPTER TWO

ORGIASTIC CELEBRATION AND
HOLY EMACIATION

What then will become of you a young girl physically sound, dainty stout, and ruddy, if you allow yourself free range among flesh-dishes, wines, and baths, not to mention married men and bachelors?

If, as you lie on your couch after a meal you are excited by the alluring train of sensual desires; then seize the shield of faith.

JEROME

PAGAN LANDS are lands of nature, based on life and survival; on the rain, the spring, the summer. When winter howls in the branches, whips snow like iced-muslin stifling your breath, who is to know that life will come again? That again there will be dappled summer shades, the red of radishes, purple asparagus, freedom of movement? Pagan lands are lands of make-believe peopled with imaginary spirits: spirits of vegetation, tree and corn and water gods. When the young breezes rustle through the beeches, the rivers roar again with spring, it is the spirit of vegetation returning.

But for all their magic and make-believe pagan lands are practical; their religion corresponds to their needs. The Italian deities were quite simply protectors of the state, each with his own special function allotted him. At first, the Italians being largely men of the country, their gods were primarily agri-cultural—gods and goddesses of the seasons, of springtime and daybreak, of fertility. They protected the crops and flocks; pre-sided over the manuring of the fields, the sowing of the corn, over the prosperity of the cattle, the clearing of the land and making of new pastures. They presided over marriages and child-birth; they controlled the elements and warned and punished men by hurling thunderbolts and withholding the rain and the sun.

The rhythm of the seasons was part of the Romans, as it is part of all ethnic people. It beat with their hearts in the innermost part of their bodies, throbbed like the pulse of distended organs. For pagan life is an intercourse with nature—intercourse with the gods. The sowing of the seed in December in the bare brown earth; its wakening, the magic of a Mediterranean spring when all the earth moves up in green; the long hot summers of heavy trees, full-blown grasses and swollen seed pods; and then the parturition, the harvesting, the reds, the golds, the sadness and fulfilment of autumn, the smell of the earth, of fallen leaves, of returning winter; its bleak, bare dreaming bones waiting again for the seed to penetrate once more.

As Italy became more urbanized some of the rural deities adopted other duties besides their agricultural ones: trade and travel, war and commerce. Every year there was a festival celebrated in honour of each god, at which sacrifices were offered to ensure his goodwill, protection and purification for the coming year. They were joyous occasions, often licentious, often degenerating into orgies, symbolizing new life and growth, fertilization and fruition. And because the majority of Italians had originally been husbandmen, the calendar of festivals is largely that of a farmer, the celebrations falling to celebrate the planting, the sprouting, the harvesting of seed.

For example each March there was the Liberalia in honour of the god Liber Pater—god of vegetation and fecundity—who protected the growing seed. During the celebrations a chariot travelled through the cities and fields supporting a large wooden phallus; this was pursued by a procession of rejoicing naked prostitutes and men, each one sustaining dummy genitalia on the ends of long poles; afterwards there were great debauches, singing and promiscuity.

To encourage the buried seed there was the fertility cult of Fauna, celebrated by ladies at the beginning of December with mysterious festival; the participators were, according to Juvenal, to be seen processing, howling and drunken, through the streets, tossing their heads, whinnying and grinding their thighs together in mounting lust until they achieved such frenzies that they itched for men—boy-friends, water carriers or slaves—and if there were not enough to go round they entertained donkeys. And there was the Saturnalia: a series of rural festivals in the name of Saturn, a working god, a vine-grower and manurer of fields, they lasted for seven days, over the birth of the new year, from December 17, seven days of unrestrained festivity and feasting when all laws and conventions were dismissed.

But worst and wildest of all had been the Bacchanalia, in honour of the wine god, Bacchus, or Dionysus. The places of worship, it was said, resounded nightly with shrieks, uproar, thrilling music and wild dances; anyone who refused to be initiated was bound to a windlass and snatched away out of sight, either to be persuaded, or violated. Such were the cries, the beating of drums and the hymns that no one could hear the victims crying for help. When notice of these proceedings was brought to the senate in 186 B.C. it was deeply shocked and disgusted, pronouncing the caves and grottoes to be abodes of corruption, and prohibiting for ever the Bacchanalia. Something extremely serious must have been going on to have roused the senate into taking such drastic action. Grounds of bibulous licentiousness would not have been enough. Roman policy distrusted any private associations among its people and considered any body that separated itself from public worship suspicious and dangerous. But in this case it would seem the Bacchanalia was terminated on grounds that the worshippers were indulging in human sacrifice and cannibalism—rituals not at all approved by the senate; that they had reverted to more primitive days.

It is now believed that the Eleusinian mysteries were originally inspired by hallucinogenic mushrooms. Gordon Wasson in his *Soma: Divine Mushroom of Immortality* has proved most lucidly and conclusively that Soma the divine drink in the *Rig Veda* is the juice of *Amanita Muscaria*. This was imbibed in two ways: directly by pressing the juice out and mixing it with milk, water, herbs or alcohol; or second-hand from the urine of someone who had drunk it. It was in this way, Robert Graves believes, that the divine knowledge came to Greece from India, locked up in Aryan thighs. Dionysus is the counterpart not only of the Mexican god Tlaloc (inspired, Wasson has proved, by the hallucinogenic mushroom *psilocybe*) but of the Vedic god Agni; Agni, as Wasson has shown, is Soma, as Soma is the hallucinogenic *Amanita Muscaria*. This as Robert Graves points out, would explain Dionysus's hitherto inexplicable nickname 'Mero-traphes' ('thigh-nursed') and also the legend of his double birth, which relates how he was first born from Semele, a moon-earth-and-underworld goddess whom Zeus (Indra, the god of lightning's counterpart) 'thunderously impregnated'. 'His light-ning destroyed her,' writes Graves, 'but her spirit was later elevated to Olympus under the name of Thyone. The infant Dionysus, untouched by lightning, had been sewn up in Zeus's thigh.' Ambrosia, the legendary food of the gods, gave its name, Graves tells us, to the October festival of Dionysus, which was also known as *Mysterion*, probably meaning 'uprising of toad-stools'. Ambrosia and Soma were one and the same thing. By mixing it with barley or spruce beer, or possibly, Graves suggests, yellow ivy, the worshippers would have received powers of potency and the necessary muscular strength with which to tear fawns, kids, children and even men apart; later, he believes, the *Amanita Muscaria* was replaced by an alternative hallucinogenic mushroom, one easier to handle 'that could be baked in sacrificial cakes shaped like pigs or phalli, without losing its hallucinogenic powers'.

The nervous system would have been paralysed, the feasters become delirious, while by eating the milder entrancing *panaeolus papilionaceus* coloured visions would have been supplied by which the feaster became as a god. At the beginning of the first century B.C. it appears that the Bacchantes, in the isolation of their caves, returned to enacting the full passion of Dionysus and eucharistic-ally consuming the god, forcing their victims to undergo every circumstance of his death. One version of the story tells us that the god-child was cut up limb by limb, boiled with herbs and eaten.

Ironically, one of the reasons the early Christians were so

disliked and feared was because they were suspected of imitating precisely those Eleusinian mysteries that had shocked the senate. It seems, from Professor Allegro's thesis *The Sacred Mushroom and the Cross* that these suspicions were not so ill-founded or fantastic after all. Professor Allegro believes that Christianity is rooted, along with the other Holy Mysteries, in a sacred mushroom fertility cult, and that Christ was no person but a code-name, a form of word-play, concealing the identity of the real god—the sacred mushroom. Like Soma, Christ was the hallucinogenic *Amanita Muscaria*. '. . . what could be more logical than to link the Soma and Dionysiac nonsenses with the sacred meal of the Christians, and now philologically we can see just how they do tie up,' he wrote to me in a recent letter. The symbolic bread and wine may have replaced, not only other more ferocious feasts, but also the drinking of Soma in its two forms—the juice itself and the urine of persons who had consumed it. The Adam and Eve legend is probably a Palestinian version of the Siberian belief, which still survives, linking the birch tree—one of *Amanita Muscaria*'s hosts—to the scarlet fruit growing at its base. It is paradise to which mushrooms take one, and, as Robert Graves points out, all paradises contain a serpent: 'supposedly because a bright serpent apparition is one of the brain's natural reactions to the cutting off of its full oxygen supply. The serpent may be glorious or terrifying according to one's state of mind: the advanced alcoholic state also sees snakes; so do certain sufferers from meningitis.'

All kinds of horrid tales circulated concerning the primitive Christians and their celebrations. A new-born infant, it was whispered, entirely covered with flour, was slaughtered, everyone greedily drinking the blood and tearing asunder the quivering limbs. The sacrifice was succeeded by suitable entertainment, drink whipping up lust until the lights were suddenly extinguished and the darkness was polluted by incestuous commerce, sisters and brothers, sons and mothers all enjoying one another.

To the Romans the early Christians seemed a gloomy, lazy, unreasonable bunch; a rude, dirty, malevolent crew, possibly dangerous, with no interest at all in the good of the community;

moreover they seemed astonishing—abandoning the temples of the gods and heroes who had protected their land and sponsored everything that was good and beautiful, to worship instead 'nothing but clouds and the numen of heaven', choosing for their leader no brave hero, but an obsolete workman, a condemned criminal, who had very properly been crucified. 'It was not in this world,' Gibbon remarked, 'that the primitive Christians were desirous of making themselves agreeable or useful.' To the temporal Romans, who preferred to gather their sweets while they might in a world of which they were certain, the Christian promises of eternal love, of the good to come in the *next* world, while disregarding the present, seemed impractical and un-attractive.

Above all the Christians appeared obstinate. 'Whatever may be the principle of their conduct,' Pliny said, 'their inflexible obstinacy appeared deserving of punishment.' And punished, as we all know, they were along with other miscreants in many unpleasant ways in the arenas and amphitheatres for the sport of the populace.

Excitement—the satisfaction of blood-thirstiness and lust for violence—together with plenty of food had long been recognized as a way of keeping a large urbanized population peaceful. It was the imperial recipe of Bread and Circuses. There is no doubt that the sadistic streak lying inside most Romans was exploited and expanded by these circuses. In every city large amphitheatres were built where the inhabitants could go to watch massacres, violence, gladiatorial contests and the slaughter of thousands of rare wild animals.

Victories, accessions of emperors and other causes for festival were celebrated by mass bloodshed. The arenas provided different means of sport for some: the horrid Caligula diverted himself by removing the canopies at the hottest hour of the day and forbidding anyone to leave, while Commodus, to the embarrassment of the people, actually entered the arena himself slaying such harmless creatures as ostriches and giraffes. Once the dens of the amphitheatres disgorged as many as a hundred lions at one time; elephants, bears, crocodiles and rhinoceroses were all transported from the furthest shores of the Empire to consume prisoners, fight gladiators and finally to die for the delight of the people.

These circuses, together with the slave system, probably were responsible for redirecting the currency and awareness of pain and channelling it so deeply towards sadism. The slave system was taken for granted by everyone, based as it was on the Roman view that men were far from equal in the sight of heaven, whose favour was preserved for the well-born and the well-educated. To be poor was a sign of ill-luck and, what was more, was infectious. Until Hadrian and the Antonines revised the laws, slave owners had the legal power to torture and kill their slaves over any crime. There were of course a great many men who treated their slaves kindly, who trusted them, made them part of their families and granted them their freedom when they earned it; but also there were a great many who treated them appallingly, reducing them to dreadful misery, keeping them in stables and sties, lashing them with whips, forcing them to undergo public tortures, floggings and crucifixions. Death was regarded as a liberation, thus it was not so much the termination of life that was the punishment as the pain that went before it. All kinds of excruciating means were devised for miscreants to make their suffering worse and ostensibly to afford more pleasure to the spectators who were invited along to gloat. It is true that Vedius Pollio, rumoured to have fattened his lampreys upon the bodies of his slaves to make them more succulent, was frowned upon in the street, but nobody moved to stop him.

The rise of the Christians in Rome, it has been suggested, was a natural reaction to the luxury and vice of the rich. The majority of early converts were drawn from the slave-class, many of whose worldly lot was appalling and who had little hope of improving their position. A doctrine that could dismiss the comforts of the body, earthly riches and ambition, and offer in exchange for a pure soul a shining gold eternity was an attractive one, especially when it was indicated that qualifications for this promised land were earthly poverty and squalid conditions. That in itself was heavenly, and made even more delicious, perhaps, by reports that the rich, who had spent their earthly lives so arrogantly, so comfortably indulging their bodies in every possible way, were to be eternally damned; their once pampered sensations would be tortured forever by the most frightful pains imaginable. Thus from out of a class-consciousness and a pride in poverty and simplicity the hatred of the body was born. In fear of the ghastly pain of hell the Christians spent the greater part of their lives with body and soul in conflict. The body *had* to be broken; it had to be abused and maltreated, its reactions, sensations and natural functions became to the Christians a real and terrible neurosis. It was a weak and dreadful pulp that would, at the drop of a hat, succumb to the devil and his temptations and precipitate the soul into hell. It was a skin-cage; their souls were trapped in skin. Through the round holes in their heads they gazed out in terror at the snares of hell, their open mouths, black O's, blowing black winds of terror; seas of faces, faces of devils, voices like surf roaring on sand, towards them, up, then back again, leaving pools of words to tempt the body, pools of terror. There must be no sleep, no hunger, the prison must be always watched. The flesh must be deprived. And when the skin hung blackened, an empty sack upon the bones, the soul burned bright within. But unfortunately those eternally damned Roman citizens inside their plump well-cared-for prisons knew nothing of this inner radiance, thought nothing of their doom. They saw only some squalid grimy creatures. They found it hard to understand why they could not *wash*. 'To induce you to take baths,' Jerome warned his band, 'they will speak of dirt with disgust.' Who did not know that baths were vile sinks of iniquity? Washing was synonymous with luxury and sin. 'The purity of the body and its garments means the impurity of the soul,' Jerome said. All agreeable sensations were damned, all harmonies of taste and smell, sound, sight and feel, the candidate for heaven must resist them all. Pleasure was synonymous with guilt, it was synonymous with Hell.

For the Christian his daily life was beset by obstacles. The first and most important thing that he must do was preserve himself pure and undefiled from idolatry. In Rome this meant he was bound to withdraw almost entirely from society. Hardly any daily activity could take place without transactions being made to the gods, and even more inconvenient was the fact that most money carried images of the gods and was therefore unacceptable. As for creations of art, they were out of the question: music, painting, eloquence and poetry were seen to be of the same disagreeable fiction that inspired the rich ornaments of houses, dress and furniture.

To the terrified Christians it seemed they were hedged on every side by the anathemas of luxury. And as the years passed and the Empire entered the fourth century the temptations were no less. From the moment they stepped into the street wickedness enticed them. There were men to be avoided, who thought of nothing but their clothes: clad in ornamental chains, long hair and beards like goats', they breathed out heady perfumes like dragons contaminating the air; their fingers glistened with rings, their long hair showed the trace of tongs. Furthermore when they traversed a damp road they walked on tiptoe, so as not to splash their feet. Then there were the *nouveaux riches*, puffed up with ambition, accompanied by troops of eunuchs, galloping about the streets, their purple robes fastened by many glittering clasps and so light in weight they billowed out like balloons behind, revealing their tunics, which it is dreadful to relate were embroidered with brightly coloured animals and fringes.

As for the women, they crammed their wardrobes with dresses. The widows were the worst, seen travelling in capacious litters, red-cloaked, plump and inviting with rows of eunuchs walking before them. The eyes must be averted from such people. 'Let your companions be women pale and thin with fasting,' instructed Jerome. If the cup of salvation was to be gained there could be no pleasure in this life and no passing the time with troupes of laughing girls. 'I prefer Paula and Melanium who weep,' noted Jerome. The way to heaven led through hell: through melancholy, paleness and emaciation. There were to be no savoury breakfasts of plump young cranes for aspiring Christians, no mouth-watering smoking dishes—steaming pheasants served on massive silver platters. For 'who does not know that gluttony is the mother of avarice,' thundered Jerome, 'and fetters the heart and keeps it pressed down upon the earth? For the sake of a temporary gratification of the appetite, land and sea are ransacked—that we may send down our throats honey-wine and costly food . . . The fact is that my native land is a prey to barbarism, that in it men's only God is their belly.'

The revellers seemed everywhere, in the towns and provinces of the Roman Empire. As the days went by and the seasons changed, men with names like Gluturius and Pordaca—their very appellations seeming to exude gluttony—luxuriously stretched themselves and lived, 'intent on stuffing themselves, they follow their noses and the shrieking women's voices to the kitchen,' growled Ammianus Marcellinus, 'and like a flock of starving peacocks they stand on the tips of their toes biting their finger-nails waiting for the food to cool'.

While rivers slid past and spring breezes trembled in the elms, men like Ausonius entertained his friends to luncheons and dinners, and in the high country houses perched above the Moselle they ate and drank too much. 'You slumber on because you drink deep,' Ausonius wrote, 'and swell out your paunch with too great a mass of food.' There was hot gravy and bubbling pots and in the distance vineyards; and all the while the sloping river waters streamed through the green water grasses, under the overhanging river banks and the roofs of houses.

It was as it had always been. There were gambling parties and brothels and public spectacles, and whirlpools of long unwholesome banquets, according to Ammianus Marcellinus, when, in the middle, scales would be demanded to see who had the largest fish, the fattest dormouse, the plumpest bird. And this was not all; 'some go so far as to take potions,' wrote Jerome, 'that they may insure barrenness, and thus murder human beings almost before their conception. Some, when they find themselves with child through their sin, use drugs to obtain abortion, and when (as often happens) they die with their offspring, they enter the lower world laden with the guilt . . . of suicide and child murder.' The guilt, the controversy over contraceptives and abortions, was born.

Looking back over the years of the Roman Empire one sees the same instances of luxury in the fourth century as those satirized by

Juvenal in the first. Apologies have been made for the declining
years, men like Samuel Dill have asserted it was in fact an austere
time, that Ammianus and Jerome have exaggerated the vice and
luxury. Ammianus, Mr. Dill explains, was a general accustomed
to the hardness of battlefields, unused to civilian life. And Jerome
had a gift for words, they snatched the pen from his fingers and
bolted away with him, over-drawing his pictures, smudging them
out in great black shadows. There may be some truth in this;
thunder is more frightening than a pop. Nevertheless if it were
entirely the case it is hard to explain why so many Christians
became so fanatical, harping always on abstinence and fasting, and
denouncing so fervently all pleasures of the flesh. If times were
austere this would surely have been unnecessary. Unless it was to
renounce temptation why did so many flee to the deserts and
wildernesses of Egypt, discarding society completely?

And flee to the deserts and wildernesses they did. Once there
no one could describe the life as pleasant, even the redoubtable
Jerome seemed to falter and look back nostalgically to the softness
of Rome. 'Oh, how many times did I, set in the desert, in that
vast solitude parched with the fires of the sun that offers a dread
abiding to the monk, how often did I think myself back in the old
Roman enchantments. There I sat solitary, full of bitterness; my
disfigured limbs shuddered away from the sackcloth, my dirty
skin was taking on the hue of the Ethiopian's flesh: every day
tears, every day sighing: and if in spite of my struggles sleep would
tower over and sink upon me, my battered body ached on the
naked earth. Of food and drink I say nothing, since even a sick
monk uses only cold water, and to take anything cooked is wanton
luxury. Yet that same I, who for fear of hell condemned myself
to such a prison, I, the comrade of scorpions and wild beasts, was
there, watching the maidens in their dances: my face haggard
with fasting, my mind burnt with desire in my frigid body, and
the fires of lust alone leaped before a man prematurely dead ... I
do not blush to confess the misery of my hapless days ...'

Among the sand and heat hazes some ascetic Christians
established regular communities of the same sex and disposition;
they were the first hermits and monks. Of these the Anachorets

were the most fanatical. 'The aspect of a genuine anachoret was horrid and disgusting,' wrote Gibbon: 'every sensation that is offensive to man was thought acceptable to God.' Some confined their emaciated limbs in collars, bracelets and gauntlets; some sank under the painful weight of crosses, some entirely cast their clothes away and wore only their long hair, some buried themselves away in gloomy caverns; the most perfect were supposed to have passed many days without food, many nights without sleeping. 'Glorious was the *man* who contrived any cell, or seat, of a peculiar construction which might expose him in the most inconvenient posture to the inclemency of the seasons.' Glorious was Simon Stylites who took up his residence on top of a pillar nine feet high, which height he annually raised until it reached sixty feet.

In the silence of their caves and the solitariness of their uncomfortable beds the holy fathers were besieged by naked women who appeared to them in mirage, and sumptuous feasts that spread steaming before them. Very soon astonishing reports came in of the miracles they were performing. But as Gibbon pointed out: 'the golden legend of their lives was embellished by the artful credulity of their interested brethren; and a believing age was easily persuaded that the slightest caprice of an Egyptian or a Syrian monk had been sufficient to interrupt the eternal laws of the universe. The favourites of Heaven were accustomed to cure inveterate diseases with a touch, a word, or a distant message; and to expel the most obstinate demons from the souls or bodies which they possessed. They familiarly accosted, or imperiously commanded, the lions and serpents of the desert; infused vegetation into a sapless trunk; suspended iron on the surface of the water; passed the Nile on the back of a crocodile; and refreshed themselves in a fiery furnace. These extravagant tales which display the fiction without the genius of poetry have seriously affected the reason, the faith, and the morals of the Christians.'

No doubt the holy fathers in their isolation did indeed experience visions, shimmering mirages in the haze. These mirages would have been considerably sharpened by the receiver's exhaustion and lack of food and sleep. There are two interesting

scientific points to be made here. Fasting—deprivation of food—
can have the effect of lowering the body's supply of blood sugar,
deficiency of which will cause hallucination and illusion. Lack
of sleep can cause a break-up of the system producing in the
conscious mind waking dreams that would otherwise have been
experienced during sleep; often the visionary cannot differentiate
between the dream and the reality. No doubt the holy fathers
really did experience and perform some of the miracles that their
brothers so eagerly noted down, but the question is how many of
them were performed in dreams—none the less real in their
emotional content—and how many were actually physical?

Jerome gives us an account of the menu and miracles of Saint
Hilarion, one of the most devout and vigorous fathers conforming
to all discomforts: sleeping on bare ground and assuming sackcloth which he never washed. For three years his food was half a
pint of lentils moistened with cold water; for the next three, dry
bread with salt and water; the following three he enjoyed wild
herbs and the raw roots of shrubs; and again the three following
he supported himself upon barley bread and vegetables slightly
cooked. However noticing his eyes growing dim and his whole
body shrivelling with a scabby eruption and dry mange he added
oil to his former food; he lasted until eighty. During his time he
performed many miracles. One of these was to drive out a grievous
demon from a powerful youth called Marsitas. On account of
this grievous demon Marsitas could not endure his chains and
fetters; he had broken the bars and bolts of doors; bitten off the
noses and ears of many of his companions, and broken the feet
and legs of others. Everyone, not surprisingly, was terrified of him.
Laden with chains he was dragged like a wild bull to the monastery.
When the brethren saw this heaving mass approaching they were
horrified, for the man was of a gigantic size. Hilarion however
was undaunted. 'Bow down your head and come,' he said. The
man began to tremble, laid aside his fierceness and began to lick
the holy father's feet. On the seventh day, the text records, the
demon came forth, tortured by the saint's abjurations; it omits
however to relate the demon's reaction to the saint's feet.

When the holy fathers died crowds of penitents flocked to

worship at their tombs. No church was complete without some relic, some portion of a saint or martyr preserved in pickle. The number of miracles ascribed to the conserved members, the phials of blessed milk, the drops of holy blood, the fragments of clothing, exceeded those exploits of their lives. The remaining pagans were disgusted.

'The monks [a race of filthy animals, to whom he is tempted to refuse the name of man],' Eunapius writes in the fourth century, 'are the authors of the new worship, which, in the place of those deities, who are conceived by the understanding, had substituted the meanest and most contemptible slaves. The heads, salted and pickled, of those infamous malefactors . . . are the gods which the earth produces in our days . . .'

CHAPTER THREE

A WORLD APART

Better sleep with a sober cannibal than a drunken Christian.
HERMAN MELVILLE

I

Man Eating Men

FOUR HUNDRED years before Eunapius the inhabitants of Celtic Britain also venerated preserved heads. They were headhunters. They were cannibals. Stuart Piggott when summing up the situation tells us 'that the Windmill Hill folk in England, in common with their continental relations in the Western Neolithic practised some form of cannibalism, utilitarian or ritual, while the abundance of skulls represented may point to its sometimes at least taking the form of headhunting'.

The Britain that confronted the Romans was a wild green magic island. A land of stone circles, of warriors, high-priests and kings. A land of tribes, of small independent republics, each one ruled over by its own king and largely hostile to its neighbours. A thin ribbon of comparative civilization sprawled along the coast opposite the continent, sometimes sixty or seventy miles thick, but proceeded into a turbulent interior. By far the most advanced people belonged to a large tribe called the Belgae which originated from Gaul and occupied the greater part of Kent. Here, historians record, the land was densely populated, the ground thickly studded with circular thatched buildings, cattle and cornfields. 'Forests are their homes,' Strabo wrote, 'for having enclosed an ample place with felled trees, they make themselves huts therein and lodge their cattle.' Dion Cassius describes them at home, lying upon wolf- or dog-skins before fireplaces heaped up with coals where cauldrons bubbled and whole pieces of meat sizzled on spits, waited upon by their children. Excavations reveal con- tinuous rings of mutton bones around the great fire-pits, which suggest the family threw their gnawed bones over their shoulders into the dark cold shadows beyond the flickering cosy circle.

These Belgae were the most civilized people, yet although they tended their animals, grew flax and wheat, baked their corn to preserve it and dug huge granaries lining them with timber and skins; although their cattle produced plenty of milk, they were not skilled enough to turn it to cheese, they knew nothing of horticulture and other matters of husbandry, nothing of manuring to maintain the fertility of the soil. It is likely that every two years new soil would have to be broken. But with an estimated popu- lation of half a million at the time of the Roman conquest there would have been plenty available.

The men, according to Strabo—he had seen some in a Roman slave market—were tall and slight with bowed legs and made asymmetrically. The women they shared between groups of ten or twelve men, especially between father and sons, but the children of these unions evidently counted as belonging to the man under whom each woman had lost her virginity. It was thought impolite for a boy to be seen out in public with his father until he was of an age to be some use in the battlefield. Their hair was worn long, their bodies were shaved—all except the head and the upper lip. The richest wore dyed garments besprinkled with gold, the rest supported skins. They were a simple, high-spirited, vain people who loved to deck themselves with bright shining colours and baubles—gold bracelets on their arms and wrists, rings upon their toes—who loved to appear terrifying in wartime and to this end turned themselves blue with the famous woad. 'It is this vanity which makes them unbearable in victory and so completely down- cast in defeat,' noted Strabo. They were dangerous and noisy op- ponents whirling down from the woods naked and blue on their small war chariots which they manipulated with astonishing agility. And when they died they were buried with their chariots, accom- panied by their jewels, their utensils, their food and drink ready for the joys of the otherworld. The divine high-priests—the Druids—were men of wisdom, they knew the best incentives to bravery. They preached that the soul was immortal and described the most delicious place into which it would pass on death. The otherworld was an ingenious fiction carefully constructed to meet the demands of warriors who loved above all else feasting and fighting. It was an ecstatic place where there was no punishment, fatigue or satiation, only delight: an unceasing procession of orgies: of feasts, sweet music and love-making punctuated with victorious and glorious battles.

To the west the tribes lived in causeway camps, well organized and vigorous societies of powerful chieftains and high-priests, but towards the interior and the north the tribes became smaller, more primitive and savage. They lived, many of them, in the shadow of great hill-forts some, like White Horse Castle at Uffington, enclosing considerable areas of land, as much as forty-five to a hundred acres within their great defence ditches, their sheer walls. They travelled high up along exposed ridgeways on the crest of hills, the steep sides falling away from the plateaus and uplands, naked to reveal would-be attackers and ambush-men.

In the early 1920s a brewer from Hereford, Alfred Watkins, claims that while he was riding one hot afternoon over the Bred-wardine hill suddenly in an instant he saw through the surface of the landscape to a prehistoric level. A web of straight lines stretched across the country linking the sacred places.[1] Mounds, stone circles, holy wells, hallowed tree-clumps and standing stones stood in exact alignment, streaking out past sacred moun-tains over whose point the sun rose on the longest day, past banked-up streams, mirrors wherein the moon, or the light from beacons, flashed through the longest night. Tracks were cut deep into hillsides and crags to show as notched landmarks faraway, ponds were dug to reflect the stars. It seemed that these alignments were arteries down which at certain significant times of the year

---

[1] Watkins's intuition has never been thoroughly investigated, but as John Michel points out in *The View over Atlantis*, ordinance survey maps show remarkable alignments of churches often erected on the old sacred sites, stone circles, tumuli and Roman roads, which frequently followed the original straight tracks.

—the autumn and spring equinoxes, the summer and winter solstices—the spirit of nature, the giant earth goddess, the White Goddess of Robert Graves, rose up from her chains among the hills and valleys and passed through her land in a great current of fertility.

Like all ethnic people the Celt was essentially of nature. His life was spent between fighting, producing and hunting food. His kings and his deities were for the purposes of fertility and war. He lived in a damp and magic land of mists and sacred springs against a black and jagged forest where wild boars roamed and the howl of wolves echoed on frosty nights. He lived like a child in an uncharted hayfield making tunnels through the stalks.

The groves of creaking trees, the black pools, the rushing rivers pouring down through steep-banked forests—foaming with chalk, or wide and silent in the valleys—the round eye of the sun: all these were sacred. Professor Thom has shown how the stone circles are temples to the firmament, geometrically arranged to refer to the positions of the celestial bodies as they cross the horizon; many, like Avebury, continued outwards in stone avenues which, like the sacred ways, directed the flow of fertility. Certain animals too were revered—the hare, the goose and the cock according to Caesar—for the deities, it was believed, had the powers to metamorphose and reveal themselves. There, in the early autumn evening, the new stubble shining white like frost under the rising moon, the men advanced with their sickles to cut the last of the corn; over the still night air the distant barks of the hunting dogs carried, and there bolting out from the last stalks, in great leaps, was the spirit of the corn. And on October nights when the geese and the cranes whirred overhead to the marshes—this was no slaughter-stained melody. These birds were no food for men; with their outstretched wings, their strange wild bird-song, they were the magic signs from the gods—they *were* the gods, foretelling the future, reminding the beholders of the happy otherworld that lay before them.

The horse too was sacred. Under the goddess Epona the horse-cult was widespread; represented by a white mare it symbolized—

like the king of a tribe—fertility. The carving of the white horse
at Uffington is well known, and a white mare figures in the
description given by Giraldus Cambrensis of an inauguration of
a king in Ulster—a region where Celtic tradition still remains and
whence comes most of its literature. Before an assembly of people
a white mare is led in. The King-Elect then emerges on hands and
knees. Declaring himself to be a beast he enjoys, in pantomime,
sexual intercourse with the mare which is then killed, cut into
pieces and cooked. The King-Elect next sits in the pot with the
pottage, bathes in the broth, eats the flesh and drinks the liquid.
He is then proclaimed King. 'Here,' writes Anne Ross, 'we seem
to have a description of a rite which is both genuine and archaic.
Sexual vigour and fecundity are characteristic of the horse, and in
this scene we supposedly must visualize the animal to be symbolic
of the powers of fertility, very important to a king, whose own
potency was believed to affect the fecundity of the entire tribe and
stock possessed by it. By imitating the stallion mating with the
mare, the king invokes these powers.' The king, as James Laver
remarked, was the personified penis of the community, while the
insertion of his head into the crown was a symbolic coitus. In
some cases a tribe could be ruled by a Queen—Cartimandua,[1]
Queen of the Brigantes, for example; her role was no less symbolic.

This inauguration ceremony links with the ritual of the ancient
Sun-Worship, when at Midsummer the Sun God, who was one
with the reigning king, was sacrificed by the priests and
eucharistically consumed by the new king, who, having assimilated
his virtues, became himself the Sun-God.

This act of bestowing on the sacrifice divine qualities, then
consuming it in order to digest and assume them, is at the heart of
ethnic sacrifice.[2] It is at the heart of the Christian Communion

[1] Sleek Pony.
[2] It is also generally at the heart of most cannibalism, especially in cases where
white people—missionaries for example—have been eaten by coloured tribes. The
missionary is seen as a god and a hero, his consumer believes that by eating him he
too will grow brave and strong and wise. In 1824 Ashantee chiefs ate the heart of
Sir Charles McCarthy, whose courage they admired. In the course of my researches
a letter was sent to me suggesting that certain organs of Dr. Livingstone were not,
as history relates, buried by his devoted and faithful attendants, but were eaten.

service, which reflects also the ferocious sacrifices of the Hebrews, who for the good of their nation would offer their sons up to Moloch to be consumed in holocausts. 'Dogmatic Christians,' wrote F. W. Ghillany, in his *Les Sacrifices humains chez les Hébreux de l'antiquité*, 'do not only eat men, or only gods: no, they eat the flesh and drink the blood of the Man-God, of a man and a god at the same time. This is cannibalism taken to its extreme limits . . .'

Caesar reports incidents of human sacrifice being carried out in Britain on a large scale. So important evidently was the role that sacrifice played in a Celt's life that the worst of all punishments was to be banned from taking part. 'Some tribes have colossal images made of wickerwork, the limbs of which they fill with

---

'You may remember that after his rescue by Stanley . . . Livingstone returned to the Lake Bangweulu area in what is now Zambia still looking for the source of the Nile. When he died of sickness and exhaustion, his faithful followers were supposed to have taken out his heart and viscera, buried them under a tree, allowed the body to dry out and then transported it wrapped in bark several hundred miles back to the Coast whence it was taken to Westminster Abbey for burial. . . .

'Where this touches on cannibalism is the theory that his heart etc. were not buried but eaten by his followers as a sort of act of transubstantiation for the absorption of his qualities and greatness. The grounds for this theory are that burying a heart under a tree is an entirely European act and response and nothing like it is known to be part of the customs and rituals of the African peoples in this region. It would however come very natural to his followers (a group of three or four faithfuls who had been with him a long time) to wish to keep his influence and virtues by eating the heart, kidney, liver, etc. They would not look on the heart as more significant than other organs. The idea of the heart as the seat of emotions etc. is purely European, more commonly primitive people find mysterious force in the liver and kidneys since physiologically they have no obvious purpose like the heart. Susi and Chuma, the two famous followers, came from tribal groups with a habit of ritual cannibalism. . . .

'. . . the whole series of events, as it has gone down in history, is so remote from traditional ways of behaving among these people. I think it is however conceivable that the decision to take the body to the Coast without the organs was a simple practical one. There was only a handful of white people in this whole region. There was a close bond between Livingstone and his small group of followers. He had been cut off totally from contact with the Coast, and his followers with the remarkable personal loyalty which Africans can show might have wanted to prove that they had not left him to die, or failed him. I doubt if they had any idea that his body was something the Western world would want to entomb and revere—this is quite alien to thought in Central Africa—but they would want to prove their actions by physically producing the body at the Coast. It would therefore have been natural to remove the organs subject to rapid decomposition and to take his dried up flesh and skeleton.'

living men; they are then set on fire, and the victims burnt to death.' The sacrifice of another life, he says, was a precaution taken by those suffering from serious diseases, or about to go into battle. They believed that the only way to save their own life was to offer another in its place. Most conveniently, the gods expressed a preference for brigands and thieves rather than law-abiding inhabitants. Mannhardt offers a further suggestion. In damp climates, such as England, success of the crops would largely depend on the sun.[1] The men in the wickerwork images, he suggests, represented spirits of vegetation, the fires charms to ensure sunshine—the light and heat necessary to the crops; the more men there were to be consumed by the fire the greater would be the fertility of the crops.

Over all sacrifices it was the Druids who must supervise. They were more than high-priests. They were teachers, they were inspired poets who foretold the future through visions. It was they who at coronations climbed the oak-trees to cut down with golden sickles the sacred mistletoe, the prime phallic emblem, symbolizing the emasculation of the king by his successor; it was they who severed mountain ash branches against the witches, watched the marsh birds flying through the mist, listened to the voice of the wind in the ivy, in the willows; and attempted divination by stabbing a man above his midriff, foretelling the future by the convulsions of his limbs and the pouring of his blood—'a form of divination,' Diodorus Siculus tells us, 'in which they have full confidence, as it is of old tradition'. Then, in the old tradition, they devoured him.

Did they consume mushrooms to give them inspiration as was the case with the Mexican and Eleusinian mysteries? Certainly these would have abounded in the sacred groves: the spotted *amanita muscaria* with its ensuing muscular power, delirious visions and gifts of prophecy, the *panaeolus papilionaceus* with an effect similar to mescalin, and the *psilocybe* which gives visions of

[1] It is probable that on certain dates of the year, to ensure the sun's heat, special consecrated cakes and blazing circles were rolled down sacred mounds like Silbury Hill, Dunstable Down, White Horse Hill and Cooper's Hill in Gloucestershire. Later these were replaced by wooden cartwheels and cheeses, the customs continuing for thousands of years to die only lately.

transcendent beauty. The Celt poet Gwion implies this could have been so.

So powerful were the Druids that to eradicate them was one of the first major tasks the Romans, on their arrival, set themselves. This, in such a tolerant polytheistic nation, seems surprising until on closer examination one sees that the government's reasons are closely connected with both the Bacchic and Christian celebrations. Not only were the Druids a dangerous and influential private body but their celebrations involved human sacrifice of which we know the senate took a dim view. They were pursued to Anglesey. There, howling curses, their arms lifted like bones to the sky, the women brandishing flaming branches, they were exterminated. 'We cannot,' wrote Pliny the Elder, 'too highly appreciate our debt to the Romans for having put an end to this monstrous cult, whereby to murder a man was an act of the greatest devotion, and to eat his flesh most beneficial.'

The head, also, was a symbol of divinity. It was recognized as the seat of emotions, the case of mysterious force. Incorporated with the penis it was the simple symbolization of life: emotion and fertility. Severed from their bodies, heads play a prominent part in Celtic literature. They rise from wells; they wink and blush; sing sweetly; sing horribly; leap about in buckets making grinding noises; float about encircled in fire and make delightful companions presiding at feasts. During hostile raids on neighbouring tribes the heads of enemies were booty of the highest degree. 'We are told [by Diodorus Siculus, Strabo and Livy],' writes Anne Ross, 'that the heads of prized enemies were taken, impaled on spears or fastened to the saddle of horses and borne home in triumph. They were thereafter impaled about the houses and fortresses of the Celtic chiefs and placed in their temples.'

Archaeologists have discovered that the remains of Celtic skulls are densest around the region where Hadrian's wall now is. A region where the inhabitants were likely to be primitive and savage; a region turbulent and open to attack where it would be logical to suppose the natives would retain a barbarity and rapaciousness. There is evidence to indicate that in some cases the brain itself was located and consumed. Sir Mortimer Wheeler describes a burial at Maiden Castle in Dorset, one of the most famous of hill-forts: 'At its eastern end were found . . . three burials on the old surface, two of children and the third a young man who had been systematically dismembered immediately after death. The bones bore many axe-marks, and the whole body had been cut up as by a butcher for the stew-pot. The skull had been hacked into pieces as though for extraction of the brain . . . The impression given . . . was that the body had been cooked and eaten.'

It is reasonable then to assume that human sacrifice and cannibalism were practised extensively throughout the Iron Age in Britain. Strabo reports the inhabitants of Ireland 'feeding on human flesh, and enormous eaters, and deeming it commendable to devour their deceased fathers . . .' And it appears that in the more isolated outposts the habits may have lingered, for we have in the fourth century Jerome repeating rumours 'that the Atticotti, a British tribe [from northern Scotland], eat human flesh, and that although they find herds of swine, and droves of large or small cattle in the woods, it is their custom to cut off the buttocks of the shepherds and the breasts of their women, and to regard them as the greatest delicacies'.

2

A Small Reflection

This then was the island which confronted the Romans: one of thick forests and sacred springs, of kings and hostile tribes, of warrior-knights housed in sheer hill-forts perched high on cliffs and hills; its composition, social structure and degree of civilization varying considerably; a wild and untapped land.

The Romans, as we have seen, came not to develop the country, but to milk it, to skim off the cream. Merchants had carried the word: how the southern fields had waved with corn, the richness of the minerals. It was the glitter and sparkle of metals, the pearls and silver and gold arching up through the mists that caught the Romans' gaze.

Julius Caesar, it was said, came for the fresh-water pearls. With two swift invasions in successive years—55 and 56 B.C.— he had come, seen, and gone. There had been penalties, the tides and the chariot warfare had taken their toll, but there had been rewards: some tribes had accepted Roman protection, footholds had been established, long thin diving boards from which to spring into the cool green unknown depths. For the British kings a new horizon had opened up with the Roman trade. Oil came in great jars, humped over the steep moats of their fortresses, and wine in great quantities, for the warriors high up in their castles drank it deep and untempered. There was new silver tableware, bronze plated furniture, ivory bracelets, necklaces, amber and glass. And in return they sent out shiploads of corn and cattle, gold, silver, iron and slaves.

Caesar had shown that Britain was within grasp, the first steps had been taken, but almost a century passed before anything further happened. It was not until Claudius had dribbled so late up to the seat of fame that the full occupation took place. Claudius longed to win honours, perform brave deeds and gain respect for a courage he lacked so dreadfully. From his lofty and precarious throne he searched unceasingly for a chance to prove himself; his attention was caught by Britain. Here it seemed was the answer to his wishes; here he could win fame and booty.

His start was inauspicious. To his soldiers the promised land seemed so mysterious a place, so outside the inhabited world they refused to embark. And when at last they were persuaded even the seas seemed strange, quite unlike the clear blue waters they knew; this was a sluggish, heaving mass 'of stagnated water, hardly yielding to the stroke of an oar'.

They landed again as Caesar had done in the south-east. They advanced north over the Medway. Once the Thames had been crossed Claudius himself led the command. He fought a pitched battle with the natives and triumphantly limped into King Cunobelinus's capital, on the site of Colchester. Here he forced several tribes to surrender; he received the voluntary submission of others and established treaty relationships. And then came the moment poor Claudius must have longed for; he could return at the head of his victorious armies; he could process triumphantly through the streets of Rome, victor and hero in decorated carriages and purple-bordered robes, his war hostages going before him. He had added another province to the Empire.

One of the kings who had asked for a treaty was Cogidumnus, whose kingdom was Verica in Sussex. It would seem likely that it was from here that Vespasian led the attack into the west. One of the main features of this aggression was Maiden Castle. Excavations have shown the solidity which confronted the Romans: the great defence ditches, the steep stone walls, the massive wooden doors overshadowed by two great towers. They have also revealed the heavy casualties of the inhabitants; the emergency cemetery where the Celtic bodies were hastily interred. Slashed by auxiliaries' swords, stabbed by the legionaries, their heads penetrated by the throwing spears, their spines paralysed by bolts from the field guns, they were buried, their limbs still embraced with the bright shining baubles they loved, the toe-rings, the ivory bracelets: the ornaments of savages.

In return for his loyalty to the Roman government, by whom he was thought of very highly, Cogidumnus received many rewards. He accepted the unique title of *rex et legatus Augusti in Britannia*— by this he was not only a native prince, but a Roman official. He did his best to romanize his realm. His own palace, which has only recently been excavated, was of a size and magnificence to compare with Nero's Golden House, and built at approximately the same time. Set just outside his capital—Noviomagus (Chichester)—the site covered six acres. The palace consisted of four wings: there were centrally heated reception chambers, banqueting halls, kitchens, guest suites, bath-houses, the earliest known mosaic floors in Britain, rare imported marbles and painted walls. It was built round a great garden, set out with ornamental curving box hedges, beds of acanthus, roses and yew trees, while the king's own apartments in the south side led down over lawns to the sheltered waters of the sea.

But kingdoms of men like Cogidumnus were only pockets in a

3A. Venus at Rudston. It is interesting to compare the British workmanship of this mosaic with that of the Roman doves illustrated on the endpapers

3B. Apollo and Marsyas in concert at Sherborne

4A. Illustration from Gerard's *Herbal* showing usnea, the moss that grew on the skulls of men especially those of hanged criminals exposed to the elements, which was believed by early doctors to be a sovereign remedy for many diseases

4B. Celtic Phallic Head, the symbolization of life, emotion and fertility—from Eype, Dorset

4C. The ferocious mouth of Hell swallowing souls that had steeped themselves in bodily pleasures

largely hostile land. They were like heads of thistledown caught in a thorn hedge. The first years were not easy for the Romans. These were years of guerilla warfare, partisan quarrels, slave raids and frontiers: years when the warriors fought from forests and hill-traps, whirling down from the mist and the mountains; years of clashing knives, stabs and thrusts, slashing cuts, when the earth drummed with war-ponies and the rattle of war-chariots; years of blood. The assumption is that Britain must have provided a large quantity of valuable commodities to make it worth all the expense and bloodshed. For the occupation of Britain was purely on a business basis. The worse a tribe behaved, the harder it fought, the more, when eventually it was subdued, it was penalized, or set to work in labour gangs. It was calculated that the farmers of Cranborne Chase—members of the Belgae who had fought so hard originally—were deprived of three-fifths of their corn; and the Iceni, who rose under Boudicca, were put to work draining the fenlands and cutting canals for waterways.

In order to tame the Britons the Romans built towns, pink brick cages for the savages: a sort of zoo, wherein the government could keep an eye upon the suitably romanized tribal festivals, the markets and general behaviour, while at the same time them-selves enjoying all the accessories of comfort, baths, banquets and theatres. The scheme at first was not a success. The Britons had to move from their original homes to make way for the towns, and many of the ordinary well-behaved people, as well as recalcitrants, had to toil in labour gangs upon the buildings, or on the new farm estates. Tacitus tells us of the insulting arrogance with which they were treated. Knowing the traits of the Roman character, its cruelty, pompous vanity and greed, it would have been unlikely for the labour gangs to be treated with much compassion or gentleness.

The humiliation engendered by their vanquishers' attitude expanded into a savage rage against their masters; against their baths, their food, their luxurious ways; against their cruelty. Some of the Britons revolted.

Probably the most famous of these risings was that of Boudicca. Dion Cassius describes her adorned with gold necklaces and grasping a spear. Standing gaunt and severe, her fierce eyes flashing, a great mass of tawny hair falling to her hips, she delivers an acid speech against the luxury of their conquerors. 'We ought to term these people men, who bathe in warm water, eat artificial dainties, drink unmixed wine, anoint themselves with myrrh, sleep on soft couches with boys for bed fellows, boys past their prime at that,' she adds crisply. Whereupon she leads her armies to plunder two of the newly established cities, one of which was Camulodunum (Colchester).

The frightful revenge the tribes took on the Roman women seems to indicate that their own had been subjected to some especially disgusting indignities. They hung up naked the noblest and most distinguished ladies, cut off their breasts and sewed them to their mouths to appear as though they were eating them. Then accompanied by sacrifices, banquets and wanton behaviour they impaled them on sharp skewers which ran lengthwise through their bodies.

All this had to stop. Britain formed part of a World Empire. And if the Empire was to be efficient, the province must be properly assimilated into the Roman way of life, with none of these distressing and expensive rebellions. Britain must be productive and peaceful. It was Agricola, with his culture drive, who achieved this.

On his arrival in A.D. 77, he found 'a fierce and savage people running wild in the woods'. With public assistance he encouraged them to emerge, build temples, courts of justice and commodious dwelling houses. 'The result was Roman apparel seen without prejudice . . . the toga became a fashionable part of dress. By degrees the charms of vice gained admission to their hearts; baths and porticoes, and elegant banquets grew into vogue: and the new manners . . . were by the unsuspecting Britons called the arts of polished humanity.'

By degrees the Britons were tamed. The columns rose, both stone and brick, limestone and chalk, decorated with Corinthian capitals, supporting low sloping roofs. Slowly the towns grew, chessboard towns with names like Calleva, Petuaria and Aquae Sulis. By the end of the second century not only were they established

but they had reached some degree of refinement. In the streets the
vendors hawked their wares, there were markets in the forum and
oyster-bars, tragedies at the theatre, death in the amphitheatre
and at the baths thick green water steamed. Half-timbered houses
sprawled round gardens where there were vegetables, herbs and
fountains. The aristocracy was educated in Latin. The Roman
day, the eating and the meeting, was in full swing, under the heavy
damp skies, the baked tile roofs.

And in all directions the roads streaked out, straight like
ribbons, through the virgin valleys, the thick forests, over the
plains and the small square fields, out to the quarries, gravel and
clay pits, mines and other towns. In many cases diggings and
alignments on ordinance survey maps reveal that they followed
the sacred lines of the Druids. They were built up high, grass
banks sloping down so that the legions marched above the colour
of butterflies and wildflowers, the sound of grasshoppers and
crickets.

And out in the country the rooks cawed in autumn and the
sea-birds settled white on the brown furrowed fields while the
ox-drawn ploughs lumbered heavily on. Cattle were fed on hay
made not only from grasses, but sheaves of leaves—elm and ash
and poplar. Farm houses—villas—varied from small squalid
cottages to luxurious mansions, whose standard of living was not
equalled again in Britain until well after the Norman conquest.
The villa-system established an arrangement of land from which
emanated the manorial allotments of the Normans.

To a people who had known only the euphoria and satiation
of animal-feasting, of stuffing themselves with food and drink
until no more would go in, the Romans introduced the refinements of pleasure: a sophisticated kitchen, elaborate tableware,
lofty bath-houses, and fine decorations. Gradually they raised
their standard of dwellings from simple farmhouses, little more
than barns, to comfortable abodes. Walls were painted in reds and
browns and blacks. There were yellow trees and bunches of
scarlet fruit, dancing girls, baskets of flowers, garlands, and on
the floors elaborate mosaic pavements. These, together with the
walls and drinking cups, often bore delightful inscriptions: 'we

wish you happiness' and 'enjoy yourselves'. That their inhabitants were not under-nourished is proved by excavation, which shows no evidence of rickets, and little tooth-decay.

The Romans in Britain were no less anxious to be fashionable, and impress their neighbours, than their friends at home—a fact which is proved by the house decorations. These were highly complicated designs, not suitable for most of the inexperienced native workmen whose standard of work shows they could have far better executed the conventional and simple abstract designs that were available. But large, complicated mythological designs were more sensational, and large, complicated designs there had to be. The Wolf and Twins appeared in mosaic at Aldborough,[1] Medusa at Fishbourne, while Apollo leered, piped and gavorted before a po-faced Marsyas at Sherborne and Venus put in a dubious appearance at Rudston.[2]

'It is a reasonable supposition,' writes A. L. F. Rivet, 'that where nothing is reported to the contrary the British way of life and thought did not differ fundamentally from the Gallic, or even the Italian, except that it was set in a lower key.'

Law and order were guarded in the same way: brigands were crucified, or lacerated by wild beasts; children were exposed.[3] The tables bore the ornate embossed platters, the succulent recipes. The peas, parsnips, turnips and celery were served in plates adorned with hunting scenes, naked deities, animals and scrolls. Salads, vegetables and fruit were served in big red bowls. Much of the tableware came in from abroad, creaking in heavily laden galleys, the slaves rising forwards and falling back on their oars, the noise of their chains rattling, the roaring of beaten waters disturbing the gulls waiting in herds for fish. And while the silver jugs were unloaded, the dishes, cups and goblets, the bronze table-lamps, the candelabra, the heated dishes, the finger bowls,

[1] Situated in the West Riding of Yorkshire, Aldborough is on the site of the Roman capital Isurium.

[2] Situated in the East Riding of Yorkshire.

[3] Evidence of this is given by A. H. Cocks who describes an excavation of a Romano British farmhouse in Hambledon: 'A remarkable feature of this excavation was the ground . . . was positively littered with babies. They number ninety-seven, and most of them are newly born, but an occasional one is rather older.'

the red glazed pottery, the glass decanters and bowls, the gulls circled and cried above the sea. Wine came, too, and oil, stone pines, incense, ginger and cinnamon; new plants for medicine and foods were introduced: nettles, fir and beech, snails, cherries, ground elder and hemlock.

The ministers of government were often as depraved as any in Rome. Against Clodius Albinus there are charges of almost every known vice. He was unjust to servants, unbearable to his wife, brutal with his soldiers; he was dishonourable, unprincipled, covetous and extravagant; moreover he was one of the world's great gluttons. Cordus tells us he could swallow of a morning five hundred figs, a hundred peaches, ten melons, twenty pounds of grapes, a hundred figpeckers and four hundred oysters.

And so the Roman days passed in light and in shadow. Britain had become a small grey reflection thrown out from the glittering Mediterranean. Although there were some barbarian raids there was nothing to compare with those that ransacked Gaul. The fourth century was a time not of desolation, but of positive economic development.

Then suddenly in the early part of the fifth century the Romans buried their treasure, withdrew their armies and went, removing with them the cream of British youth.

CHAPTER FOUR

WHERE ARE THE JOYS OF HALL?

But woe is me. There is death in the pot. O man of God. The wine
is gone from our wineskins and bitter beer rageth in our bellies.

ALCUIN

WITHOUT THE strength, energy and organization of
the Roman armies, without their young men, the Britons
were left hopeless and disorganized; they could do
nothing without supervision. The western and northern garrisons
quaked with fright within their fortifications. The towns and the
rich farms, the hopeless inhabitants with their ornamental tableware, were meat for the Picts and the Scots who itched to
get among the cattle and iron, the gold and the jewels. They
were not long in realizing that the Romans had gone for good.
They poured down from their fastnesses, harassing the Britons
with hooked weapons, worrying them, infiltrating the country like
poison in a wound. The Britons abandoned their walls, their
cities and their farms and fled into the mountains and forests.
Without an organized harvest, without the spring and winter
sowings and ploughings, there was famine.

In the more protected south the inhabitants continued their
lives fatly, in Roman style, unable to halt the enemy. In desperation they sent to Rome a letter known as the 'groans of the
Britons'. 'The barbarians drive us into the sea, and the sea
drives us back to the barbarians. Between these, two deadly
alternatives confront us, drowning or slaughter.' But the Romans
were themselves too harassed, too occupied to help.

In the year 449 King Vortigern had a brainwave. He was,
noted William of Malmesbury disapprovingly, a king 'wholly
given to the lusts of the flesh, the slave of every vice'; he had

defiled his own daughter; he was awake only to the blandishments of abandoned women. Leering through this red haze of lust he had spotted a brilliant solution.

Instead of the Romans he would invite to the country the Angles and the Saxons to fight against the Picts and the Scots. In return he would grant them the poorest land no one else wanted. They with their own uncertain living conditions would be grate/ ful; the kindness of the Britons would soften their natural ferocity; they would never quarrel with their benefactors. The system seemed infallible, the future rosy and assured. Hengist and Horsa arrived but unfortunately sent back immediately messages relating the opulence of the land and the indolence of the people. Six years later their reinforcements were not only fighting the Picts and the Scots but the Britons as well.

The cities were devastated; buildings destroyed. Excavations show their inhabitants living a miserable existence squatting in the ruins of their houses, in the one remaining room, throwing debris and garbage into those roofless yawning rooms next door. Slowly the cities and farms sank and crumbled. The Saxons did not move in. For one thing they believed the cities to be the work of giants, and haunted by them; for another they knew nothing of stone work and preferred to build their own dwellings in wood.

The invasion of the English, their settlement and establishment, was a gradual process; fierce fighting against the Britons dragged on and the whole of the country was not occupied for two hundred years. Ivy, plants and trees grew over the buildings, wild animals moved in, wolves made their lairs under the bricks and marbles; those that had built them were forgotten.

About a hundred years later Bede writes of the crumbled, once glittering cities: the columns, the pillars, the winding porticoes still remarkable in their size. 'Wondrous is this wall/stone,' wrote a poet gazing about the ruins of Aquae Sulis; 'broken by fate the castles have decayed; the work of giants is crumbling.' The roofs had fallen, the towers and the gate; frost crunched and glittered in the cement. Grey lichen and wild convolvulus grew over the pink brick. 'Bright were the castle dwellings, many the bath/houses, lofty the host of pinnacles, great the tumult of men, many a mead-hall full of the joys of men, till Fate the mighty overturned that. The wide walls fell; days of pestilence came; death swept away all the bravery of men; their fortresses became waste places; the city fell to ruin.'

The new race—the English—was again a race of warriors: warriors, noblemen, peasants and slaves.[1] Primitives who loved above all things bright and shining objects; whose supreme felicity lay in success in battle with its rewards of glistening jewels and gold treasure and feasts, where the twisted gold horns brimmed over with wine and mead, and there was the din of merry-making and friendship, poetry and the rippling music of the harp; where 'many a man light of heart and bright with gold, adorned with splendours, proud and flushed with wine, shone in war trappings, gazed on treasure, on silver, on precious stones, on riches, on possessions, on costly gems, on this bright castle of the broad kingdom'.

To the English jewels were like sweets. Now, the same lights shine translucent through the greens and reds of wine-gums and boiled sweets as those that illuminated the greenness of emeralds then; that lit green suns in the eyes of their possessors, showed the thickness of gold, the carvings on the wine-cups—so subtle the cornfields seemed to wave, the vines to bud, the men to move.

When they fought—these men—they armed themselves with jewelled swords and shields, swords with names of their own like Noegling; they decked themselves in shining war gear. And when they moved, held together by streets of brown sand, passed through little-known country by string-thin paths down windswept head-lands and plunging wolf-slopes, the sun flashed on their shields and the links of chainmail, the gold-plated bridles clinked, the bright saddles inlaid with jewels sparkled and creaked, the ash spears made a grey-tipped forest and overhead the raven and eagles waited, eager for carrion.

For their livelihood these warriors depended upon the land.

---

[1] The Anglo-Saxon slave system worked under the same principles as the Roman. A slave could earn his manumission, but until that time he was a chattel. The usual price for buying a slave was a pound, Dorothy Whitelock tells us—the equivalent of eight oxen. Slaves were either Britons—the word itself means slave—or were prisoners captured in wars, or condemned to slavery for crimes or debts.

They were above all a race of farmers. Their existence was feudal, living in groups centred round the lord,[1] in various degrees of servility, and working the land. Evidence of these long-vanished kingdoms remains in the place names; 'ing' meant the place where the followers and relations of the lord lived, 'fold' an enclosure in woodland. Thus Steyning was Stane's people's place, Worthing was Wurd's people's, and so on with Ditchling and Chidding-fold; there are many examples. Each group was incredibly loyal, families repaid the killing of any member with vendettas, and followers were bound to guard their lord with their lives. Isolation from the lord, separation from the home-group, was the ultimate dread. The poem 'The Wanderer' speaks of the desolation when the lord is dead, when one belongs to no group and is forced to flee abroad.

> Often I must bewail my sorrows in my loneliness at the dawn of each day; there is none of living men now to whom I dare speak my heart openly ... So I, sundered from my native land, far from noble kinsmen, often sad at heart, had to fetter my mind, when in years gone by the darkness of the earth covered my gold-friend, and I went thence in wretchedness with wintry care upon me over the frozen waves, gloomily sought the hall of a treasure-giver wherever I could find him far or near, who might know me in the mead hall or comfort me, left without friends, treat me with kindness.

It was a shaggy, heavily forested land still, woodland continued in great stretches unbroken. There were large areas of undrained marshland where the cranes and geese flew and little grew but silver-grey willow, bull-rushes and reeds for making flutes. The chalk and oolite downlands grew corn, the river valleys were deserted. Bede describes it as a land of grain and timber and good pasturage; vines were cultivated in various localities. There were many land- and sea-birds and plentiful springs, and rivers abounding in fish. 'Salmon and eels are especially plentiful, while seals, dolphins and sometimes whales are caught. There are also many varieties of shell-fish, such as mussels, in which are often found excellent pearls of several colours, red, purple, violet and

---

[1] W. W. Skeat shows that 'lord' is a compound word deriving from 'loaf ward', meaning 'loaf keeper', 'master of the house', while 'lady' derives from 'loaf kneader', 'maker of bread'.

green, but mainly white. Whelks are abundant, and a beautiful scarlet dye is extracted from them which remains unfaded by sunshine or rain; indeed, the older the cloth, the more beautiful its colour. The country has both salt springs and hot springs, and the waters flowing from them provide hot baths, in which the people bathe separately according to age and sex.'

The year passed in a procession of seasons, sowing, weeding, harvesting and ploughing. It was an orgy of work. No sooner was the harvest gathered in, then the fallow must be ploughed. The success of the system depended upon a steady rhythm being maintained; if this were broken the result was serious food shortage. This became especially evident in the latter years of Viking invasions when the land was plundered, all routine disrupted and serious famines ensued.[1] How the English introduced the plough —so wide and heavy it needed a team of eight or ten oxen to draw it—how they tilled the land, the great curving furrows of the open-strip system, is well known. Wheat, barley and rye were cultivated in two-year rotations with peas and beans, the third year the strip rested and lay fallow.

For the peasants working in bondage it was a long day. At daybreak the shepherds and the swineherds moved out with their flocks from their night-folds. The oxen left their night-mangers and toiled before the ploughmen up the open fields. The swineherds watched the pigs, rootling, grazing, crunching acorns and truffles in the oak-forests; the shepherds saw that no wolf entered their flocks, and twice daily milked their ewes, making from the milk white butter and cheese.

In the forests, deep in their hearts where the wild beasts lingered, the huntsmen stretched their nets and set their dogs to the chase. Into the meshes came boar, fallow deer, roe buck and hares. And the fowler lured in small birds with nets, or lime, or traps: thrushes and blackbirds, duck, pigeons and waterfowl. Apart from these, peacocks, swans and barn-door fowl were

---

[1] This, according to the Church, was the Will of God. 'The Almighty Ruler,' explained Archbishop Aelfric, 'sometimes withdraws sustenance from men on account of sins, but nevertheless, we believe that he whom hunger takes goes to God unless he was particularly sinful.'

raised for the table. Hawking was a favourite sport, while hunting was more to obtain food than pleasure.

Out under the broad headlands, the steep cliffs, in the sea, the rivers, the streams, the fishermen made net-traps and took their catch to sell. Deep-sea fishing was not so popular, it was dangerous and more expensive, the sea was a hostile waste and needed big ships to sail upon it; but there were herrings to be had, porpoises, sturgeon, oysters and crab, mussels, plaice, soles and lobsters, and there were Bede's whales—particularly dangerous and difficult to kill, but profitable on account of their teeth, which were used instead of ivory.

New wooded cities sprang up on harbours, navigable rivers and the junctions of important roads. They were rural establish-ments where nightingales sang, pigs rootled in the streets and smoke hung grey over the roofs, where the peasants lived in one end of a single room while their animals lived at the other. There were gardens where herbs grew: rue and hyssop, onions, lovage, parsley, fennel, mustard, elecampane, southernwood, rosemary, coriander, lupin, chervil, flax, celandine, radishes and cummin. And there were fruit trees: pear and cherry and medlar—which bore the singular name of open-aerse. And there was mandrake, a magic root used for aphrodisiacal purposes.[1]

The lords lived in lofty gabled houses consisting of one huge hall, with small chambers leading out. The Ramsey Chronicle describes one such mansion situated most beautifully—the surrounding countryside spread out like a tapestry from the door of the hall. They were furnished with trestle tables and fixed benches, which at night were strewn with mattresses and pillows. Floors had tesselated pavements, walls were hung with woven hangings—tapestries worked in gold—benches had elaborately carved ends, table legs curved and had faces.

Abroad, the English carried a dreadful reputation; from Italy they were viewed by the Christians as a barbarous and fierce nation. Highly superstitious, they lived in a land surrounded by monsters; dragons wheeled through the midnight sky setting buildings on fire with their breath, smoked in prehistoric burial

[1] See Appendix I, pages 237, 238.

mounds guarding piles of jewels and wine-cups; monster vampires came in with the mist, stalked in off the moor, bit necks, drank blood and devoured flesh. Like frightened children the English carried magic charms against the bogeymen. Boniface who was born among them could like neither them nor their habits. They 'utterly despise matrimony,' he complained, 'utterly refused to have legitimate wives and continue to live in lechery and adultery after the manner of neighing horses and braying asses'. They were people to be avoided. Gregory, however, according to the traditional rather sickening story, thought differently. Visiting the market place in Rome he spotted among some merchandise several boys exposed for sale. Their fair complexions, fine-cut features and beautiful hair filled him with interest. On enquiring from whence they came he was informed the island of Britain, where, alas, the population were still ignorant heathens. 'They are called Angles,' he was told. 'That is appropriate,' said he, 'for they have angelic faces, and it is right that they should become joint-heirs with the angels in heaven.'

Inspired by God, the Pope sent Augustine and several other God-fearing monks to spread into England the Good Word. The God-fearing monks and Augustine were appalled to go to what seemed to them a seething mass of awfulness. Nevertheless, in 597, the Word of Christ landed in England and slowly spread through the land. The establishment of Christianity under the tactful eye of Gregory was not traumatic. The temples remained, only the idols were removed, and relics of saints inserted in their lieu. 'They are no longer to sacrifice beasts to the Devil,' Gregory instructed, 'but they may kill them for food to the praise of God … And since they have the custom of sacrificing many oxen to demons … on such occasions they might well construct shelters of boughs for themselves around the churches that were once temples and celebrate the solemnity with devout feasting.'[1]

In this Gregory displayed equanimity and some of the Roman

[1] The Anglo-Saxon abhorrence of horsemeat has been traced back to Gregory, who apparently in 732 ordered Boniface to forbid the consumption of horseflesh so that the Christians could be seen to be different from the surrounding pagans, who very practically put to good use all available food and consumed large quantities of horse.

genius for adaptation and conversion. However, now, instead of the comfortable domestic gods who saw to all fertility and manuring of fields, and who were saluted with joyous feasting, here rose a dour anthropocentric god, who with one hand dangled carrots and delights before the bewildered noses of his men, offering all living creatures and plants for their use, but with the other exposed the dreadful terrors of hell, were his gifts to be employed towards enjoyment. Pleasure, as we have seen, was sin.

The old deities, it was taught, were devils.[1] Spring still came, 'groves put forth blossoms; cities grow beautiful; the fields are fair; the world revives'. But no longer was it the tree spirits and the corn gods who were uniting to make the green. No, they had become, overnight, bad and hostile. Nature had become riddled with devils. Wicked spirits flew about the island; water spirits, instead of lobster harvests, provoked shipwreck; satyrs and fauns danced on heath and green making inundations, or sat by the highways exciting horses to stumble, men to fall; fiery devils worked by blazing stars; aerial spirits stimulated lightning, thunder and tempests, struck men, beasts and steeples, affected whirlwinds, corrupted the air bringing plague, sickness and fire, caused copulation between witches and ordinary men— begetting further devils. Bedtime was a time to be frightened. Beds heaved with incubi and succubi.

Primitive religions believe that death is an aggressive force; that corpses rise from graves to suck blood, that witches wait to enchant you to death so that at midnight they can employ your body, or eat it; that men by night change to wolves, strangle dogs and children and eat them 'with excellent appetite'. The new Christianity did nothing to dispel these ghosts. It was unequal to root out superstition, rather it tried to fling a cloak of religion over it all, introducing holy names and incantations to the old charms and trying to exorcize devils with holy relics, saints and water. In some cases the recommendations were delightful: cattle should be sung to each evening to help them—religious themes

---

[1] Hot Cross Buns, it is believed, date from about this time. They were originally cakes eaten by the Anglo-Saxons in honour of the goddess Eastre, which the clergy, endeavouring to expel paganism, exorcised and marked with a cross.

like the Tersanctus—and should the unhappy event occur that they vanished from their grazing then there were proper charms to bring them home. Having recalled the saints and Christ upon the Cross one murmured:

> So I think to find these beeves,[1] not to have them go far, and to know *where they are*, not to work them from mischief, and to love them, not to lead them astray. Garmund, servant of God, find me those beeves, and fetch me those beeves, and have those beeves, and hold those beeves, and bring home those beeves, so that he, *the misdoer*, may never have any land, to lead them to, nor ground to bring them to, nor houses to keep them in . . . Amen.

But in others the Church endorsed the old fears: as late as the fifteenth century Sigismund held an inquiry into werewolves. The learned assembly of theologians declared that anyone who denied a man could transform himself into a werewolf was guilty of heresy; Guillaume de Lure, at Poitiers, was burnt for not believing it.

Like all ethnic races, the English placed great trust in magic amulets and charms against disease and evil spirits. 'Lay a wolf's head under the pillow, the unhealthy shall sleep,' the leech books recommend against insomnia. If the holy bishops had had their way it would have been no wolf's head below the bolster but that of a saint. The remains of saints and martyrs united with wolf-dung, wolves' heads, live foxes' tongues and red rags as protections and remedies. Caskets were suspended round bishops' necks; ambassadors begging the hands of princesses in marriage brought presents of them. They were as good a currency as gold and precious jewels. There were swords that had driven into Our Lord's Side, parts of the True Cross and of the Crown of Thorns besides the usual blessed members and body secretions. People became collectors of relics. In her book, *The Vampire*, Ornella Volta has a nice point to make on this ghoulish Anglo-Saxon cult. She puts their talismans down not to piety but a derangement of the sex instinct, which she explains has deviated to the 'death-instinct'.

---

[1] Dorothy Hartley tells us that beeves are castrated males, bred on poor hill pasture, which gives them a strong constitution and firm bone so that they would be good doers and put on flesh rapidly when brought down to lower richer pastures.

Daily, miracles—many of which were no more than pious forgeries to show the superiority of the Christian saints over the heathen gods—were noted and ascribed to the relics. Through their power legs bent with disease straightened, children's sight exploded with light, withered limbs filled, storms were quelled, epidemics halted, wind and fires averted, stone sarcophagi too small to admit their bodies suddenly expanded.[1]

The same kind of miracles and visions as those recorded by the desert fathers are experienced by the early English bishops and brethren, many of whom endured the same rigid vigils and fasting. Scribes in the Anglo-Saxon Chronicle report instances of the sign of the holy cross appearing in the moon; milk, butter and rain turning to blood and fiery dragons flying past. There were many cases of people being engaged by evil spirits, crying out, grinding teeth, foaming at the mouth and tossing limbs in wild contortions. Such a case is reported by Bede as occurring after supper. None evidently could hold the victim, or bind him, until a casket containing holy dust was revealed. It is probable that these possessions were often no more inspirited than ordinary fits caused by the consumption of certain bacteria or minerals in impure water.

Medicine was a mixture of mumbo-jumbo and herbal cures. No plant was without its use and it was the women's job to gather the herbs and roots for remedies. But recoveries to health were seen mainly as the direct intervention of God. With agues, distempers and pestilences—malaria, erysipelas, epilepsy and

---

[1] Bede tells us that the young bloods would gallop to and fro on their spirited palfreys, leaping for wagers such huge cavities in the roads—for by now the Roman roads were in bad repair—that they often fell and broke their thumbs and cracked their skulls. Then it was not so much the bandage of the surgeons that cured their wounds as the bishop's breath fanning their faces, or a sprinkling of holy earth. There is a story that Oswald, a very holy king, was killed in a seventh-century battle while fighting for his country against the heathens. The spot where he died appeared to cure all sick men and beasts so efficiently that people started removing the dust from the site so that they could mix it with water into potions. Gradually quite a hole was dug, a pit in which a man could stand. All sorts of distressed animals and people either climbed or were lowered into it, when all pain ceased and, restored to perfect health, they were able to rise, tidy their hair, adjust their headgear or graze as the case might have been.

leprosy—raging, sometimes to survive was indeed a miracle. Symptoms were treated as diseases. Somewhat of a hindrance to practising, or even studying, medicine was that a surgeon who failed to cure his patient was liable either to pay his value, or die himself. So that such complaints as the wagging of teeth and inward worms were more inclined to be treated with a mixture of charms, sympathetic magic and decoctions of herbs; as were monstrous nocturnal visitors (indigestion according to the Reverend Oswald Cockayne), and the bite of a mad dog for which the remedy was to eat the head of the mad dog itself, 'sodden'.[1] Against a paroxysm of colic you should wear some wolf-dung with bits of bone in it enclosed in a pipe; you could also cut out the tongue of a live fox, dry it, tie it up in a red rag and suspend it round the neck. If something caused annoyance to the eye 'with five fingers of the same side as the eye run the eye over and fumble at it saying three times: tetunc, resonco, bregan gresso and spit thrice'; while against toothache 'spit in a frog's mouth and request him to make off with the toothache'.

It was, as everyone knows, the monks who were responsible for recording the ancient remedies. By the beginning of the eighth century there were several established convents.[2] Their inhabitants were mostly sincere: gentle and religious men who were learned in gardening and medicinal herb cures, who copied down and translated manuscripts from the Greek, copying most brilliantly the texts, illuminating the pages so that they crackled and glinted with gold, shone vivid with reds and blues and greens. An arduous, exacting work, and in the winter Bede gives the picture of the monks wrapped in sheepskins, their hands frozen with cold.

It was a life not suited to everyone, all were not learned men producing works of erudition under appalling conditions; some possessed little or no genius for the rigorous life and looked for drinks and comforts to pass the time away. Even Bede repeated

---

[1] Mediaeval term for 'boiled'.

[2] Once founded it was the inhabitants' most important duty to pray for the founder and his family's souls. They must also provide board and lodging for the founder whenever he chose to stop by.

the rumour that monasteries were sometimes founded by men for no better reason than to exempt their lands from taxes by using them for religious purposes. Mysterious strangers were often emerging from texts, entering monasteries by night and revealing themselves to the one member of the community, the one man of God, who was up keeping the vigil and reading the psalter. 'I have visited every room and every bed of this monastery,' said such a stranger, as evoked by Bede, 'and entered every building and dormitory. Nowhere have I found anyone except yourself concerned with the health of his own soul. All of them, men and women alike, are either sunk in unprofitable sleep, or else awake only to sin. Even the cells, which were built for prayer and study, are now converted into places for eating, drinking, gossip, or other amusements . . .'

Later, the Viking invasions caused serious disruptions to the religious. It was found necessary to publish canons forbidding drinking in church. It was the custom to hold wakes on saints' days. People assembled in church the evening before and kneeled in prayer through the following night. This was inclined to become boring; instead 'the people fell to lecherie, and song, and dances with harping and piping and also to glotony and sinne'.

It was no easy task that the Church had in hand controlling this unruly bunch of people who behaved little better than wild, ill-mannered children. It used the edict that hundreds of years later Dr. Johnson pronounced: 'children, being not reasonable, can be governed only by fear'. Terror was the medium by which they should be disciplined. A terror of hell. 'Warn them of the terrible judgement of God lest for their bodily desires they incur the pains of eternal punishment,' Gregory had said. 'If they cannot contain, let them marry,' the Apostle Paul had said, but there should be no lust about the marriage: it was to obtain children, not to satisfy. Because you had indulged yourself with luxuries, your flesh with sweetness, syrups, the hell you understood was pain, eternal pain and bitterness. The most uncomfortable, unbearable discomforts imaginable were described and forecast; those that gorged down food and drink, it was said, suffered the worst agony of all in their tongues, likewise adulterers were afflicted in their nether regions.

The Sutton Hoo ship burial, dated at the early part of the seventh century, reveals the forbidden luxuries and earthly treasures a pagan king would require in the next world. Here is a gold-hoard that had been enclosed in a delicious garnet-encrusted purse, and a wealth of jewels and harness—buckles and hinged shoulder clasps, studs and a helmet; for war, there is a sword and a shield shining with red and green enamel; for his food and drink two silver spoons, wonderful embossed hanging bowls and drinking horns; and to accompany his words of poetry a stringed instrument. It is believed that the most likely candidate, for whose use these treasures were put away, would have been Redwald, King of the East Angles. One of the Wuffingas, he was kinsman to Anna, a devout Christian who, a few years after the death of Redwald, also became King of the East Angles. One of his main virtues, according to Bede, was his excellent family, one of his daughters being Etheldrida. Through her it may be seen that the Christian attitude towards the whole subject of luxury, sensuality and worldly goods was no less fanatical than it had been under the desert fathers.

She was a sort of dotty, early *sans-culotte*, always at the front fighting her anti-luxury campaigns, and usually involving her patient family in them as well. For twelve years she lived married to King Egfrid who, devout man that he was, noble in mind and deed, longed to sleep with his queen; indeed so much did he long for this that he contrived bribes, promised the good Bishop Wilfrid—of blessed memory—estates and much wealth if only he could persuade her. But no, she must preserve the glory of per-petual virginity. She must forever urge the necessity of 'bidding adieu to earthly things' and beg the unfortunate king to allow her to retreat from worldly affairs so that she might serve the Only True King—in a convent. The tapestries dipped in Sidonian dyes, the sculptures, the vessels overwhelming the tables with their weight in gold, the delicacies so anxiously sought through land and sea to pamper the appetite, the bodies indulged with luxury and con-stantly gorged—were not these things smoke and vapour? To prove her point she liked to play crazed pranks upon the long-suffering king. She arranged with a servant to splash the palace, where she and the king had just been staying, with heaps of filth and piles of excrement, and put in the bed—whence they had risen that morning—a sow which had just farrowed. She waited until their journey was well underway, then persuaded her patient husband ro retrace his steps to the palace where, not surprisingly, he 'was astonished at seeing a place which yesterday might have vied with Assyrian luxury, now filthily disgusting'. After this she obtained his reluctant consent and entered a convent, soon becoming the Abbess of Ely,[1] where on that island— floating it seemed above the undrained fens—it was said she wore only woollen garments and would seldom wash in hot water. And when she died her body remained uncorrupted in the grave; devils were expelled at the touch of her shroud, and her coffin relieved diseases of the eye and pain of the head.

Less fanatic was the Virgin herself, who had been known to descend and lend a hand with the groceries. It was the custom for the king to travel from estate to estate—accompanied by his court— feasting off the land, at some expense to his hosts. There is a story that when King Athelstan promised to pay a visit to Aethelflaed—a lady of royal rank—his purveyors went ahead to inspect her provisions. All was in order apart from the mead-store, which was inadequate. The hostess however prayed to the Virgin, whereupon the mead never failed in spite of the butlers over- whelming the drinking horns and goblets all day 'as is the custom at royal banquets'.

English habits and manners up until the Norman invasion are veiled; the English are dark shapes looming behind the shade; now and again the greyness lifts to expose unclouded glimpses of daily life. We see them spreading their cloths, at the ninth hour of the day, upon the tables, sitting up to the beef and mutton which had grazed on the salt marshes, or the aromatic hill pastures, the pigs, goats, calves, deer and wild boar, the peacock, swan, duck, pigeon, water and domestic fowl, the geese. We see from the Monastic Colloquy the young boys in the frater pulling up their benches to worts, fish, cheese, butter, beans, flesh meat and gruel

[1] Deriving its name apparently from the vast quantity of eels that were caught in the marshes.

'as cooks ken to do'. But what did the cooks 'ken'? What was the standard of English cooking really like?

According to the Reverend Oswald Cockayne, who studied an enormous quantity of Anglo-Saxon manuscripts, it was excellent. Cookery, he says, was an admired art, the cooks professors of cookery who could make oyster patties and delicious stuffings, who were conversant with preparations of milk-junkets, goose-giblets, pigs-trotters and invalid food (concoctions of bread and goat's milk), pigeon cooked with a piquant sauce of vinegar, peas sweetened with honey, broths of cabbage, beef and marrow boiled with young swine, nettles cooked in water.

Through etymology we find the only Anglo-Saxon words for cook and kitchen are derived from the Latin, which would suggest that before the Roman influence the Saxon standard of cooking was rude; this in its turn suggests that some of the Roman sophistication and technique would have been absorbed into the kitchens.

Contemporary illustrations indicate that much of the cooking took place out of doors. Meat broths and stews containing pot-herbs were concocted in giant cauldrons; meat was also fried, steamed or roasted and brought to the table on long spits. Much is often made of the poverty of diet through history, of the un-pleasantness of winter meat owing to the necessity of salting down huge quantities of beasts because of lack of winter fodder. To put this in its proper perspective several facts should be listed: facts that are often not taken into account. Cattle were not reared primarily for meat; oxen were draught animals, cows were for milk; sheep were for wool and dairy produce. The diet was largely one of dairy produce, legumes, cereals, game, fish, wild fowl and *young* animals. There were few forest laws and no enclosures, game, fish, fuel and fodder were there for the taking. With a population estimated at two million at the time of the Norman invasion a very small proportion of the land was cultivated, there were huge areas of wasteland for the cattle to browse—on tree loppings and shrubs as well as on herbage. The advent of Lent prohibited the eating of meat; before the eighth or ninth centuries, when Ash Wednesday was nominated as the official day that fasting should begin, it had been known to start as soon as fifty or sixty days before Easter, which made a total of approximately two months when no meat was consumed; by Easter the young green would be sprouting, there would be suckling pigs and kids, spring would be there once more. Easter was a complicated festival. Originally one in honour of Eastre, the goddess of spring and dawn, it depended for the date of its celebration on the position of an imaginary moon. It was a subject of constant vexation with the different branches of the Church. Wars and famines could rage, the earth could shake, and still the major concern was the pig-headedness of the beloved brothers in the western outposts, who despite all letters of instruction were at variance with their calculations and kept a different Easter, contrary to paschal numerations.

From a glossary Archbishop Aelfric produced to revive the use of Latin we get a further insight into the life and tastes of the early English. Salt was greatly liked, without it food was considered insipid. Cheese and butter were churned with it; it was eaten with all bread and meat. 'What man', asks the salter, 'enjoys sweet meat without the taste of salt?' Fat was especially valued and it seems vegetables were considered unwholesome unless boiled quite pale. 'If you expel me from your company,' says the cook, 'you'll chew your cabbage green . . . nor can you have fat broth without my art.' This in our over-fed, overweight, sedentary age sounds disgusting; but it must be remembered that such a broth would have been rich and sustaining in days without hot sweet tea and fatty chips, chocolates and toffees, and that the humid chilly climate demanded sustaining, comforting meals, and a heavy fatty diet based on bread and pulses.

Purple palls were imported and silk, precious gems and gold, rare vestments, drugs, oil, ivory, brass, brimstone and glass, dishes sometimes silver, sometimes glass, cinnamon, ginger, myrrh, frankincense, aloes, vermilion and wine. This was drink for the rich; everyone drank ale, sweet ale, sweetened with honey to counteract any sourness in the brewing. All families brewed their own ale, this, like the herb harvest, was woman's work, success depended on individual skill and judgement in assessing the correct temperature of the malt. Ale and bread were essentials of life, their prices were strictly controlled and often they comprised much of the rent a tenant must pay to his lord. In the eleventh century at Hurstbourne Priors for each hide of land they worked the tenants had to pay six church mittans of ale and three sesters of bread and wheat. Estates were passed in favour of people provided they gave to the community each year one day's food. Such a will, in 958, in favour of Aethelyrd stated he should enjoy the estate at a rent of five pounds provided he paid annually forty sesters of ale, sixty loaves, a wether sheep, a flitch of bacon, an ox's haunch, two cheeses and four hens.

And when they died, having lived a life of sin, having enjoyed luxury and the sensual pleasures of food and sex, that dreadful hell awaited them. The battle, the neurosis between the soul and the body, was concluded. This theme of a soul's anger against the sinful body is a common one in Old English poetry. 'Thou wert proud in thy food and glutted with wine ... and I was athirst for the body of God, for spiritual drink,' moans the soul, returning after death to visit its body.

To those early English with their love of warmth, of bright shining things, gaiety and friends, their dread of estrangement, the hell the Church painted could not have been more nightmarish. It was one of icy darkness and isolation: a death filled with oval white shapes, heads hanging crookedly on bodies as though on pieces of string, of dark ravenous earth-worms that stripped the ribs and drank the blood. The body had become a ghastly spectre. 'The head is cleft, hands disjointed, jaws gaping, mouth rent open; sinews are slackened, the neck gnawed through, fingers decayed, feet broken ...'

Now there was no home. The soul, a small pale disc, was buffeted eternally from side to side in a terrible valley. From a dreadful cold, a whirling hail and snow, it was thrown to the blast of white-hot searing heat: ceaseless flames leaping and falling, tongues rising filled with the souls of men flying like sparks high into the air. Eternally. From the whole there exuded a foul stench, there howled lamentations and harsh laughter.

Whither had gone the horse then? Whither had gone the man?

'Whither has gone the giver of treasure? Whither has gone the place of feasting? Where are the joys of hall? Alas, the bright cup! Alas, the warrior in his corselet! Alas, the glory of the prince! How that time has passed away, has grown dark under the shadow of night, as if it had never been!'

CHAPTER FIVE

MEDIAEVAL SUMMER

Woe unto thee, O Land, when thy Princes eat in the morning.

DOCTOR HUNTER OF YORK

I

New Avenues of Satisfaction

The herbs were springing in the vale;
Green ginger plants and liquorice pale
        And cloves their sweetness offered,
With nutmegs too, to put in ale
No matter whether fresh or stale,
        Or else to be kept coffered.

                        Canterbury Tales—CHAUCER
                        (translated by Neville Coghill)

THE ONE real date school leaves in the mind is 1066. That September, when nights were lengthening, days swirling with mist, when there was the smell of brown leaves and yellow quinces, the bellow of red stags in rut, the Normans came. In Normandy there was a land hunger; already large numbers of adventurers had gone to Southern Italy, towards the seductive riches of the East. Now William moved his armies across the thick channel waters to Pevensey and Hastings, and 'at the grey apple tree' fought, slaughtered and conquered quantities of English. It was an aristocratic conquest. William of Normandy had won a kingdom for himself and he distributed the lands of the previous inhabitants among his barons.

Like the Roman villa-system each estate was an economic unit; each tenant was bound to his lord—in the English manner—labouring in his fields in return for his land and his abode.

William's future depended on efficient control of the country. Under each lord there was a garrison, a company of knights, to serve in war and to provide an escort for the baron and his house/ hold as he travelled about the land from one to another of his places.

A holocaust had swept through the island, as it had often done before. But this one was ruthlessly efficient. Like octopi, their slimy arms running into every valley, every homestead, every wood, the Normans went to compile a vast survey—the Domesday Book—their aim to bleed the people and take all the wealth into their own pockets; so very thoroughly did William 'have the inquiry carried out,' the Anglo/Saxon Chronicle relates, 'that there was not a single "hide", not one virgate of land, not even—it is shameful to record . . .—not even one ox, nor one cow, nor one pig which escaped notice in his survey'.

'Alas! how wretched and how unhappy the times were then!' Never had there been so many portents, so many pools seen bubbling with blood, so many black hounds and he/goats careering about, eyes round like saucers, so many famines and pestilences, such thunder and lightning.

One of the bitterest blows the English had to endure was the Law of the Forest. This decreed that in certain forests none but the court should hunt the meat, nor take the greenwood. What seemed particularly unfair was that not everywhere came under this jurisdiction which mostly touched the thick forests en/ circling London; most of Essex was included, and from the Thames passing westerly through the woods of Windsor and Bagshot the trees continued on into the New Forest. Villagers in these environs could do nothing. They could hear the cry of the pheasants echoing down the glades, the plop of the trout as they rose in the quiet water, the hum of the bees, the step of the deer through the undergrowth; but the extra meats, the honey, the acorns for the swine were forbidden. No longer when they had the time and energy could they supplement their rations and their firewood. They could toil only up the fields, graze their cattle on the commons and listen with hate to the sound of the royal hunting horn, the thunder of hooves as the detested William II 'sunken in greed, given up to avarice' galloped down the glades pursued by his long-haired effeminate court, his troupes of catamites and harlots.

Rules, they say, are made to be broken and the Forest Laws were no exception. People of all classes were to be seen abroad—especially on Sundays when they should have been properly at Divine Service—with coloured greyhounds, bows, arrows, mounds of leaves and branches camouflaging the stolen venison. But the penalties were severe; under William II 'whoever slew a hart or a hind was to be blinded'.

The barons filled the land with great stone castles and forced the English to work at their building, hauling the heavy materials up the hills. Their treatment of the people was no better than the Romans'. They behaved with appalling cruelty. Those they believed to have wealth they seized, put them in dungeons with snakes and toads and excruciated them with unspeakable tortures. They levied taxes on the villagers known as 'protection money'. 'When the wretched people had no more to give, they plundered and burned all the villages,' the Anglo-Saxon Chronicle tells us, 'so that you could easily go a day's journey without ever finding a village inhabited or a field cultivated.' Some people were reduced to stealing for a living; were they discovered the penalty was blinding and castration, or, more mercifully, hanging.[1]

Ironically the system under which these knights and barons operated was the Order of Chivalry: a European movement whose functions were to protect the Church, fight against treachery, reverence the priesthood and fend off injustice. Of this, romantic literature presents an idealized and brilliant fiction: knights—with some gallantry—gallop about in flashing armour at tournaments and elsewhere fighting falsehood, upon their sleeves favours from their ladies broadcasting an ideal love never to be consummated; the ladies meanwhile, swathed in crimson, flutter tissues from the walls and swoon. Unfortunately on close examination the tinsel

[1] Some tried forgery as an alternative means of income. But in 1125 all 'moneyers' were ordered to assemble at Winchester. 'When they came thither,' noted the Anglo-Saxon Chronicle, 'they were then taken one by one and each deprived of the right hand and the testicles below. All this was done in the twelve days between Christmas and Epiphany. . . ,'

woven through the myth falls away to reveal some crude truth: greedy, rough, illiterate men who exercised themselves with wars, nuns, eating, drinking and blowing horns; and rather rumpled buxom ladies interfering with swarthy labourers in the hedge.[1] As for the ideal love, according to Alexander Neckham—whose mother had the doubtful pleasure of simultaneously giving suck to Richard I with her right breast and Alexander with her left— wives were constantly palming bastards off upon their husbands; a crowd of lovers or pigs—from the manuscript evidently it is not clear which (*porcorum* or *procorum*)—would pursue them 'hotly standing over, urging their suit, sweating and swearing': an affair that sounds anything but ideal especially were the suitors swine.

But these gallants made one startling if oblique impact upon the western kitchens. They re-established, for the rich, a luxurious classical cuisine which lasted more or less unchanged until the seventeenth century. Great numbers attached the sign of the cross to their sleeves and departed towards the East in search of Crusades and adventure; for the miserable peasants it was an opportunity to escape from their lords and their grim, impoverished homes; eager not only for the slaughter of the unfaithful and the liberation of the Holy Land they were hungry for the riches they supposed to abound, the pavements lined with gold, the 'odiferous groves

[1] Matters did not improve as the Middle Ages drew on. One discovers appalling accounts in the chronicles. In 1379 Sir John Arundel, Marshal of England, who owned 'two and fiftie new sutes of apparell of cloth of gold or tissue', was due, with his company, to set sail for France. However, first on account of financial difficulties and then contrary winds he was delayed for some months. In spite of the head begging him to desist he billeted his men in a convent of virgin nuns where, inspired it is thought by the devil, his company burst into the cloister and ran amok among the rooms violating various daughters and maidens of the neighbourhood as they sat awaiting their morning lessons. From these the chivalrous company moved on to ravish some widows, and finished the exercise by leaping upon the nuns also. After this, encouraged by the brave Sir John Arundel, they pillaged the countryside, carrying off the plate from the altar of the church, for which they were excommunicated. Undaunted they set sail, carrying with them a number of lamenting and groaning widows and erstwhile virgins from the abbey. A dreadful storm blew up and they threw everything, women and all, overboard. The ships were driven before the storm to the coast of Ireland, whereupon Sir John's sank, together with Sir John and all his finery.

of cinnamon and frankincense', the milk and honey, gold and diamonds. Dazzled, they set forth. And a very extraordinary sight they must have looked, more like a travelling gypsy encampment than a brave army, supporting ovens, forges, cornmills, boats for fishing and falcons, hawks, hounds, and coursing dogs for sport en route; their beasts, said Peter of Blois, were 'laden not with steel but with wine, not with spears but with cheeses, not with swords but with wine-skins, not with javelins but with spits. You would think they were on their way to feast, and not to fight.'

To the citizens of Constantinople they appeared rough and unruly brigands. Their behaviour as they passed to the Holy Land—encouraged by visions of white-horsed knights waving white banners—was despicable. They ravaged and plundered in the name of Christ. After each battle the soldiers were given licence to sack the cities, and the slaughter they accomplished was often incredible. 'You could not walk on the streets,' wrote Steven Runciman of the capture of Antioch, 'without treading on corpses, all of them rotting rapidly away in the summer heat.' Sometimes food shortage and famine was so great the Christian soldiers were obliged to roast and devour their unfaithful captives. Among the Turks and the Saracens they gained the reputation of odious cannibals; when spies infiltrated to their kitchens they were shown several bodies turning on a pit. To the Arabs their conduct was barbarous: they amused themselves by setting old women to run after greased pigs.

If the spiritual advantages of the Crusades appear dubious, the material ones are evident. To the rapacious pilgrims the cleaner, better built towns of the East gave an appearance of opulence. They and the Frankish settlers could buy silk garments, indulge in scents and spices in a way that only the very rich had done in Western Europe. When they returned home they introduced many of the improvements they had seen into their houses; trade increased, especially the demand for Eastern goods: dyes, scented woods, silks, porcelains and spices from the Arab world—cinnamon, cardamom, musk, mace, cloves, galingale and nutmeg. Besides these newly accessible corridors to delight the oral senses, Dr. Dingwall claims that the Crusaders discovered in the vicinity of the Holy Land another avenue to sexual satisfaction. They returned, he said, with Sodomy.

2

Manners and Mealtimes

They fetched him first the sweetest wine,
Then mead in mazers they combine
　　With lots of royal spice,
And gingerbread, exceeding fine,
And liquorice and eglantyne
　　And sugar, very nice.
Canterbury Tales—CHAUCER

For the rich, mediaeval life was a curious mixture of astonishing splendour and hospitality, and dreadful squalor. The castles were draughty and uncomfortable, their inhabitants doing the best they could to disguise cold stone, primitive drains and privy seats with brilliant cloths that shone vivid like painted glass.

It is possible to reconstruct their lives and surroundings from the old account books. We see Bishop Swinfield of Hereford at the head of his all-male household with his chain of retainers, his huntsmen, larderers, falconers, porters, bakers, farriers, threshers, carters, sumpturers and sumpturers' boys. Proceeding through the year from one estate to the next, passing in through the silent gates and walls of the empty manors carrying their pots and pans, linen and food stores; fishing in the ponds and rivers through their duration, hunting in the forests, drawing from the farms. The accounts show they did not go short of food. At the end of October one finds all the great households—the Dowager Countess of Pembroke in Goodrich Castle, Eleanor de Montfort and the Bishop—at work slaughtering, salting and curing, making up their larders, not so much against the winter as the great feast of Christmas. Venison was soused in vinegar, nutmeg, cloves and mace and covered with butter; the tripes and offal were pickled in ale for spiced umble-pie,[1] the tallow turned to candles, the hides to leather, the fruit dried and preserved. Each item, no matter whether it came from the farms, the markets, the herb garden, from hunting or from the larder, was carefully entered in the accounts, its consumption noted. Nothing that entered the kitchens went unmarked. Royal children, like Henry de Bray the small son of Edward I, often had their own castles. Henry reigned at the centre of a splendid household, surrounded by his retainers, his nurses, cooks, butlers and chamberlain. He had a fine new walled herb garden built in 1297 for sixty-two shillings and fourpence; a new dove-house, white-washed pigsties and fowl-houses, sheepfolds, granaries and a bake-house together with a splendid kitchen and a grand fountain, costing forty-one shillings, which played outside the door. But Henry was a sickly child, always falling ill. His parents were busy and often abroad, they paid him visits when they could and sent him presents. In his last illness his mother sent him a white palfrey; the surrounding countryside was ransacked by his servants for herbs to make restoring and healing conconctions; masses and prayers were said, but to no avail. Henry never rode the white palfrey, never lived to enjoy his fountain, the voices of his doves, the aromatic scents of his herb garden. He died at the age of seven.

The attitude towards children in general was unsentimental. At an early age they were sent away to other people's establishments on the pretext that they learnt manners and individuality. Andrea Trevisano, however, visiting England in 1497 had a different opinion as to the motives which lay behind the English scheme:

> . . . I, for my part, believe that they do it because they like to enjoy all their comforts themselves, and that they are better served by strangers than they would be by their own children. Besides which the English being great epicures, and very avaricious by nature, indulge in the most delicate fare

---

[1] Umble-pie originally was made from the 'umbles' of the deer—the heart, liver, tongue, feet, palates, kidneys, brain and ears. Later on umble-pies incorporated other meats. They were economical and practical compositions. Stewing beef, kidney, liver, heart, brains and oysters were contained inside shortcrust pastry, likewise fat bacon and rabbit together with its offal, or hare. Alternatively mutton and pork, in which case often the pie included a layer of fruit—apples or rowan berries—laid below the pastry lid.

themselves and give their household the coarsest bread and beer, and cold meat baked on Sunday for the week, which however they allow them in great abundance that if they had their own children at home, they would be obliged to give them the same food as they made use of themselves . . .

Before they left home and as soon as they were able they must busy themselves round the castle. They were instructed not to run in heaps like a swarm of bees, but to salute their parents reverently and, if they were big enough, to bring the food to the table, but not to fill the dishes so as to spill over the parents' clothes or the parents would be angry. And when the meal was finished they must clear away, cover the salt, serve the wine, fold the tablecloth, spread the towel and sweep the crumbs.

The manners of both children and adults seem to have been the cause of some concern. Etiquette books were written to try and check the worst faults. 'Let not they privy members be lay'd open to be view'd,' warns the *Booke of Demeanor*, 'it is most shameful and abhorr'd, detestable and rude.'

There were cautions not to scrape while at table, scrub or claw your dog, your head or your back; not to prowl round your head searching for lice. You were not to pick your nose, 'or let it drop', blow it on the tablecloth, or too loud lest your sovereign heard. Neither were you recommended to put your hands in your hosen 'your codware for to claw', and if 'thou sit by a right good man . . . under his thigh thy knee not fit'. You were not to use your mouth to squirt or to spout, put your tongue into a dish to pick the dust out, belch or hiccup. Above all you must always 'beware of thy hinder part from guns blasting'. Ladies were particularly recommended not to let men put their hands into their breasts, or to kiss them on the mouth as it might lead to greater familiarities. Often it was the custom to share trenchers[1] of food at the table in which case ladies were further recommended to turn the nicest bits towards the gentleman, and not to go picking out the finest and largest for themselves. No doubt many,

[1] A trencher could be made either of wood, or pieces of four-day-old bread which were pared smooth and cut into thick squares by the pantler. Probably the English custom of serving various dishes such as mushrooms, herring roes, tinned spaghetti and beans on toast roots from the bread trenchers.

unlike Chaucer's Madam Eglantyne, dipped their fingers too deep in the sauce and splashed themselves and their neighbours. Forks were not common until the seventeenth century; indeed during the Middles Ages there were those like Isaac D'Israeli who viewed their use as heresy: 'God in his wisdom has provided man with natural forks, it is considered impious to substitute them by metallic artificial forks when eating.'

The lord of the manor was looked after like a child, literally waited upon hand and foot by the chamberlain acting as a nanny. His duties were to brush his lord carefully, beat his feather-bed, keep his 'privy-house for easement' clean and sweet, hand him his clothes well warmed in the morning while his master sat upon a cushioned chair. When the lord wished to go to bed, his shoes, socks and breeches were pulled off, he was set upon his footsheet while the nice chamberlain combed his head, put on his nightcap, drew the curtains and drove out the dogs and the cats. Should the lord require a bath there was a tremendous commotion; sheets full of herbs were suspended round the room, while the lord sat and leaned on several sponges and was washed with a basinful of hot herbs and rinsed with rose-water.

Before he could sit up to dinner there were ceremonies. There was the ceremony of washing which involved basins, pots, napkins, aromatic waters and a great deal of gliding about and conveying towels and tablecloths, getting them absolutely smooth, folding them precisely a foot this way, a foot that. 'Bow when you leave your lord. Cough not nor spit . . .' conclude the instructions. If the lord was of royal blood then there was the ceremony of testing the food for poison. Each cornet of bread must be dipped thrice into the dish under assay, flourished thrice over the head of the server then put to the lips of the chief officers. Next, each dish was covered, more to keep the poison out than the heat in, while the pantler watched lest an intruder should creep in and make off with one of the dishes.

There is the scene of the mediaeval feast. The low tables along the sides of the hall, the high one along the top laid ready by the pantler with the well-washed spoons, the bright knives, the sweet, clean linen, the trenchers pared, smoothed and squared, the before-

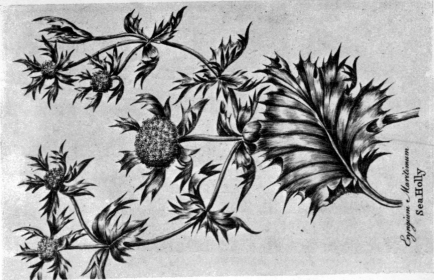

Eryngium Maritimum
SeaHolly

(*left*) Leaf from Nicholas Culpeper's *Herbal* showing the Dwarf May Thistle —the tender young stalks of the thistle were eaten in the spring with butter, like asparagus

(*right*) The Eringoe or Sea Holly's Root was supposed to hold erotic properties and was often eaten candied
Culpeper's 'Herbal'

Polycantha Acaulos
Dwarf May Thistle

6A. Illumination from the Queen Mary Psalter showing how a hungry dog was used to harvest the mandrake

6B. Swineherds knocking down apples for their hogs. *Queen Mary Psalter*

6C. Illumination from the Luttrell Psalter showing oxen and ploughmen tilling the fields

7A. Sickling and Binding Corn. *Luttrell Psalter*

7B. A lady feeding her tethered hen and their young. *Luttrell Psalter*

7C. A horse rake. It is interesting to note that the horse and the four oxen in plate 6C appear to be plump and well-covered. *Luttrell Psalter*

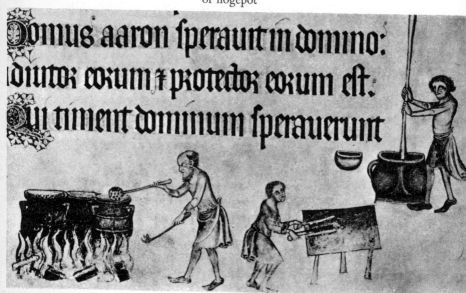

8A. Part of a medieval cookery manuscript, attributed to the late fifteenth century (*Peniarth, 394 from the National Library of Wales*), showing a recipe for gees in hotchpot, or hogepot

8B. The great iron pots in which the puddings were boiled, the hotchpots and pottages bubbled. Here three cooks are at work: one is pounding herbs and meat fine in a pestle and mortar, one is "smiting" the joints into pieces and one is tasting to see whether his seasoning needs adjusting. *Luttrell Psalter*

8C. Here the carver is "unlacing" the cony, which is then taken to the next table where his assistant adds the correct sauce before the dishes are conveyed away to the tables by servitors. *Luttrell Psalter*

dinner apéritif waiting, according to the season, of plums, damsons, cherries or grapes. The great fire smoking in the centre of the hall, attacking one side only of the feasters, draughts whistling behind, the candles, the mutton-fat rush-lights spattering up suddenly to illuminate the grease shining on flushed faces, or a lady surreptitiously about to wipe her nose upon the tablecloth; the colours of the clothes[1]—the crimsons, the scarlets, the powdered ermines, the yellows and the green silks; the dogs glaring under the tables; the pages and servers tripping over bones and loose rushes and between the courses scratching, spitting and searching for fleas and lice; the minstrels singing against the dogs' crunching of bones, or 'the sharp cry of some ill-bred falcon for many lords at dinner kept their favourite birds on a perch behind them'. The floors cannot have been very hygienic what with the dogs and birds and 'the harbouring there below' of spit, vomit and urine together with beer and the remnants of fishes from which in the opinion of Erasmus 'a vapour exhales which in my judgement is far from wholesome for the human body'.

Mediaeval people had large appetites. Theirs was a vigorous life of open air and exercise, they were unafraid to consume large mounds of food. And consume them they did, mainly all at one meal of the day: dinner which was celebrated in the morning between eleven and midday. Then later they would enjoy a supper of wine, ale and spiced cakes.

Mediaeval food, like Roman, is supposed to have been un-palatable, the recipes uncookable and uneatable. The scholars seem to have envisaged putrid messes made of curious lumps resembling vomit, writhing upon every trencher. Much of this view is an emotional one. We have come to believe it because it

[1] Husbands were inclined to dress themselves and their wives richly to enhance their prestige and display evidence of their wealth. In 'The Parson's Tale' Chaucer describes the gentlemen's dress as being rather odd—padded shoulders, high collars, long pointed shoes and hose so skin tight that 'the wretched swollen membres' departed their hosen in white and red so that it 'semeth that half hir shameful privee membres were flaine'. Sometimes they departed their hosen in other colours as well, white and blue, white and black, or black and red, in which case it seemeth that the privy membres were corrupted by St. Anthony's fire. As for the other side of their hosen, it was horrible to see, 'eke the buttokkes' were as 'the hinder part of a she ape in the ful of the mone'.

has been stated firmly as truth for the last two hundred years. Much of it is exaggerated. Mediaeval recipes and cooking techniques are of course based on the Roman; from them we can see how our English tradition had evolved from the Mediterranean, and how most of the contemporary terms derived from either the Latin or the old French. There were the same sweet and sour combinations, again very like Creole and Eastern dishes, the same techniques with honey, herbs and spices; the same forced meats, custards, stews and spiced glazed joints, farinaceous pottages, peas boiled with bacon, liaisons of ground nuts and savoury puddings roasted or boiled in cauls; and the delicious piquant sauces from which emanate our well-known bread- and mint-sauce. As Jeaffreson said: 'The cuisine of feudal England was Roman in its principles and details ... The mediaeval broths, brewets and mortrews were the pultes, patinae and minutalia of the more ancient cuisine.'

Until the end of the fourteenth century culinary detail is frag-mented. There is the story narrated by Peter of Blois of how William the Conqueror, who could not bear tough meat, was one day so outraged by the opposition of a half-roasted crane that he was about to strike his favourite cook when a friend stepped in and diverted the ghastly blow. Descriptions of the food served in the twelfth century at the Court of Henry II are not encouraging. There, evidently, it was quantity rather than quality. Henry was a patron of the arts, his halls were packed and many scholars and poets were to be seen, but the quality of the ale and dinner was so frightful that people dreaded attending. The bread was hastily made from the yeast in the ale-tub, the wine served so sour and muddy 'that a man need close his eyes, and clench his teeth, wry-mouthed and shuddering, and filtering the stuff rather than drinking. There, also, such is the concourse of people that sick and whole beasts are sold at random, with fishes even four days old; yet shall not all this corruption and stench abate one penny of the price; for all the servants reck not whether an unhappy guest fall sick and die, so that their lords' tables be served with a multitude of dishes; thus we who sit at meat needs fill our bellies with carrion, and become graves ... for sundry corpses.'

So unappetizing are the viands in this picture that the worst fears of the scholars would seem to be justified. But the fact that Peter of Blois finds this scene unusual enough to describe argues that such low-quality fare was not common. And we find Henry's chaplain, Giraldus Cambrensis, noting with disapproval the excellence of the 'sixteen very costly dishes' set before him by the monks during his visit to Canterbury. So substantial was the dinner there that when the pot-herbs were finally brought in they were 'little tasted. For you might see so many kinds of fish, roast, boiled, stuffed and fried, so many sauces contrived with eggs and pepper by dexterous cooks, so many flavourings and condiments, compounded with like dexterity to tickle gluttony and awaken appetite.'

Alexander Neckham writing from St. Albans, about ten years after Henry's death, transcribes very simple recipes: pork was to be roasted, or broiled on red embers requiring no sauce but salt and garlic; capon was to be well peppered; goose roasted on a spit and served with garlic sauce mixed with a little verjuice; fish was simmered in wine and water and strewn with herbs and garlic. There is no mention here of spices—St. Albans apparently kept a plain table—but by the middle of the thirteenth century the returning Crusaders carried back eastern influences, and spices are prominent in the store cupboards and account books of rich housekeepers like Eleanor de Montfort, whose lists show ginger, cinnamon, cloves, galingale, mace, nutmegs, cubebs, coriander and cummin.

By the end of the fourteenth century we see from an elaborate manuscript roll—'The Forme of Cury'—compiled by the cooks of Richard II, that for those who could afford it a sophisticated standard of cooking had been gained.

The court of Richard II was European. England formed part of Europe; her habits, manners and cooking were similar to both the French and the Italian; her houses were filled with rich hostages from the French wars who lived as honoured guests surrounded by their personal servants. The spoken language was French, the written Latin; people kissed when they met and departed. The court was at the heart of England, the throbbing centre of patronage, art, learning, knowledge and ambition; to find favour with the king was the only means of self-advancement, a good attendance at court won rewards. The standard of royal meals, hospitality to foreign ambassadors and other travellers of note, had to be advertisements of the prosperity, politeness and stability of the king and his country. Richard held the reputation of a gourmet, his guests it was said were well entertained; as many as ten thousand would come daily to eat at his board, to serve them two thousand cooks were employed and three hundred henchmen.

Mealtimes of the rich were not only for the purposes of feeding; they were remedies against ennui, long successions of dishes punctuated with entertainments, parties offering opportunity to meet people. Mealtimes were vehicles in which to parade the host's wealth and benevolence. Furthermore it was not only the king who advertised his prosperity. As early as the reign of Edward II the government had tried to take measures against extravagant spending. Sumptuary laws[1] were passed to prevent excess in banquets, dress and private expenditure. Statute 10 in the reign of Edward III, chapter 3, records that 'through the excessive and over-many costly meats which the people of this realm have used more than elsewhere many mischiefs have happened; for the great men by these excesses have been sore grieved, and the lesser people, who only endeavour to imitate the great ones in such sorts of meat, are much impoverished . . . no man, of whatever condition or estate, shall be allowed more than two courses at dinner or supper, or more than two kinds of food in each course, except on principal festivals of the year, when three courses at the utmost are to be allowed'.

From all accounts these laws do not seem to have been taken too seriously. Of all principal festivals Christmas was the great set-piece of the year stretching over several days; it was the climax of all the housekeepers' autumn preparations: the Christmas pies were baked; the pork, the pickled umbles, the neats' tongues were enclosed in elaborate paste coffins;[2] the spiced fruit mixtures were preserved in wine and ale; the boar's head had been smoked

---

[1] Shades of these laws still remain in the taxation of our luxury goods such as tobacco, spirits and wine.
[2] Mediaeval term for pastry cases.

and glazed, or enforced and endored; the chickens, capons, peacocks, game and small birds from the forest had been roasted, or inserted one into the other for the famous Grete Pye; the swans had been upped, slaughtered, enclosed in paste and baked, and now everyone could sit down and enjoy themselves. No less delicious was the rejoicing at Easter, when the brown stretch of Lent had been done and everything was a new green once more. In the year 1290 at Bishop Swinfield's great Easter Feast at Colwell an enormous amount of food vanished down the relieved abstainers' throats: one fresh ox and three quarters of a fresh beef, one and a half carcasses of salt beef (from this it can be seen that salt meat was no less esteemed than fresh), one bacon, three boar, four and a half calves, twenty-two kids, four pigs, eighteen capons, one hundred and fifty-six pigeons. But greatest and most tremendous of all are the marriage and engagement feasts to mark arrangements of convenience and mutual cunning on the part of the brides' and bridegrooms' families. Stories of these jump out of the past—massive, glistening, malodorous occasions; how thirty thousand dishes were served at the marriage feast of Richard, Henry III's brother; how the meats that were brought to the banquet of the Duke of Clarence—one of Edward III's sons—would have served ten thousand men. Not only did the host bear the cost of all the food, but also of the presents which he must apportion between the courses. This, when one considers that at the banquet of the Duke of Clarence there were thirty courses, must have been colossal. Between two courses alone seventy horses clattered in to be distributed, adorned with silk and silver furniture; between two others, silver vessels, falcons, hounds, armour for horses, coats of mail, breast-plates, glittering steel helmets and corselets, jewels, purple cloth and cloths of gold were administered. Henry V at his coronation feast, undaunted by freezing weather and falling snow, had the conduit of Palace Yard running with claret and Rhine wine; inside the hall armoured and plumed marshals and heralds rode astride horses controlling the guests, while the food was served by mounted officers of state, who, requiring both hands to hold the dishes, left nothing with which to steer their chargers.

To construct a picture of the food and atmosphere at one of these feasts one has only to look down the great lists of food and consult the recipes.

In October of 1399 the following feast of three courses was served on the occasion of the first marriage of Henry IV. The menu was written in a mixture of French and early English and it will be seen that there are comparatively few made dishes.[1]

Course 1

Braun[2] en peuerade	—slices of meat cooked in a spiced sweet and sour sauce
Viaund Ryal	—a purée of rice and mulberries sweetened with honey, flavoured with wine and spices
Test de senglere enarmez	—boar's head and tusks
Graunde chare	—a large piece of roasted meat
Syngnettys	—cygnets
Capoun de haute grece	—capon which has been crammed in the same manner as the foie gras geese
Fesaunte	—pheasants
Heroun	—herons
Crustarde Lumbarde	—a pie made from cream, eggs, dates, prunes and sugar
Storieoun, graunt luces	—sturgeon and great pike
Subtlety	

Course 2

Venyson en furmenty	—a famous dish of venison served with a spiced gruel of cream and wheat and eggs
Gely	—calves' foot jelly with white wine and vinegar
Porcelle farce enforce	—stuffed sucking pigs
Pokokkys	—peacocks served in their plumage
Cranys	—cranes
Venyson roste	—roast venison
Conyng	—rabbits over a year old
Byttore	—bitterns
Pulle endore	—glazed chicken
Graunt tartez	—great pies of meat, game and poultry
Braun fryez	—fritters of meat
Leche lumbard	—small spiced cakes of dates originating in Lombardy
Subtlety	

[1] See Appendix II, pages 247–252, for the made dishes listed here.
[2] During the Middle Ages the word 'brawn' means flesh. Only later does it become particular to pork meats.

Course 3

Blaundesorye	—an almond and chicken mousse
Quyncys in comfyte	—quinces preserved in syrup
Egretez	—a kind of heron
Curlewys	—curlews
Pertrych	—partridges
Pyionys	—pigeons
Quaylys	—quails
Snytys	—snipe
Rabettys	—young rabbits
Smal byrdys	—small birds
Pome Dorreng	—rissoles of pork roasted on a spit, basted with spices and herbs to make a spicy crust
Braun blanke leche	—meat in a white sauce
Eyroun engele	—eggs in jelly
Frytourys	—fritters
Doucettys	—custard tarts
Pety perneux	—small spiced tarts of eggs, cream and raisins
Subtlety	

As can be seen from the list, at the end of each course a subtlety was presented. These were moulded devices, often of great complexity, made from sugar and almond paste. There could be brightly coloured sylvan and hunting scenes, or religious motives—interiors of abbey churches with a multitude of altars, the Virgin and Child with St. George and St. Denis kneeling on either side—or fully armed ships with the barons of the cinque ports aboard, or more modestly there were doctors of law, eagles and tigers looking into mirrors.

Of course, rich and royal feasts such as Henry IV's marriage celebrations are not representative. The meat ration as we have seen was supplemented whenever possible by pigeons from dove-cotes, especially fattened barnyard poultry and encooped partridges, game and small birds. The peasantry lived—like the Saxon—on what they could produce from the land and glean from the hedges: herbs, legumes, cereals, eggs and white meats, gruels and porridges made from oats. Barley and wheat together with coarse bread formed their bulk; bread was made largely with bran for although the peasant grew his own corn he had to pay the miller to have it milled. Millers were shrewd, often dishonest men, like Chaucer's, who was 'a master hand at stealing grain', feeling it with his thumb and taking three times his due.

Ordinary rather impoverished people like Oxford and Cam bridge scholars generally lived on a plain, somewhat dull diet and not too much either for, says William Nelson's fifteenth-century school book, 'it is selde sean that they which ffyll their belys overmych be disposede to their bookys'. It was a gala day for the one who 'suppyde yesternyght with sum of my cuntreymenn wher we faryde well, for beside rostyde chekyns and other grosse disshes we were servede with swanys, pococks, venson, which is not accordynge for scholars to be servede with such delicate disshes . . .'; and again 'after oure frumenty, we were servede with gose, pige, capoun, pococke, crane, swane and such other delicates that longeth to a goode feste'. As for butcher's meat: 'I have no delyte in beffe and motyn and such daily metes. I wolde onys have a partridge set before us, or sum other such . . .'

At the end of each winter, stock was carefully examined to see which cow was barren and weak, which sheep; which ox could no longer pull the plough. They were then put out to pasture through the summer, to grow fat and soft on the new grass, the tender young shoots of gorse growing up through the burnt, prepared ground, until slaughter time at Martinmas. Swine at all time—unless a sow was in trouble farrowing—rootled and foddered for themselves. At slaughter time the meat was salted, then either hung up in the smoke to cure—beef, mutton and pork hams and bacons—or it was stored away in great tubs.[1]

Meat both raw and cooked—sold from the cook shop—was surprisingly cheap. Prices were strictly controlled through the mediaeval scheme of Just Price—a precaution instigated by the

---

[1] This system is still used in Iceland, where each winter the snow creates mediaeval conditions with the difficulty in communications, the lack of fodder and storage space, so that each farm must be a self-sufficient unit. Every autumn, Loftur Johannson told me, the meat is cut up into large joints, put into air-tight barrels and packed in thick layers of salt. It is stored inside the house, and, depending on how well it has been salted, can last through the winter. It is eaten served in soup with beans, or it is boiled and dished with a cream sauce, potatoes and carrots. It is, according to Loftur Johannson, extremely delicious.

Church permitting no man to make more than a bare living from the sale of his produce and merchandise. Because of a lack of cooking facilities many of the poorer townspeople would buy ready cooked meat from the cook shops; the following lists show that cooks were allowed to charge only a penny for the trouble of enclosing a capon or a rabbit in a crust, and that cooked meats were only slightly more expensive than raw.

Cooked meats 1378
Best roast pig 8d, best roast goose 7d, best roast capon 6d, hen 4d, river mallard 4½d, dunghill mallard 3½d, 5 roast larks 1½d, woodcock 2½d, partridge 3d, plover 2½d, pheasant 13d, curlew 6½d, 3 roast thrushes 2d, 10 roast finches 1d, best roast heron 18d, bittern 20d, 3 roast pigeons 2½d, 10 eggs 2d
In pastry capon 8d, hen 5d.

Raw meats 1383
goose 6d, capon 6d, pullet 2d, rabbit 4d, river mallard 3d, dunghill mallard 2d, woodcock 3d, partridge 4d, plover 3d, pheasant 12d, curlew 6d, 12 thrushes 6d, 12 finches 1d, heron 16d, bittern 18d, 12 pigeons 8d.

Comparatively, swan was one of the most expensive meats, not available in the ordinary cook shops and selling in 1380 at three shillings and fourpence a bird. It is interesting that there is no mention of beef or mutton on these lists, which proves that these were not so much valued for food as for their living powers of draught, wool and dairy produce.

The authorities did their best to keep up the standard and quality of food. Just as in these days there were prosecutions. But whereas in the hygienic year of 1956 there were 2,019 instances reported of selling bad meat, in 1366 there seems only to have been one: John Russell at Billingsgate was prosecuted for exposing for sale thirty-seven pigeons 'putrid, rotten, stinking and abominable' to the human race. He was duly sentenced to the pillory and the pigeons were burnt beneath him. This, which was the standard practice against such malefactors, could, depending on the mood of the crowd, be more than a mere degradation. Criers would announce when anyone was going to be exhibited in the pillory and people would assemble armed with baskets of bad eggs, decaying vegetables, balls and rocks. As soon as the prisoner was locked into the pillory the hangman had to start running to escape the fusilade. Rich prisoners paid for someone to wipe their faces clean with a cloth on a long pole, for it was possible to suffocate under the wealth of decomposed matter.

Usually meat and fish were not enjoyed at the same meal; fishdays and fleshdays were set apart from one another. It is not generally recognized to what extent fish featured in the mediaeval diet; in fact throughout the Middle Ages more of it was eaten than meat. This was on account of the numerous fishdays decreed by the Church, which numbered through the year more than fleshdays. In every week Tuesday, Friday and Saturday were fishdays, together with all the ember days and all the days through Lent. There were special dinners listed for fishday feasts and many recipes given for meat could be adapted by inserting fish, milk or almonds in its place. Even inland a great variety of fish was available. Bishop Swinfield's household in Hereford consumed, according to the accounts, salmon, sturgeon, red and white herrings, cod, haddock, hake, gurnet, ling, plaice, mackerel, barr, shad, sprats, stockfish, eels, bream, pike, tench, trout, minnows, perch, dace, roach, gudgeon, lampreys. At Coulsdon in Surrey excavations have discovered in the kitchen areas great quantities of oyster and mussel shells. But for those with uninspired cooks, like the poor fifteenth-century scholar, Lent must have become very monotonous: 'Thou wyll not beleve how wery I am off fysshe,' he complains, 'and how much I desir that flesch wer cum in ageyn, for I have ete non other but salt fysshe this Lent . . .'

3

Spices, Strong Words and Beer for Breakfast

> O gluttony, it is to thee we owe
> Our griefs!
>
> *Canterbury Tales*—CHAUCER

The English haute cuisine, as we have seen, was European, originating from the Classical Roman source. Consulting the Italian and French cookery books of the period we find the same recipes, the same ingredients: the rich light pastry crusts for pies, from which emanated the Italian pastas, the English pasties and suet paste; the same savoury white jellies—almond and meat mousses—called *blamangers*,[1] which only later turn to sweet puddings; the meat and game pies, the broths, pottages and *soppes* (from which soup, 'broth wherein there is a store of sops or sippets', emanated); the *mortrews* and *ryschewys* (forcemeat balls), *crustades*, *doucetes* (sweetmeats), *frittours*, *garbures*, sauces, possets, *viaunds* and *charlottes*; the *herbelades* (minced herb tarts), nut custards and cakes, the *compostes* (afterwards the French compôte, salads of fruit or vegetables), the *civeys* (delicious piquant stews) and above all the excellent sauces, of which the *pièce de résistance* is a *sauce verte*, comprising bread, vinegar, chopped sage, mint, garlic, thyme and parsley—a cross between bread- and mint-sauce—excellent under baked eggs or mixed with grapes for pigeon.

'Woe to the cook whose sauces had no sting,' said Chaucer, and many of our appetizing pungent sauces still survive: horse-radish, which was originally gathered from roots growing wild in the hedges, mustard, caper and all the fruit jellies, mixtures again of the sweet and the sour. Verjuice was served at the most refined tables. This was the juice of any sour fruit or vegetable: sorrel, gooseberries, crab-apples, apples and rowan-berries. Less refined tables used the solid vegetable or fruit as accompaniment, hence the familiar redcurrant jellies, and gooseberry and sorrel sauces.

[1] See Appendix II, page 250.

The system is a world-wide one. All meats are improved by the
addition of fruit and combinations may be found in all national
cookery—cherries and pineapple with pork from America, duck
with orange from France, melon with ham from Italy, and so on.
The list is endless.

Joints of meat and poultry and rabbit were filled with savoury
stuffings, strewn with herbs and spices and basted so that a crisp
crust formed. Sometimes the sauce was served in the same way
that we serve mashed potatoes, chicken or meat was accompanied
by a purée of bread flavoured with stock, mixed with grapes, or
raisins or green herbs. Pottages and broths were simmered in
great cauldrons, the meat being removed by huge flesh-hooks.
There were spiced quince pies, syrups, date puddings, eggs
poached and served with the delicious *sauce verte*; fillets of steak
were stuffed with parsley, egg yolks and onions, and roasted in
a herb crust on a spit and glazed with honey; there were roasted
veal balls, apple, sage-leaf, parsnip, vine-leaf and elderflower
fritters, pancakes sprinkled with sugar, chops baked with nuts,
small birds wrapped in vine-leaves. New white cheese was
whipped up with eggs and served with sugar; mushrooms were
simmered with leeks; chickens and pork were garnished with
roses, primroses and violets, gilded with saffron, or dyed blue
with heliotrope. Flowers were used a great deal, together with
their essences, for flavouring or colouring dishes. There are
recipes for hawthorn-bud puddings, primrose, violet and rose
pies. Comforting dishes were served: white bread with a sauce of
cream and egg yolks, flavoured with nutmeg and cinnamon,
perhaps a few raisins and sprinkled with sugar—a cross between
bread and butter pudding and bread and milk.

The kitchens clanked with well-buckets drawing up the spring
waters, echoed with the sound of chopping and pounding, were
redolent with the aromatic smells of fresh-pounded spices, fresh-
roasted joints. The Luttrell Psalter shows among the roasters one
who might better be termed a *toaster*; habited in a rag round his
middle he exposes his meat to the flames at the end of a utensil
the length of a hayfork. Small boys or dogs rotated the spits
slowly before the great oak logs. They were poor beasts, the most

wretched of creatures; dejected and abused they were kicked around the kitchens and ran to turn the spit with a live coal at their heels.

Mediaeval people loved marrow; Chaucer's cook stood alone 'for boiling chicken with a marrow bone, sharp flavouring pow-der and a spice for savour'. He could roast and seethe and boil and fry, make good thick soup and bake a tasty pie. In many of the patties and pies, suet was used for the pastry instead of butter; it was also used as a lubrication inside the pie. White sauce had not been invented, the most usual liaisons were achieved by employing almonds or breadcrumbs, cream and eggs, or blood, for fine-ground flour was a luxury. Puddings during the Middle Ages were either enclosed in intestines, like our sausages, or in cauls and bladders, like haggis, or cooked inside the beast itself; it was only later they removed into cloths. Many of the very com-plicated dishes were only curiosities to be set before the court and king as illustrations of the cook's skill, not to be undertaken by ordinary people. 'There is too much to do,' says the 'Goodman of Paris' about one intricate dish which involves inflating a chicken, removing the flesh, filling it with another meat and colouring it, 'it is not the work for a citizen's cook, nor even a simple knight's.'

Each region specialized in the foods that the local soil could produce best. In Pontefract[1] there was liquorice, saffron came from Saffron Walden; lampreys were baked in a special way at Worcester; mountain sheep were served with rowan-berry jelly and the aromatic herbs on which they had grazed, those from the salt-marshes were eaten with laver, or samphire salad; herrings along the shores were caught and smoked over oak chips; snails were simmered in the Cotswolds; pork and geese were dressed with apples from the orchards where they had rooted; from the lush green valleys and the yellow cream of Devon came White

---

[1] Besides its liquorice fields Pontefract benefited from another attraction. Thomas of Lancaster's felt hat was housed in a shrine to which many penitents flocked on pilgrimage. The shrine was one of many that during the Middle Ages were centres of thriving businesses, receiving thousands of people who, hoping for absolution, endured long and tiresome journeys in order to visit in addition to the holy relics at Pontefract such devotionals as the body of Thomas Beckett at Canterbury and Simon de Montfort's foot at Alnwick Abbey.

Pot;[1] and everywhere there were warming dishes of dried peas and beans, greedy for pork and goose fat. They had different names in different regions: in Staffordshire they were known as Blanks and Prizes and were eaten with small lumps of bacon, in Northumberland there was a special Lenten dish of peas, called Carlings.

In Bedfordshire and Hertfordshire black cherries grew wild and abundantly in the fields; when these were ripe they were gathered in great purple-stained baskets for black cherry pasty feasts. In Kent it was the custom to go holidaying at Easter to eat pudding-pies and drink cherry beer. The pies were the size of a teacup, flat, made with a raised crust and lightly sprinkled with currants. All down the road to Canterbury travellers would stop 'to taste the pudding-pies'. In Hereford it was the method to make Simnel cakes during Christmas, Lent and Easter. They were hard raised cakes, made from a paste of simnella flour, water and saffron, filled with a very stiff, very rich, plum cake mixture tied up in a cloth and boiled for several hours. By the seventeenth century it became fashionable for young people in Gloucestershire to carry Simnels to their mothers on Mothering Sunday. Often the crust emerged from the cloth as hard as wood. One lady, story tells us, not evidently in the habit of receiving Simnel cakes, took hers to be a footstool and employed it accordingly. But these regional dishes, this comforting native peasant cooking does not emerge to be recorded until several hundred years later, in the sixteenth and seventeenth centuries, for it was a practical not literate knowledge handed down from family to family. Yet the food, as Dorothy Hartley says in her delightful book *Food in England*, was of good quality.

How is it that such strong and unsavoury opinions have been formed against mediaeval food? How is it that our national cooking has never, apart from Dorothy Hartley's work, been traced back to its sources? Scholars have based their arguments on three main facts: the lack of vegetables, the absence of forks, which necessitated a general unpleasantness of texture and sloshiness, and the poor quality of the meat which required the lavish use of spices

[1] See Appendix II, page 247.

to mask its rankness. 'Even ale was frequently used in cooking,' one savant remarks in surprise, betraying his own lack of knowledge in the matter, for again, these learned gentlemen are no cooks. They made wild conjectures on subjects like the mediaeval palate which are based on no facts. 'Fortunately for the cooks,' mumbles William Edward Mead, author of *The English Medieval Feast*, 'who prided themselves upon the number of incongruous elements they could combine in one dish . . . they catered for men and women who were coarse-feeders, whose palates were dulled by sharp sauces, by spiced wines and by peppers, mustard and ginger and cubebs and cardamom and cinnamon with which the most innocent meats and fruits were concocted.' Chaucer's cook however had the reputation of owning a particularly fine palate, so sensitive it could detect in which part of the country ale was brewed by its flavour.

Mr. Mead has also fallen into the spice and quantity trap. 'One of the most characteristic features of the old receipts,' he grumbles, 'is the vagueness. In our own time all cookery books worthy of the name prescribe that every ingredient shall be carefully weighed or measured. But, as a rule, in the old books no definite quantity of meat or fish, or of anything else is specified, and the proportions are left to the cook.' This—as with the Romans—was precisely the case, the recipes were rough guides only. The master cook was an experienced and influential person who had many lesser cooks beneath his supervision, he could earn a salary equivalent to three thousand pounds. Besides which it was only the skilled and educated men who would have been able to read and write the recipes at all, the rest were illiterate and learnt domesticity at their mother's knee.

There is however one book which is an exception to this rule. It was written by 'the Goodman of Paris', a gentle, kind book to instruct his young fifteen-year-old wife into the secrets of cooking and housekeeping so that his old age might be comfortable and serene. For a young girl to be ignorant in these matters was unusual, but this child was an orphan and since she had received no basic training her husband tells her the quantities that should be added. Even though the recipes are on rather a large scale—for the

Goodman was a rich merchant, he had a large household and had to entertain extensively—we can see that the dishes far from being heavily spiced would have been mild. For a giant pottage for a large fishday feast the Goodman recommends his wife should take six salmon, six tench, six freshwater eels, three stockfish,[1] a quarter[2] of white herring and green porray[3]—herbs including onions and spinach; the spices he recommends should be purchased for this quantity are 6 lb almonds, which blanched and ground were used instead of flour for thickening, ½ oz of saffron, 2 oz of small spices, ¼ lb cinnamon and ½ lb ginger. This when added to the weight and volume of pottage would have the effect of a mild background seasoning. Spices were expensive; they were kept carefully under lock and key and rationed out when required; it is unlikely they would have been thrown lavishly into the pots. Cooking techniques remained the same until the seventeenth century and we find many clues as to spice quantities from the household accounts. From the years 1536/7 the household books of the nuns of Syon show them preparing their provisions for Lent: these included 749½ lb sugar, 18 lb nutmeg, 500 lb almonds, 4 lb currants, 6 lb ginger, 100 lb isinglass, 6 lb pepper, 1 lb cinnamon, 1 lb cloves, 1 lb mace, 2 lb saffron, 3 quarters of rice. From this it can be seen spice was in comparatively very small quantity indeed.

One of the scholars' main troubles was the unappetizing vocabularies of the cookery books. The dishes *sounded* unsavoury and foreign, meat was hewed, hacked, smitten, ground and brayed into gobbets, bread into sops and sippets, cast into pots, seethed in fresh grease and finally messed up. Mr. Mead's distaste and confusion is illustrated perfectly in his attitude to the following recipe for a pear custard. 'A comparatively simple but horrible example,'

[1] Stockfish was fish that had been dried and salted. The nuns of St. Radegund kept their dried stockfish in layers in canvas; it was so dry and hard it had to be beaten before use. It was supposed to have derived its name from the stock, or post, on which it was beaten.

[2] It is important to realize this signifies 28 lb, not ¼ lb.

[3] Porray can also mean puréed leeks. The word is a muddled one and is probably the result of scribes becoming confused over *porée* or *porrata*, which is the Old French for leeks, and *purée* or *purata* meaning strained, or sieved.

he writes, 'of what to avoid appears in the directions for making charewarden, "Take warden pears and boil them in wine or clean water. Then take and grind them in a mortar and draw them through a strainer without any liquor, and put them in a pot with sugar and clarified honey and cinnamon enough and let them boil. Then take them from the fire and let them cool, and cast thereto yolks of raw eggs till it be thick. And cast thereto powdered ginger enough and serve in the manner of fish. . . ." Could anyone imagine from the taste that this jumble of incongruities was a preparation of a choice fruit?' But this recipe when translated into modern language is nothing more than a simple one for pears, simmered in wine or water, sieved, sweetened, spiced with cinnamon 'to taste', thickened with egg yolks and sprinkled with ginger. What has clearly thrown Mr. Mead are the instructions to the server, and the manner of the dish's presentation. The majority of dishes served at meals were not made dishes. These were served only to vary the textures of roast meat, while the sweet dishes—the fruit purées, fritters, creams, curds, custards, the tarts and spiced nut cakes—were breathing spaces between the heavier viands: semi-colons, as Waverley Root has remarked. The presence and importance of the carver proves the bulk of solid joints, whole birds and fish. The carver was an officer second only to the pantler. Before his lord he cut and served, with some ceremony, the birds, fish, joints and pies. The books on manners and etiquette include full instructions of how the carver must go to work; with flourishes and ritual he should 'disfigure' the peacocks, 'unlace' the conies, dismember the herons, open the pies, touch the venison with his left hand, pare the mutton and mince the partridges. He must also add the finishing touches to dishes, he must see the right sauce went with the right meats; worts with hens, rabbits, beef or hare, frumenty with venison, pease with bacon. Whelks, shrimps and crab were to be served with vinegar, grilled beef or venison steaks were sprinkled with vinegar and ginger, herrings with mustard.

It has often been claimed that mediaeval tables were not served with vegetables. Seeds, it is explained, do not appear on the account lists as having been purchased each spring for the gardens, and vegetables are hardly ever mentioned at meal times. But there were vegetables, and in abundance. 'We shall dine today,' says the fifteenth-century school book, 'with wortes, garlyke and onyons.' This misunderstanding has come about because of two facts. Seeds for the vegetable gardens were *not* purchased, they were collected carefully each autumn by the women and guarded until the sowing time—this appears as one of the 'Goodman of Paris's' instructions; thus they are never included in the account books. Pot herbs were so commonplace a food they do not appear at the great feasts which are the main records to which academic scholars have resource when discussing mediaeval food. They were not the most favourite of foods. At Canterbury, Giraldus Cambrensis describes them as being served at the end of the meal when everyone was so filled with the delicious dishes that had gone before they could make no space to eat them; at that luxurious table Giraldus Cambrensis said they stood as low among the other dishes as ale stood among the spiced and sweetened wines, the strong drinks of pigment and claret. Part of the misunder-standing again comes through vocabulary; apart from pulses, which stood on their own, vegetables were usually classed together under the name of pot-herb, porray or worts. Up to the end of the last century pot-herbs were sold in the markets at a penny a bundle, consisting of onions, parsnips, carrots, parsley and thyme to flavour the stew. Many castles and monasteries had gardens as did many town-houses, for cities were rural communities where the food was grown locally and swine rooted in the streets. That their gardens were productive is shown by Miss Abram who writes that before 1345 the London gardeners of earls, bishops and citizens were in the habit of standing by the side of the gate of St. Paul's churchyard to sell the vegetables and fruit produce of their masters—pulses, cherries and other wares.

Alexander Neckham lists the herbs and vegetables a good garden in his day should contain. It should be adorned with roses and lilies, heliotrope, violets and mandrake; parsley, cost, fennel, southernwood, coriander, sage, hyssop, savoury, mint, rue, dittany, smallage, pellitory, lettuce, garden cress and peonies. There should also be beds planted with onions, leeks, garlic, pumpkins and shallots, beets, herb-mercury, orach, sorrel and mallow, poppy and daffodil. There were fruit trees and saffron crocuses, thyme, pennyroyal and borage. The Goodman advises his wife to entertain a continual sowing of cabbages through the year so that she would have a continual supply of green, carefully saving the seed at the correct time. In September cabbages were cut down to a stump which then shot new green five or six times during the autumn and winter. In December and January, he notes, the winter weather would have killed the leaves but these would spring again in February, followed a fortnight later by spinach and sorrel.

Gardens to the mediaeval people were fragrant living store-cupboards. There was not a plant that did not have its use and purpose. The lupins poking up coloured to the sky expelled dead children, voideth worms, provoketh urine. Roses were not only delicious in cakes, sauces and scented wafers, but the juice of them was profitable to make the belly loose and soluable, while the musk leaves eaten as a salad with vinegar purgeth the body very noticably of waterish and choleric humours. Roots were pounded, leaves eaten in salad or made into pastes. Flowers were distilled or their sweet oils extracted. Even plants that nowadays are seen as tiresome weeds were valued. Daisies and celandines were cultivated in the hedges to heal ulcers, help sore eyes and teeth; groundsel cured gout; dandelions were eaten in the spring together with dock leaves, the budding leaves of hawthorn and nettles, which when older were carded into thread and spun into fine nettle linen. 'Every hedge,' John Evelyn remarked hundreds of years later, 'affords a sallet.' There were wild parsnips and carrots—more delicious and greater than domestic ones grown in the gardens—whose seeds were gathered to be sown; there were the roots of couch grass, sow thistle; fungi and snails; and out over the sea samphire hung on the cliffs or sprang up from the black mud of the salt marshes.

There is delightful description of rural London given in the twelfth century, by FitzStephen. It lies, renowned for its wealth, its extensive trade and commerce, its grandeur, in the green bowl of the hills, a large whitewashed village with trees and gardens and church spires, fringed by forests and cornfields. The sound of the church bells calling the Angelus, the clack of the mill sails carry over the red poppies in the corn. There are the smells of roasting meat, the cries of the cook-shop knaves: 'Hot pies, hot pies,' they cry, 'good pigs and geese, come and dine.' There are the calls of the taverners: 'White wine of Alsace, red wine of Gascony to wash down the roast.' Its citizens were the politest in England, in their dress, their manners and the elegance and splendour of their tables. For those that dwelt in the suburbs gardens lay all round: 'which are well furnished with trees, are spacious and beautiful. On the north are corn-fields, pastures and delightful meadows, intermixed with pleasant streams, on which stands many a mill, whose clack is so grateful to the ear. Beyond them an immense forest extends itself, beautified with woods and groves, full of the lairs and coverts of beasts and game, stags, bucks, boars and wild bulls . . .' There were excellent springs whose waters ran sweet, salubrious and clear: Holywell and Clerkenwell where the scholars and youths of the city sauntered on a summer's evening. 'And moreover, on the bank of the river . . . there is a public eating-house or cook-shop. Here, according to the season, you may find victuals of all kinds. Roasted, baked, fried or boiled. Fish large and small, with coarse viands for the poorer sort, and more delicate ones for the rich such as venison, fowls and small birds. In case a friend should arrive at a citizen's house, much wearied with his journey, and choses not to wait anhungered as he is, for the buying and cooking of meat . . . recourse is immediately had to the bank above-mentioned . . . Those who have a mind to indulge, need not hanker after sturgeon, or a Guinea fowl . . . for there are delicacies enough to gratify their palates.'

Towns and villages were self-supporting, self-sufficient units. It was necessary that they should be, communications between them were dreadful. The Roman roads had broken and gone, now there were dust baths in summer, mud tracks in winter. So precarious and badly managed were they that in 1499 a miller was able to set two men to dig clay from the middle of the road to mend his mill; unhindered, they caused a chasm eight feet deep, ten feet wide and eight feet broad into which an unfortunate glover fell with his horse when returning from the market through the dusk, and drowned. It was not perhaps surprising that many people never left their villages where they were born. They lived dominated by the church-bells chiming the hours, the rhythm of agriculture: the wind and the rain, the harvests and the seasons. Their days were filled with hard work, beginning at the first crow of the cock, ending with the curfew.

They were villages peopled with men and women from the pages of Langland and Chaucer. The ploughman wearily carry-ing his dung in the early morning, past the church, its walls yellow with wallflowers, knobbly with stonecrop, past the small meadow, silver-still with dew, sheltered by trees where the widow lived with sows, three cows and a sheep called Molly. Hers was not a comfortable house but it gives a view into mediaeval interiors: dark, melancholy and sooty, the fire burning in the centre of the room, smoke perpetually lingering, staining the rafters, curling through a hole in the roof for as yet there were no chimneys and the ceiling was used as storage space, hanging with bacons, black puddings, muttons and beef hams which slowly seasoned in the swirling smoke. Seven hens and a frowning handsome cock called Chanticleer perched in the hall. That cock was the widow's pride, he was the vainest, most beautiful cock, of the most ex-cellent burnished gold feathers, who sauntered on azure toes and lily-white nails; as for his comb, never had there been one finer— redder than coral, battlemented like a castle wall. Never had there been such a crow either—jollier than the organ blowing; the way he stood on his toes, stretched his neck closing his eyes, opening his beak—the performance was masterly. Close-by where the butterflies fluttered over the cabbages, the hens took dust baths in the sun.

But the ploughman continued on, down past the franklin's[1] house where his table stood always ready in the hall for unexpected guests, past the reeve's[2] (where it snowed food and drink and all the dainties a man could think), and there passing the ricks where the swallows perched were two nasty-looking people, meandering

---

[1] A landowner, who was free by birth, but not noble.
[2] A steward on an estate.

down the thin dusty track. A pardoner,[1] all yellow rat's tail hair and bulging eye-balls, covered with a rubble of relics—one even in his hat—with which to astonish the parson (these included all manner of strange things from a glass of pig's bones to a pillow-case which he claimed was Our Lady's veil). Beside him strode the summoner,[2] a bogeyman of a person, with plenty of carbuncles and black scabby brows overhanging a lecherous face, exuding stales fumes of garlic, red wine, onions and leeks. They passed the hedges where the honeysuckle wound with traveller's joy and met Absalon with his grey eyes, gold hair and light-blue jacket going along with jars of honey, spicy ale and piping hot wafers: goodies with which to seduce the miller's wife, a delicious piece with her broad rump and high round breasts. Beside them in the meadows peonies and canterbury bells swayed; in autumn there would be purple and white saffron crocuses.

Poverty varied from village to village. In a good summer life was not too bad. For growing his corn and his legumes each man had a plot of land, and for white meats, leather and wool his cow, goat or sheep grazed on the village common, while his poultry and swine foraged in the wastes and in the village street. He had a constant supply of animal fat, milk products and eggs; he lived on a diet of rye bread, bacon, pease and bean pottage, eggs, cheese and milk[3] with fresh herbs and fruits from the hedges. But winter could be hard, everyone worn with cold and hunger. Burdened with children and the landlord's rent, the women were often not able to spin enough to cover the expenses: the long cold nights spent rocking the cradle, the thin exhausting cries of hungry children, the combing, the carding, the washing and the rubbing; the drudgery attached to everything—even the laborious process required to provide light when rushes must be peeled, cutting and whipping the hands, and dipped in the mutton fat.

It was a difficult life, especially in those distressed years when

[1] One who had authority from the Pope to sell pardons and indulgences.

[2] One paid to summon sinners to trial before an ecclesiastical court.

[3] Mediaeval people in general did not use or drink milk whole, that would have been wasteful. They separated it, using the curds for butter, cheese or sweet dishes and drinking the whey, thus manufacturing two products from the one.

the harvest was poor, or there was murrain among the cattle. The famous passage from Langland shows the worry and the sustenance of the fifteenth-century labourer. 'I have no penny,' said Piers Plowman, 'to buy pullets, nor geese, nor pigs, but I have two green cheeses,[1] a few curds and cream, and an oat-cake, and two loaves of beans and bran baked for my children. And yet I say, by my soul, I have no salt-bacon, nor no eggs, forsooth, to make collops, but I have parsley and leeks and many cabbages, and eke a cow and a calf, and a cart-mare to draw my dung a-field . . . All the poor people then fetched peascods, and brought in their laps beans and baked apples, onions and chervils and many ripe cherries . . .'

Famines together with epidemics were sent down by God, it was believed, as a punishment for the wickedness of the people. Trumpets blew in the sky, pear and plum trees were blasted to the ground for warning: 'ye should do better, ye men.' But apparently they went unheeded for God sent down the Black Death and several famines. The poor, it was recorded by Troke-lowe, were so hungry they ate dogs, cats, the dung of doves and their children. Thieves starving in prisons ferociously attacked new prisoners, devouring them half alive. But the Black Death was one of the turning points in history, it had the effect of unloosening the knot of feudal ties; gradually from then onwards they unwound and fell apart. The loss of population resulted in shortage of labour and people could leave their villages, cross the forests, settle anew and demand wages for their work.

It was a rhythmical monotonous life and for an illiterate people without light and intellectual pursuits often the only way to alleviate weariness was to get drunk—especially on Church holidays. Langland's village is an amusing but squalid place populated by unsavoury characters who shout and vomit in the pub all day long. Sloth with two slimy eyes, Covetousness, hungry and hollow, beetle-browed, his cheeks trembling lower

---

[1] There were four kinds of cheeses, Drummond and Wilbraham tell us, in *The Englishman's Food*: soft cheese, hard cheese, green cheese and spermyse. The first was cream cheese, the second hard, of the cheddar type, green cheese was a very soft, very new cheese, spermyse was a cream cheese flavoured with herbs.

than his chin, his beard beslobbered with bacon, his hat lousy, his coat no less disgusting—twelve winters old—full of vermin. And Glutton, travelling feebly churchwards, but seduced easily into the tavern by the prospect of ale, gossip and hot spices. Inside we find Uncle Tom Cobbley and all: Cio the Shoemaker, Wat the Warrener and his wife, Tim the Tinker, Hugh the Needle-seller, Daw the Ditcher, Someone the Fiddle player, Someone Else the Ropemaker and masses of others besides, all sitting there early in the morning. And there they sat all day shouting and haggling for one another's clothes until evensong when Glutton, propped up by his stick, lurched to the door and tripped over the step. Clement the Cobbler kindly sat him in his lap, where Glutton was venomously sick. Finally his wife and daughter disagreeably carted him home where he passed out for two days, rising only on Sunday at sunset, to call for the bowl.

As with Saxon law, ale, together with bread, was considered an essential to life for man, woman and child, who drank very small beer. To drink water was considered a hardship—owing to the unreliability of many of the water supplies. Ale prices were strictly controlled. In the fourteenth century three strengths were brewed and sold commercially: the weakest selling at a penny a gallon, medium strength at a penny halfpenny and the strongest and best at twopence. From all points considerable quantities of alcohol were consumed. 'Drinking in particular was a universal practice,' observed William of Malmesbury, 'in which occupation they [they English] passed entire nights as well as days . . . They were accustomed to eat till they became surfeited and to drink till they were sick.'

Most estates, monasteries and individual families brewed their own ale. The malthouse at Fountains Abbey had a substantial brewing potential. With an area sixty foot square its floor would have been capable every ten days of producing sixty barrels— thirty-six gallons each—of very strong ale; with the malting process generally lasting during the six winter months this would make a brewing potential of nine hundred barrels of ale each year.

Thirty-eight vineyards are mentioned in the Domesday Book. Wine, both home-made and imported—with names like Malmesie,

Vernage and Bastard[1]—was also available. The 'abundance of wine and strong drink, pigment and claret, of all intoxicating liquors' was such, Giraldus Cambrensis noted disapprovingly, that even ale had no place at the luxurious meal to which he was entertained at Canterbury. From canons published at the end of the thirteenth century it appears that officers of the Church indulged quite extensively in immoderate drinkings; archdeacons deans, rural deans and priests even going so far as to hold drinking competitions. Canon No. 5 forbids the ill practice 'by which all that drink together are obliged to equal draughts and he carries away the credit who hath made most drunk and taken off the largest cups . . .' 'As I hauntede ale howses and wyn taverns, I have spende all the money that I hade in my purse,' says the fifteenth-century school book. In fact the exercises seem largely to be about hangovers and surfeits, the scholar drinking so much 'that I coulde scant stande on my fete nor my tongue coulde do me no service'; how he was then 'disposede' to his 'bookys' remains open to conjecture.

Rations of wine and beer were considerable. In 1371 soldiers in the garrison at Dover castle received as part of their daily rations five pints of wine; the nuns of Syon got seven gallons of ale each week; and the famous 'braikfaste for my lorde and my lade' recorded in the Northumberland Household Book was composed of two manchets of bread, a quart of beer, a quart of wine, two pieces of salt fish, and six baked herrings or sprats, while the nursery enjoyed one manchet, one quart of beer, a dyche of butter, a piece of salt fish, a dish of sprats or three white herrings.

Breakfast, ale-house excursions and daily consumptions such as these, though not endorsing the Victorian delusion in which dawn perpetually breaks over an England merrye with village greens, its population capering in eternal dance, must have had some effect on the national character and probably went some way to fattening the patient rustic temperament of the Middle Ages.

[1] A sweet Spanish wine.

4

Houses of Buxomness and Peace

There is a well fair abbey,
Of white monkes and of grey,
There beth bowers, and halls:
All of pasties beth the walls,
Of flesh, of fish, and a rich meat,
The likefullest that man may eat.
Flouren cakes beth the *shingles* [tiles] all
Of church, cloister, bowers and hall.
The pinnes beth fat *puddings* [sausages]
Rich meat to princes and kings.

The Land of Cokaygne—ANON

One sees the Middle Ages set out like an expensive Church controlled boarding school, supported, so that its pupils may have the best of fresh eggs, milk and butter, by its home farm. There the poor wait, soft eyed, whiskered and bovine at their troughs, before moving out to work the fields. Quite often the food is unfairly distributed, most goes to the pink skinned pupils and the plump ecclesia, little but husks remains for the farm workers. The pupils are a rowdy ill disciplined crowd, never alone, never with any privacy to work out the rules for themselves, playing together at children's games: soldiers and war, and, after dinner, blindman's buff, ball and hot cockles. The authorities behind the magnificence of their silks and velours, their chants and their incense, their *mystery*, bully and frighten them into keeping the rules, condemning any originality as heresy; threatening expulsion and hell.[1]

[1] Any deviation from conventional methods caused a thunderstorm. For example certain unfortunate 'heretics' made the fatal mistake of trying a different approach when representing Christ upon the Cross and not, as was usual, showing the body draped to the feet, both of which were nailed separately. Instead they were guilty of attempting 'to pollute the orthodox faith by painting or carving ill shaped images of saints in order that by gazing on such images the devotion of Christian folk may be turned to loathing. In derision and scorn of Christ's Cross they carved images of our Lord with one foot laid over the other so that both were pierced by a single nail thus striving either to annul or to render doubtful Men's faith in the

Everything, they claimed, all small insects and fierce animals, was in league to remind man of his Fall. Flies, for this purpose, invaded his food and drink, fleas disturbed his sleep, lice molested him. Anything new was considered dangerous—a crime against God, the Church and the king, a treason to be punished in the proper manner: racking, then burning alive, to symbolize the hellish flames in which the miscreant would shortly be roasting. Mediaeval people were no less superstitious and credulous than the Romans and Anglo-Saxons, and one of the most dangerous heresies was witchcraft. The church knew that sorcery was one of the means Satan employed to stir up other heterodoxies. Regularly witches confessed[1] that they transformed themselves into wolves and other ravenous beasts. They came to assemblies mounted on broomsticks—there was not a switch about their houses that had not carried them hundreds of miles—they took little children and reduced them, in cauldrons, to unguents mixing them with spiders and black worms to make ladies' faces horrid like goats. William of Newbury knew of one gentleman, Endo de Stella, who whizzed through the air with a multitude of followers and sat down to tables which were suddenly spread by invisible hands with rich viands and strong wines; but William of Newbury had heard the meats were not substantial.

Within the authorities themselves all was not well. There was much corruption and funds were misdirected towards the very sins against which the Church thundered. In the year of grace 1321, as investment for sacerdotal funds, an English cardinal

---

Holy Cross and the tradition of the sainted Father by superinducing these diversities or novelties.'

[1] In order to extort these confessions 'witches' were forced to endure the most appalling 'trials' which were, according to Freud, of a sadistic sexual nature. The accused were squeezed into thumbscrews, wrist and arm bands, stretched on the rack. Some were obliged to run about the room for several nights and days, or sit cross-legged on a stool, or were thrown into ponds and rivers to see if they sank. It is no wonder many marvellous confessions were extracted. Plaintiffs related experiences like those of poor Agnes Simpson, who confessed to sailing out of North Berwick in a chimney, the devil passing before her like a rick of hay, to a wonderful ship loaded with abundance of wine and good cheer; this consumed, the wonderful ship sank without trace, the devil departed, and poor Agnes Simpson and the chimney had to find their own way home.

purchased a London brothel, and, during the same century, those under the management of the Bishop of Winchester numbered no less than eighteen. Affairs were no more virtuous at the holy court of Rome. In the sixteenth century Andrew Boorde, who had himself, when a monk, been accused of keeping three whores at once in his chamber, went thither and noted: 'In every place I did se lechery and bogery, cardinals and prelates there is none of them without three or four pages trimmed like young princes; for what purpose I cannot tell . . . Rome is not without 40,000 harlots maintained for the most part by the clergy and their followers.'

Church services were often no more devout than visits to the zoo.[1] Men were especially recommended to take their hawks there in order to accustom them, while training, to noise and bustle. They arrived, said Geiter, equipped like hunters, 'bearing hawks and bells on their wrists and followed by a pack of braying hounds that trouble God's service. Here the bells jangle, there the barking of dogs echoes in our ears to the hindrance of preachers and hearers.'

The priests were the learned men of the land, it was they who taught the only letters their rustic audiences could enjoy. But unfortunately they were often themselves badly confused. 'The ignorance of the priests,' said Archbishop Peckam, 'casteth the people into the ditch of error, and the folly or unlearning of the clergy, who are bidden to instruct the faithful to the Catholic faith, doth sometimes lend rather to error than to sound doctrine.' One priest earnestly explained that *piscus assus* (broiled fish) was an ass-fish, complying with the delightful mediaeval notion that the ocean-world was in every way a counterpart of our own.

This corruption and ignorance of the Church lies at the bottom

---

[1] Eileen Power tells us of Lady Audley who lodged at Langley nunnery with her twelve dogs, all of which followed her into Divine Service where they made such an uproar that they terrified the nuns and hindered them in their psalmody. Often, even without such impediments the verses were mere mumbles, slurred and gabbled through, the pauses between the verses omitted so that one side of the choir was beginning the second half before the other side had finished the first. There was a special devil, concocted by the Church, called Tittivillus, a foul misshapen fellow who was employed on collecting the dropped syllables and gabbled verses, amassing them in a great poke as evidence for Judgement Day.

of one of the major changes in English history. It helped to disintegrate the Middle Ages and to change the diet and behaviour of the nobility from *European* to *English*. The hinge on which this change swung was the dissolution of the monasteries. For a long time the Reformers had complained at the behaviour of the clergy. Here were men, not irreligious but sincerely indignant at the corruption of the Church, the low quality of divine service and the clergy in general, at the way they conjured money from the ignorant and superstitious. But it was not so much the clergy and the potentates who received the force of the accusations, as the convents. Many of these were large landowners, who over the years had received many gifts of money and estates against eternal damnation. The trouble was that many of the abbots and abbesses were not competent. The business of managing their estates was too much for them. Some were too ambitious and were carried away by wonderful new building schemes, others were hopeless. With sorrow reports were advertised from the convents of the appalling state of affairs, that 'it raineth within and without', that 'there was not one bowl from which to drink' because they were either broken or in pawn, that the parish church by reason of its 'evident craziness' had fallen to the ground.

Poor old dim-eyed Abbot Hugh of Bury St. Edmunds was one of the most incompetent muddlers: his outdoor affairs were a disgrace; inside the parlour was stripped of its ornaments, silk copes, tablecloths and gold salt pots—they were all in pawn. On his death it was as though a whirlwind had hit the place. Abbot Samson took over. He built chapels, enclosed parks, made dwellings from barns and though never stinting himself at table —four courses for the first seven years and after that three—he was such a wizard with the accounts that allowances which Abbot Hugh could not make last for five days managed with him for eight or nine. Even so he was not without some internal trouble. His monks were forever quarrelling. So serious was this that when affairs ran amok in the town and the cellarer[1] was obliged to make

---

[1] The cellarer looked after the food of the house and domestic servants, and superintended the management of the home farm, laid in stores, ordered meals, engaged and dismissed servants.

some arrests, the sacrist, in whose care the jail lay, refused to lend it to him in order to house the malefactors. The convent cellarers were fond of trading surreptitiously at unchristian rates; they charged exorbitant prices for produce, or raised tolls by the road-side refusing passage unless the people paid. Those at Bury St. Edmunds seemed quite out of hand; abroad in the town they were observed removing doors and other equipment from the houses of the poor, while old women threatened them with sticks, or were discovered wrestling with burgesses in the road over dung-hills, snatching their carts and making away with the manure.[1]

For nuns, many of whom were quite unsuited to a cloistered life, an existence incarcerated in a convent was often more monotonous than for the monks, there being no academic diversions whatsoever. Many were often entered when small child-ren, complete with feather beds, little cupboards and cauldrons; some to the indignation of the other ladies were deformed, or idiots; some, it was rumoured, were persuaded to enter for no better reason than that the food was good. To relieve the boredom they kept monkeys, dogs and birds, while the monks had packs of hounds and hawks. For many, food, drink and sex were happy oases in the brown sand of ennui and tempered the dread accidia —that mixture between sloth, irritation and gloom. The in-junctions show exasperated bishops trying to gain control over their naughty giggling flock, who are perpetually escaping from the walls of the cloister to run down to the pawn shop with the spoons and knives. They forever enjoin the brethren to 'hold no drinkings or messes after compline', not 'to go out of the cloister precincts', or 'into the town of Bourne and hold any drinking or feastings in the same', neither must 'our beloved sons have access to the nuns at Elstow, under what colour of excuse soever, nor shall the same nuns for any reason whatever be allowed to enter the same priory'; furthermore 'with all possible speed you bring back and restore to the priory, as far as you are able, all and sundry

[1] This street manure, which was deposited by the town cattle, was a valuable commodity. One either to be laid over the fields of the home farm, or sold at pre-posterous rates.

the jewels and utensils of the house, wheresoever or to whomsoever they are in pawn'.

At table so anxious were they for satisfaction that they panted and groaned in anguish 'so that you might think they are seeking another wider orifice for their roaring maw . . .' Their hands and eyes roamed everywhere, they crumbled the bread, poured the wine into cups and goblets, drew the dishes round and mounted to the assault. Some were anxious for new delights, 'new and unwonted sorts of food'; for these a host of servants scoured the villages 'tearing up roots from wild and distant mountains', dragging 'a few little fishes from the deepest whirlpools', collecting 'untimely berries from the withering bushes'. Others paid too fastidious an attention to the preparation of their food, 'excogitating infinite sorts of stewings and frying and seasonings; now soft, now hard; now hot, now cold, now sodden, now roast; seasoned with pepper, now with garlic, now with cummin, now with salt, after the fashion of women in their pregnancy'. Some, in their anxiety to empty the dishes, wrapped the 'four square gobbets of the mess' in their napkins, 'dripping with the fat or the grease that had been poured upon them'. Others wiped their greasy hands on their garments, fished with 'bare fingers instead of spoons, for their pot-herbs . . . Others dip repeatedly into the dish their half-gnawed crusts and the sippets which they have bitten, and plunge the leavings of their own teeth, in the guise of sops, into the gobbets'.

CHAPTER SIX

THE BRITISH OAK OF COOKING

Ah gentlemen, keep a little quiet, one does not know of what one is eating.

MONTMAUR

I

Quickened by the Fruits of Adultery

THIS THEN was the situation as the sixteenth century opened: the monastics, frustrated within their cloisters, were dipping in grease, tearing at roots and gnawing at crusts while ever more magnificent, ever more extravagant the Tudor court with Henry VIII at its head rotated slowly through the seasons of the year. At Christmas the pillars in the gardens were decorated with pearls, artificial flowers of silk and gold, pomegranates and roses; the peacock was roasted, sewn into its plummage, covered with leaf gold, stuffed with spices and sweet herbs and gilded with egg yolk. It seemed at court that every season was Christmas, such was the hunting, the dancing, the dining. Never had the feasting begun so early—ten o'clock in the morning; never had the court been so adorned: 'sometimes cap, sometimes hood, now the French fashion, now the Spanish, then the Italian fashion and then the Milan fashion.' Sometimes the young bloods donned stage-beards of gold and silver wire, the better for Henry to arrive incognito and 'peruse' the incomparable beauty of the 'excellent fair dames'.

Henry wanted many things: pretty girls, good food and wine and above all a son, for which purpose he needed a divorce and a new wife. All this was expensive and close inspection of his

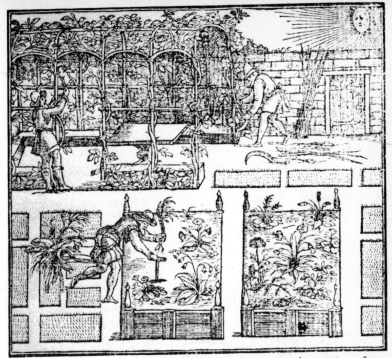

9A. Front page from *The Gardner's Labyrinth* showing the training of a sixteenth-century arbour and the planting of the garden

9B. A sixteen-century cook-maid, undressed because of the intolerable heat of the kitchen, preparing some salted fish from the store-tub on the floor

9C. The cook-maid dressed to serve the dish to the waiting gentlemen

10. A broadsheet dated 1603 entitled 'Tittle-Tattle', satirizing the idleness and gossiping habits of women. In the lower left hand corner AT THE BAKEHOUSE gossips bring their bread to bake, near the oven end of the table the master baker stands, with a feather in his cap, taking a liberty with one of the customers. Above them AT THE HOTTE-HOUSE naked ladies stand about chattering, or sit in tubs being served with food and drink, while above them AT THE CHILDBED a recently delivered lady sits bolt upright and fully dressed in bed, ignored by her companions who sit giggling, their backs to her. In the centre AT THE CHURCH everyone sits chattering among themselves not even pretending to listen to the sermon; outside, leaning against the Hottehouse Wall a gentleman is busy kissing a lady. Next door AT THE MARKET wares are being marketed fairly peacefully, but below them WASHERS AT THE RIVER find occasion to fall out and fight with the washing mallet, and AT THE CONDUITE ladies line up to draw their water not without some of them coming to blows and pulling one another's hair, while AT THE ALEHOUSE several ladies sit around drinking pots of ale

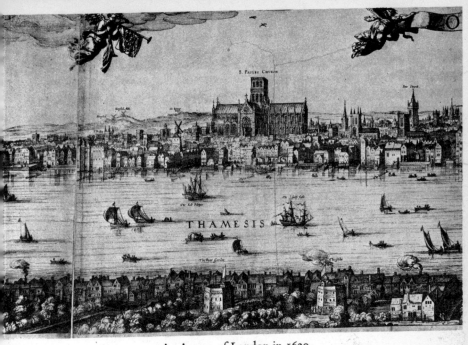

11A. A map of London in 1620

11B. The Duke of Beaufort's seventeenth-century house in Chelsea

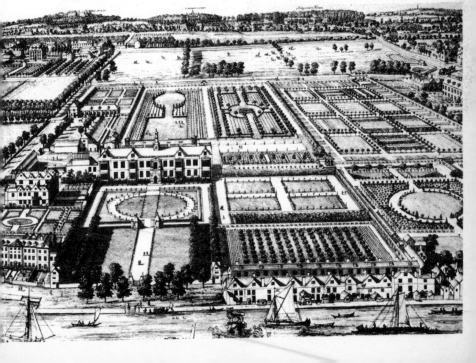

Cap: 45.

12A. Examples of carve-peeling to dignify the fruit

12B. Carême's ornamental sugar
windmill

12C. Carême's decorated sucking pig

coffers revealed a less excellent spectacle than had the 'fair dames'. Henry was nearly bankrupted. A new source of income must be found. The monasteries with their high reserves of capital, their low reputations, seemed the ideal solution. Out into the cloisters Henry sent his spies. Back came the reports: 'Ye shall also receive a bag of relicks, wherein ye shall see strange things,' wrote R. Layton dispatching at the same time some of his evidence to Thomas Cromwell; 'as God's coat, our Lady's smock, part of God's supper . . . these are all of Maiden Bradley; whereof a *holy father* Priour who hath but *six children*, and but one daughter married yet of the goods of the monastery, but trusting shortlie to marry the rest: his sons be tall men, *waiting upon him*. He thanks God, he never meddled with *married women*; but all with *maidens*, *fairest* that could be gotten . . . I send you also Our Lady's girdle of Bruton, red silke, a solemn relick sent to women in travail.'

Within four years the monasteries were all dissolved and Henry had severed his connection with the Pope and the Church of Rome. He had his divorce.[1] What a day of rejoicing there was in celebration of his wedding to Anne Boleyn. Green rushes and lighted tapers lined the way; the horses were clad in crimsons, scarlets and grained cloth; coloured banners, covered all over with bells, streamed out in the breeze; there were trumpets and silk canopies; the fountains and conduits ran all afternoon with white wine and claret and on the river great red dragons moved continuously casting fire. The Church of England was born. There were some disasters—the Abbot of Glastonbury was hanged from his own doorway—but in most cases the treatment of the monks and nuns was good. All received a pension, many nuns married and for the heads of the houses there were bishoprics and deaneries. The worst damage of all was to the beautiful carvings and statues in the churches and the monastery libraries: the thick manuscripts, the bright crackling pages shining with gold were as rubbish to be dumped, some to be lost for ever, some to be salvaged by men like Leland and Cotton. The feather beds, the little cupboards

---

[1] His divorce had been essential. Anne Boleyn was pregnant and it was vital that the child should be born in wedlock.

the nuns had brought with them, the plate and the jewellery went with the capital sums into the state coffers. The fraters where the novices had dipped their hands into their goblets, the cloisters where the monks had yawned, fermenting in accidia, stood empty. Used as quarries for building, they crumbled and stood open to the sky. Willow herb sprang from the gateway where the Abbot of Glastonbury had hanged. A nail had been banged into the coffin lid of the Middle Ages.

The monasteries had held large estates, their dissolution caused major eruptions in the land system. A new race sprang up, with a new spirit that was quite unmediaeval—business men who all tended to adopt for their own interest the new religion. The new Church of England—that had been quickened by the fruits of adultery—was as orthodox a church as the Pope's. Heresy was still not only spiritually damnable but socially dangerous. Heretics felt the rack and smelt the fire: as they burnt most surely did they pray. But there were differences. As the Tudor years advanced the notion that it was wrong to lend and make money was abandoned. The ideal of Just Price was forgotten. There evolved a religion of the home, essentially middle class, dedicating the business life, exalting the married state, reacting against the past creed that the true life was celibacy and monastic separation. These new men were business men and merchants. They were not of the feudal mind that realized the value of land for the number of men-at-arms it could furnish; now it was good for the rents it paid into the coffers, valuable for the number of sheep it could hold; it was good for profits. These were the Years of the Wool. English fleece carried a high reputation abroad, the cloth trade expanded, there was an almost insatiable demand for wool. Everywhere land was put down to grass—even those wet tracts quite unsuitable to carry sheep; everywhere land was enclosed.

The middle class rose, the conditions of the poor sank. There was unemployment, since the wool policy resulted in less demand for rural labour; the unemployed were reduced to roaming and begging for food; where the land was enclosed the people could not graze their own cows, their own sheep: there was no butter, no cheese, no whey, curds, cream or milk.

The merchants were efficient business men. In order to raise prices they stored grain. Beef and mutton became so expensive no poor man could afford them. 'Our English nature cannot live by rotes, herbys or such beggerye baggage,' shouted Sir William Forrest, '. . . give Englishmen meat after their own usage beef, mutton, veal to cheer their courage.'

Villages and towns, Starkey saw, were allowed to fall to ruin, churches were only kept because they would shelter sheep, the poor lay dying, untended and uncared for by the sides of ditches, or flitted, vague hungry shadows, eating 'when they may so to talk of order of their repast it were a needless matter'. When they could, Fynes Moryson, the famous sixteenth-century traveller, observed, the husbandmen ate barley and rye brown bread 'and prefer it to white bread as abiding longer in the stomach, and not so soon digested with their labour; but citizens and gentlemen eat most pure white bread, England yielding all kinds of corn in plenty. The English have an abundance of white meats, of all kinds of flesh, fowl and fish and of things good for food. In the seasons of the year the English eat fallow deer plentifully, as bucks in summer and does in winter, which they bake in pasties, and this venison pasty is a dainty, rarely found in any other kingdom . . . No kingdom in the world has so many dove-houses. Like-wise brawn[1] is a proper meat to the English not known to others. English cooks, in comparison with other nations, are most commended for roasted meats.'[2]

Never had so much meat been consumed. 'In number of dishes and changes of meat,' Harrison in his *Description of England* said, 'the nobility of England (whose cooks are for the most part musical-headed Frenchmen and strangers) do most exceed, sith there is no day in manner that passeth over their heads, wherein they have not only beef, mutton, veal, lamb, kid, pork, cony,

[1] Now, in the sixteenth century, we find brawn referring exclusively to pork meats.

[2] Apologists for English cooking are often explaining that the quality of English meat is so excellent that it needs no clever sauces to mask it. Here, if we adopt their argument, we have proof that mediaeval meat was good enough to stand alone roasted—the quality of Tudor meat did not differ from the mediaeval, agricultural policies were little changed.

capon, pig or so many of these as the season yieldeth but also some portion of the red or fallow deer . . .' Brought up, according to Cardinal Pole, 'in hunting, hawking, dicing, carding, eating and drinking' the English were 'more given to idle gluttony than any people in the world.' 'Never,' added Lupset,[1] 'was such feasting and banqueting and so many kinds of meat as there are now.' And as Holinshed remarked, 'the kind of meat which is obtained with most difficulty and cost, is commonly taken for the most delicate and thereupon each guest will soonest desire to feed'.

At Dover Castle, the accounts for the year between 1521 and 1533 show the king and queen together with their noblemen sitting down to a month's victuals, before embarking for France, of 700 quarters of wine, 150 tuns of French and Gascon wine, 6 butts of sweet wine, 500 tuns of beers, 340 beeves, 4,200 muttons, 800 veals, 80 hogs head of grease; while later in the century Sir William Petrie and his household at the season of Christmas consumed one ton of cheese, 17 oxen, 14 steers, 5 bacon hogs, 13 bucks, 4 cows, 29 calves, 129 sheep, 3 goats, 5 does, 54 lambs, 2 boars, 9 porks, 7 kids and 1 stag.

Never had the celebrations been so wild, so schoolboyish. At a great city feast an enormous dish was brought filled with custard; while the guests were engaged in eating as much as they could, a jester ran into the room, sprang over their astonished heads and into the quivering custard, occasioning much mirth to all those who were far enough away for their fine clothes to remain unmoistened. Never had the feasts been so prolonged: 'many hours together', said Paulius Jovius, 'and [the diners] intersperse their varied and exquisite repasts with music and jesters, and when the meal is over, they fall to dancing and indulge in the embraces of their ladies'. Here is an interesting point which is made by Kenneth Hare in 'Food and Drink': an Italian, whose own country stood at the front when it came to skill and reputation for cookery, is pronouncing the English dishes to be exquisite.

With the fall of the Church of Rome the official fishdays no

[1] Thomas Lupset was tutor to Cardinal Wolsey's son, Thomas Winter.

longer existed. The fishing industry was affected, the sea-ports fell into decay, holes appeared in the quays and jetties. Rather to promote the navy and revive the coastal towns, than as religious observance, fish-laws were passed forbidding again the consumption of meat during Lent and on Fridays. When the law was not obeyed there were prosecutions; in Dover a woman was sentenced to sit in the pillory with a shoulder of mutton before her on a spit as punishment for attempting to cook and serve it on a fast day.

2

Pudding Time, Pepys and Puritanism

During the middle years of the sixteenth century religion, balanced like a see-saw, plunging down into the black abyss of Mary's reign—six years of Catholic purges, of hangings, drawings, quarterings and burnings—to fly up among the glittering coloured stars of Elizabeth's court. The years of her reign seem to burst in relief, up from the dark depression, showering like fireworks, in gold, red and blue suns of energy and inspiration. The chroniclers seem to have a different tone, seem to have shaken themselves, stretched and relaxed in the leafy country, rested by brooks, gazing down through the moving waters. 'What should I speake of the fat and sweet salmon dailie taken in this streame,' writes Holinshed of the Thames, 'and that there is such plentie as no river in Europa is able to exceed it. What store also of barbels, trouts . . . roches, daces, gudgings, flounders, shrimps . . .'

The Thames was for Londoners the main avenue of transport. A busy, bustling scene. The barges and the watermen conveying their brightly coloured passengers to and fro; the queen travelling with her court in the morning sunshine to a banquet at Greenwich, past the banks, the stairs, the landing places where the boats waited by the steps to carry people along or across the river; the courtiers with their pendant codpieces protruding, the ladies, their dresses jagged and cut over their bosoms, their sleeves of sundry colour; the sounds coming over the water of chatter and laughter and music; the crimson velvets, the pease pottage silks, the popinjay blues; the queen's barge moving like a burnished throne into the east towards Greenwich, burning in the water, the poop like beaten gold in the morning rays, the sails purple and scented, the oars silver in the water beating time to the flutes; and the queen like Shakespeare's Cleopatra seated in a pavilion of cloth of gold, surrounded by pretty boys. Waiting at Green-wich, erected in the park, would be the banqueting houses, made with fir-poles, decked with birch-branches, roses, lavender and marigolds, the floors strewn with rushes and herbs; and there would be bear baiting and bull baiting and the Queen's Grace would look down upon the spectacles, upon the bonfires and the rejoicing; and there would be masques and great banquets and the river would grow red in the setting sun and in the dark there would be castings of fire and the shooting of guns.

It was under the Elizabethans that an Englishness emerged— an isolation of character reflecting the supreme isolation of the monarch: 'She is our God on earth.' Englishness is a curious quality, indefinable; a quality of comfortableness and solidarity, of new-green, of daffodils swaying in a south-west breeze; but a quality, too, holding a large measure of Christian guilt, of Puritanism—an essentially commercial urban movement. England was a rich self-sufficient island guarded behind a wooden wall of ships; made of merchants, who, beneath the almond blossoms and the breezes of the Elizabethan spring, constructed new self-sufficient dwelling houses. Solid black beams sunk into white plaster—feather stitching on a white wool background—holding inside wet and dry larders, bake-houses, slaughter houses, herb gardens and spiceries.

Conditions in the kitchens were often intolerable. The fires blazing before the great rotating joints made the quarters an inferno with the cook, according to Earle, 'the Divell in it, where his meate and he fry together', murdering the fowls, building towers and castles in pastry; a military man lining up his armies of dishes to be demolished by valiant (black) teeth,[1] placing strong meats to the fore, the quivering custards and tarts behind, then retiring to the cellar to drink and to sleep. Evidently the heat from Henry VIII's huge pots and smoking joints was so great that many of his kitchen staff were obliged to work naked.

Through these frightful conditions Ben Jonson shows the master cook reigning brilliant and supreme.

> A master cook! why he's the man of men,
> For a professor; he designs he draws,
> He paints, he carves, he builds, he fortifies,
> Makes citadels of curious fowl and fish.
> Some he dry-ditches, some moats round with broths,
> Mounts marrow-bones, cuts fifty angled custards,
> Rears bulwark-pies; and for his outer works,
> He raiseth ramparts of immortal crust,
> And teacheth all the tactics at one dinner—
> What ranks, what files to put his dishes in,
> The whole art military!

As the new Puritanism gathered strength it swept its inhibitions into these subterranean furnaces. There were food taboos. Spices were barred on the supposition they excited passion; Christmas was no longer recognized as an occasion for bibulous holiday. Gone were the times when Christmas stretched over several days. Finished were the years like that of 1562 when the feasts were celebrated at the Temple, the wildest taking place on December 26 with a facsimile of a hunt being staged before the important personages—among whom were the Lord Treasurer, the Lord Privy Seal and the Chief Justice. The first elaborate course had been consumed and the Earl Marshal entered 'with a fair, rich compleat harneys, white and bright, and gilt, with a nest o' feathers in his helm . . . and a like pole-axe in his hand . . .' At this, fifteen trumpeters announced the entry of the Master of the Game in green velvet and the Ranger of the Forest in green satin holding a green bow and 'divers arrows'. The two of

---

[1] Muralt writing later, in 1695, found English women almost irresistible with their delicate complexions, their gentle bashfulness, their figures, but for one thing: 'The greatest fault I find with them is that they do not take care of their teeth, the care the more necessary as, according to the custom of the country, they eat much meat and little bread . . .'

them paced about the fire three times, each blowing three 'blasts of venery' through his hunting horn. Then the Master of the Game—making three curtseys—kneeled before the Lord Chancellor whereupon 'a huntsman cometh into the hall, with a fox and a purse-net; with a cat, both bound at the end of a staff; and with them nine or ten couple of hounds, with a blowing of hunting-hornes: And the fox and the cat are by the hounds set upon and killed beneath the fire . . .' The sport concluded, the second course proceeded.

As we have seen, the Christmas fare had been rich and lavish, consisting of boar's head, peacocks, capons, swan, pheasant, frumenty, delicious spiced pies and plum porridges. But now the Puritans were on the march, prohibiting all traditional fragrant pies and broths.

> All plums the prophets' sons deny,
> And spice-broths are too hot,
> Treason's in a December pie,
> And death within the pot.

Later the Quakers took up the cause, denouncing luxuries and festivities at Christmas or any other time. 'The Christmas pie, is, in its own nature, a kind of consecrated cake, and a badge of distinction,' wrote Bickerstaffe; 'and yet it is often forbidden, the Druid of the family. Strange that a sirloin of beef, whether boiled or roasted, when entire is exposed to the utmost depredations and invasions; but if minced into small pieces, and tossed up with plumbs and sugar, it changes its property, and forsooth is meat for his master.' And Samuel Butler derided the restrictions in *Hudibras*:

> . . . They [the zealots] will
> Quarrel with *minc'd Pies*, and disparage
> Their best and dearest friend *Plum-Porridge*;
> Fat *Pig* and *Goose* it self oppose.
> And blaspheme *Custard* through the *Nose*.

Until the Civil Wars Twelfth Night was observed with great and splendid feasting, the centre of which was a magnificent cake, containing a bean. Whoever received the piece encompassing this was accepted as king of the day. After the Restoration, when the food restrictions were lifted and the fanatics prosecuted, the custom was resumed. On January 7, 1661 Pepys attended a party at his cousin Stradwick's 'and after a good supper, we had an excellent cake, where the mark for the Queen was cut . . . and the King being lost, they chose the Doctor: so we made him send for some wine . . .' Eight years later Pepys was holding his own party, and very typically—for he was, like Pliny the younger, on the mean side—he prefers his guests not to *eat* the cake to discover the winner: 'very merry we were at dinner . . . and in the evening I did bring out my cake—a noble cake—and there cut it into pieces with wine and good drink: and after a new fashion, to prevent spoiling the cake, did put so many titles into a hat, and so drew cuts: and I was the Queen, and The. Turner King . . .'

Formerly, the occasion had often been marked with the diversion of a huge pasteboard cake, the equivalent to a subtlety, except that it was required to play an active part. Confections and pies such as these were very popular with the Tudors and Stuarts. At many feasts, birds, mammals and reptiles flew, wriggled and hopped from the dishes for the astonishment of the guests. After a while birds and frogs were considered dull stuff, the revellers could be shocked only by the appearance of unusual creatures. Toy terriers, hares, foxes and dwarfs all emerged at one time or another. The preparation of these surprises was of such invention that any Roman *coctor* would have had the confidence of an amplexbride as he laid them before his Emperor. Robert May in *The Accomplisht Cook* gives instructions for a most complicated and energetic contraption. First a ship should be made from pasteboard, covered with paste, flags, streamers and guns of unbelievable intricacy and surrounded by a moat floating with egg shells and rosewater. Next a paste stag would be placed in a platter, an arrow in his side, his body filled with wine. In another a castle should be made with battlements, portcullises, gates, drawbridges, gilded bayleaves and more guns of unbelievable intricacy. Finally on either side of the stag would be placed yellow pies, gilded with egg yolks and saffron, 'in one of which let there be live frogs, in the other live birds'. The table set,

the scene in position, one of the ladies should pluck the arrow
from the stag. What then could be more exquisite than to
see the claret flowing as blood from a wound? What could be
more exciting than to hear the guns from the ship and the castle
fire and see them engage in battle, even though there was the minor
inconvenience of the room swirling with acrid gunpowder smoke
which set everyone a-choking? To 'sweeten the stink of the powder'
the ladies took the egg shells full of sweet waters to throw at one
another. Dripping and dishevelled now from the exertion and the
water fight the guests, according to the instructions, would settle
down to relax, 'all danger being over'. But the fun was not finished:
there was another jolly joke. Quickly the lids were whipped off
the pies and out bounced the frogs 'which make the ladies skip
and shout' then the birds 'who by a natural instinct flying at the
light will put out the candles so that what with the flying birds
and the skipping frogs the one above, the other beneath will
cause much delight and pleasure to the company'.

The revolt against Puritanism is shown by the excesses that
took place at court. Often important banquets and entertainments
were inclined to relapse into dissipated orgies, the honoured
guests spattered in cream and other beverages. The intemperance
at Hatfield, during the royal entertainments held early in June,
1606 in honour of King Christian of Denmark, is a fine illustration. After sports and feasting there was to be a representation of
the Coming of the Queen of Sheba before Solomon—a pantomime
designed to flatter His Majesty, who as Solomon was supposed
to represent wisdom in the act of receiving great wealth. Unfortunately, according to Sir John Harington (who invented the
water closet), all was not well '. . . alas as all earthly things fail to
poor mortals in enjoyment so proved this. The lady who was
playing the Queen's part, carried precious gifts to both their
majesties, but, forgetting the step arising to the canopy, overset her
caskets into his Danish majesty's lap, and fell at his feet, or,
rather, into his face. Much hurry and confusion ensued, and
cloths and napkins made all clean. His majesty then got up and
would dance with the Queen of Sheba, but he fell down and
humbled himself before her, and was carried to an inner chamber

and laid in a bed of state, which was not a little defiled with the presents which had been bestowed on his garments; such as wine, cream, jelly, cakes, spices, and other good matters. The entertainment and show went forward, and most of the presenters went backwards, or fell down, wine so occupied their upper chambers. Then appeared, in rich dresses, Hope, Faith and Charity. Hope tried to speak, but wine so enfeebled her endeavours, that she withdrew, and hoped the king would excuse her brevity. Faith followed her from the royal presence in a staggering condition. Charity came to the king's feet, and seeming desirous to cover the sins of her sisters, made a sort of obeisance; she brought gifts, but said she would return home again, as there was no gift which heaven had not already given his majesty: she then returned to Hope and Faith, who were both sick in the lower hall . . .' The ceremonies concluded by Victory nodding off to sleep on the steps of the ante-chamber and Peace banging some courtiers on the head with her olive branch.

Although after the Restoration and downfall of Cromwell food taboos were lifted, nothing was ever quite the same again. The seed of Puritanism was planted; gradually during the following century it swells and splits, roots protrude and grip, the green inhibitions grow up the years until by the nineteenth century the middle class walls are smothered in bright glossy hypocrisy. There is an interesting parallel in the rise of inhibition and establishment of tea and coffee as the national beverages, replacing the native alcoholic beer and ale.

As the food scholars entered the second half of the seventeenth century they heaved a sigh of relief. Something was at last emerging from the mass of recipes that they could recognize. An Englishness. A plainness. This, as Kenneth Hare remarked, was the British oak of cooking: plain fare which required no imagination. There was a middle-class hostility towards foreigners and foreign things, especially towards foreign food. Evelyn, on December 4, 1679 after dinner at the Portuguese Embassy writes: 'besides a good *olio*[1] the dishes were trifling, hash'd and condited after their way, not at all fit for an English stomac which is for

[1] See Appendix II, page 254.

solid meat'. And Rochester, without losing an opportunity to add some sexual allusions, illustrates a hearty meal at a well-known inn.

Our own plain fare, and the best *terse* [claret] the Bull
Affords, I'll give you and your bellies full.
As for French kickshaws, sillery and champagne,
Ragouts and fricasses, in troth w' have none.
Here's a good dinner towards, thought I, when straight
Up comes a piece of beef, full horseman's weight,
Hard as the arse of Mosely,[1] under which
The coachman sweats as ridden by a witch;
A dish of carrots, each of them as long
As tool that to fair countess did belong
Which her small pillow could not so well hide
But visitors his flaming head espied.
Pig, goose, and capon followed in the rear,
With all that country bumpkins call good cheer,
Served up with sauces, all of eighty-eight,
When out tough youth wrestled and threw the weight.
And now the bottle briskly flies about,
Instead of ice, wrapped in a wet clout.
A brimmer follows the third bit we eat:
Small beer becomes our drink, and wine our meat.

Examinations of a French contemporary cookery book—Varenne's *The French Cook*—show the detested ragouts and fricassés to be the old mediaeval dishes. A ragout is simply an ordinary sauce, either piquant or bland depending on the viands it accompanied, made from broth, herbs, onions and salt. A fricassé is a fried meat, again served with sauce, which is usually a white cream one. Kickshaws, or *quelque choses*, were the delicious garnishings of asparagus, mushrooms, truffles, lemon slices or pistachios—in short all the things that went towards making a dish tempting and agreeable.

It is an interesting conjecture that had it not been for this Puritan stunting, the English tradition might have blossomed as richly as that of the French. The ingredients were as fine as any in France: the cool rain-filled salt breezes, the lush green valleys, the aromatic pastures, the salt marshes, nourished cattle quite as

[1] 'Mother' Mosely kept a London brothel.

succulent even including the prized *pré-salé* mutton. The apple-fed pork, the stubble-fed geese, the wonderful drippings, the rich cream and butter, the soft and hard cheeses, the yellow corn should have blended in triumphant harmonies, made music as sweet as Purcell's; instead they seethed into a curdled nostrum. The English reputation for cooking is an international joke, as bad as any music-hall mother-in-law. 'Every country possesses, it seems, the sort of cuisine it deserves which is to say the sort of cuisine it is appreciative enough to want,' says Waverley Root in *The Food of France*. 'I used to think that the notoriously bad cooking of England was an example to the contrary, and that the English cook the way they do because, through sheer technical deficiency, they had not been able to master the art of cooking. I have discovered to my stupefaction that the English cook that way because that is the way they like it.' Hugh Kingsmill believed the English to be among the most potentially imaginative people in the world. But when it comes to physical matters—like cooking—this gift is seldom used. The native application is stunted. Where did it all go wrong? What other explanation is there than it was rusted by this Puritan mould?

But there it was. The delicious sauces, the simple pottages made from birds, meats and herbs were repelled, as very likely were the highly practical culinary methods of barding and larding. Unlike the paper food-scholars, contemporary visitors to seventeenth-century England, who had actually to eat the food, were unimpressed. 'The English,' observed Sorbière in 1663, 'are not very dainty and the greatest lords' tables, who do not keep French cooks, are covered only with large dishes of meat. They are strangers to bisks and pottage. Only I saw some milk-pottage in a large and deep dish . . . Their pastry is coarse and ill-baked, their stewed fruits and confectionery ware cannot be eat; they scarce ever make use of forks or ewers . . .' 'Gluttons at noon and abstinent at night,' said Misson, noting that they eat a great deal at dinner, rested awhile and 'to it again, till they have quite stuff'd their Paunch'. He too saw they were great flesh eaters. Some noblemen, he said, had both French and English cooks 'and these eat much after the *French* Manner: But among the middling Sort of

People . . . they have ten or twelve Sorts of common Meats, which infallibly take their Turns at their Tables, and two Dishes are their Dinners; a Pudding, for instance, and a Piece of roast Beef: Another time they will have a Piece of boil'd Beef, and then they salt it some Days beforehand, and besiege it with five or six Heaps of Cabbage, Carrots, Turnips and some other Herbs or Roots, well pepper'd and salted, and swimming in Butter: A Leg of roast or boil'd Mutton, dish'd up with the same Dainties, Fowls, Pigs, Ox-tripes, and Tongues, Rabbits, Pidgeons, all well moisten'd with Butter, without larding: Two of these Dishes, always served up one after the other, make the usual Dinner of a substantial Gentleman, or wealthy Citizen. When they have boil'd Meat, there is sometimes one of the Company that will have the *Broth*; this is a kind of Soup, with a little Oatmeal in it, and some Leaves of Thyme or Sage, or other such small Herbs . . . The *Pudding* is a Dish very difficult to be describ'd, because of the different Sorts there are of it; Flower, Milk, Eggs, Butter, Sugar, Suet, Marrow, Raisins etc. etc. are the most common Ingredients of a *Pudding*. They bake them in an Oven, they boil them with Meat, they make them fifty several Ways: BLESSED BE HE THAT INVENTED PUDDING for it is a Manna that hits the Palates of all Sorts of People; a Manna, better than that of the Wilderness, because the People are never weary of it. Ah, what an excellent Thing is an *English Pudding*! *To come in Pudding time*, is as much as to say, to come in the most lucky Moment in the World.'

Christmas was again quite the thing, with its accompanying pies and pottages. 'Every Family against *Christmas* makes a famous Pye, which they call *Christmas* Pye,' records the industrious Misson. 'It is a great Nostrum the Composition of this Pasty; it is a most learned Mixture of Neats-tongues, Chicken, Eggs, Sugar, Raisins, Lemon and Orange Peel, various kinds of Spicery etc. They also make a Sort of Soup with Plums, which is not at all inferior to the Pye, which is in their language call'd Plum-porridge.'

If there ever was such a person as a 'man of his age', Pepys was one. There is no better person with whom to observe and enjoy the food and to experience the inhibitions. We follow him through the narrow paths of Whitehall, with his wife stumbling on new soles, to eat a sack posset,[1] or drink a glass of whey;[2] we ride out to the fields of Islington, with their windmills and dairy herds, to taste a cheese-cake in the famous cheese-cake house; at Woolwich walk among the green corn and peas singing; eat buttered salmon, fritters, a barrel of pickled oysters, venison pasties, a 'hot pie made of swan' and at Christmas 'a mess of brave plum-porridge'; we stroll out into his yard to see his stock of pigeons, his turkeys newly come from Zeeland which Mrs. Pepys will have to kill, her maid not liking to. We push into the ale houses to swallow cakes and ale, and eat a wigg.[3] We sit up till four in the morning with Mrs. Pepys, busy among her mince pies—although the truth is she would far rather be dressing up pretty in her patches and her new tabby gown. We trudge off to market with her at six in the morning to buy the dinner, and before the fine feast of January 26, 1660 stay up far into the night 'making of her tarts and larding of her pullets'. And on the day there is 'a very fine dinner—viz a dish of marrow-bones, a leg of mutton, a loin of veal, a dish of fowl, three pullets, and two dozen of larks all in a dish; a great tart, a neats tongue, a dish of anchovy, a dish of prawns and cheese'. We hear the chimes from All Hallows carrying each hour into the rooms and advance with Mrs. Pepys brandishing the red-hot tongs designing to pinch her husband upon the nose so jealous, lonely and enraged is she.

It was an irregular household. Mrs. Pepys was left much on her own and felt isolated and bored. She was an erratic house-keeper. Sometimes there would be breakfast: red herrings or eggs. Sometimes dinner would be delicious, the house sweet and clean, at others the meat would be black as it emerged from the pot, the sauce too sweet, the linen foul and the new green serge hangings in

[1] Sir Walter Raleigh's recipe for Sack Posset is as follows: Boil together half a pint of sherry and half a pint of ale, and add gradually a quart of boiling cream or milk. Sweeten the mixture well, and flavour with grated nutmeg. Put it into a heated dish, cover it over, and let it stand by the fire 2 or 3 hours.

[2] It was fashionable in the seventeenth century to drink whey as a health aid.

[3] See Appendix II, page 259.

the dining room would shake with Pepys's rage at her incompetence. We can see how the great hall of the Middle Ages had
now become the entrance hall and in its place there was a smaller
more private room. The Pepyses' was very grand with gilt leather
and the famous new hangings. Dinner was now later, taking place
between eleven and midday. As Pepys became more prosperous
he would employ a mancook to arrange his more important
gustatory receptions: 'I had a pretty dinner for them: viz, a brace
of stewed carps, six roasted chickens, and a jowl of salmon, hot,
for the first course; a tansy, and two neat's tongues, and cheese,
the second; and were very merry all the afternoon, talking, and
singing, and piping on the flageolet. We had a mancook to dress
the dinner . . .'

In general Pepys's interest in food was materialistic rather than
epicurean. He wanted his table to be noble and proper to impress
other people, he minded very much what others thought. 'So to
dinner,' he writes on October 11, 1662, 'where there being nothing
but a poor breast of mutton, and that illdressed, I was much
displeased, there being Mr. Cooke there, who I invited and for
whom I was concerned to make much of.' But he was better
pleased four years later on November 28, 1666—'and so to get
things ready against dinner at home; and at noon comes my Lord
Hinchingbroke, Sir Thomas Crewe, Mr. John Crewe, Mr.
Carteret and Brisband. I had six noble dishes for them, dressed
by a mancook and commended, as indeed they deserved, for
exceeding well done. We eat with great pleasure and I enjoyed
myself in it; eating on silver plates, and all things mighty rich and
handsome about me.'

Pepys was not alone in this materialistic approach. Evelyn
was always very much interested in the cost of food. Of the consecration dinner of the Bishop of Worcester he writes: 'one of the
most plentifull and magnificent dinners, that in my life I ever saw;
it cost near 600 pounds I was assurd'.

Normally, to dress his food Pepys employed peasant girls, or
cookmaids as they were called, grumbling a little in 1663 when
he had to pay as much as four pounds a year 'the first time I ever
did give so much'. Often they were inefficient, for men maintained

the lead in the field of cookery, and the girls were commonly un-
trained, incompetent and forgetful, half-roasting the meat, ill-
dressing the fish. And Pepys would come home and fall out 'with
my wife and my maid for their sluttery', pull his wife's nose and
baste the maid with a broom till she screamed; or on another
occasion 'saw my door and hatch open, left so by Lucy, our
cook-maid, which so vexed me, that I did give her a kick in our
entry, and offered a blow at her, and was seen doing so by Sir W.
Pen's footboy, which did vex me to the heart, because I know he
will be telling their family of it; though I did put on presently a
very pleasant face to the boy, and spoke kindly to him as one
without passion, so as it may be he might not think I was angry'.

One of Pepys's troubles was that he suffered from two painful
and inconvenient ailments common at that time: dimness of the
eyes and a stone of the bladder—against which horseradish ale
was often drunk. On March 26, 1658 he endured an operation
for the calculus's removal, his recovery from which he com-
memorated every year afterwards by eating a thanksgiving dinner.
But the operation damaged the whole of his reproductory system,
resulting in his sterility and causing him intermittent pain for the
rest of his life—particularly when sexually aroused—and irritations
that probably accounted for much of his promiscuity. For all
his dalliance with girls, for all his reputation Pepys was at bottom
a Puritan. His lusting afforded him little pleasure and much guilt.
Moreover he disapproved heartily of the goings-on at court,
where the aristocrats, untempered with any Puritan wish-wash,
fornicated and wassailed away their days, 'there being so much
emulation, poverty and the vices of drinking, swearing and loose
amours, that I know not what will be the end of it but confusion'.
In February 1664 'a child was dropped by one of the ladies in
dancing; but nobody knew who, it being taken up by somebody
in their handkercher'. The king, it was rumoured, was interested.
He removed it to his closet and in the spirit of the new learning
dissected it.

Pepys's affliction of eyes afforded him so much inconvenience,
so much distress that, in 1669 at the age of thirty-six, he really
believed he was shortly going to be blind. He left his lucubrations,

illuminated by the guttering candle, never to confide his innermost secrets to his diary again. 'And so I betake myself to that course, which is almost as much as to see myself go into my grave: for which, and all the discomforts that will accompany my being blind the good God prepare me!'

But as we know he did not go blind and lived on to the age of eighty-nine, although on his death seven stones were discovered in his right kidney. Both of his malevolent afflictions were probably caused by deficiency of Vitamin A; Pepys's diet quite simply wanted in butter and green vegetables: lack of these it is now known can lead to blindness and the formation of stones in the urinary tracts. In general, prosperous urban people took a snobbish aversion to vegetables. *Meat* was a man's food. Pot-herbs and pottage belonged to peasants. Vegetables were food for the poor. A dinner of coleworts and bacon was considered by Pepys as 'poor Lenten fare'.

By now Lent was more an exercise in self-will than anything else. Everyone, as they entered the season, wondered whether they would be able to sustain some measure of abstinence throughout. Pepys could not. On March 26, 1661, an occasion which coincided with his 'great day' three years ago having been cut of the stone, he records in his diary '. . . Very merry at dinner: among other things, because Mrs. Turner and her company eat no flesh at all this Lent, and I had a great deal of good flesh which made their mouths water.' Fast-days were called sometimes by the government, but nobody really knew what they were supposed to be doing: 'This morning Mr. Berkenshaw came again, and after he had examined me and taught me something in my work, he and I went to breakfast in my chamber upon a collar of brawn; and, after we had eaten; asked me whether we had not committed a fault in eating today; telling me, that it is a fast-day ordered by the Parliament, to pray for more seasonable weather . . .'

The haut-goût of cookery—as we have seen from Pepys's household—was achieved by men. Most writers of cookery books were members of the nobility: chancellors, poets, inventors and physicians, whose imagination and food consumption was unlikely to have been coated by any Puritan rust, which was essentially a middle-class blight. Men like Sir Theodore de Mayerne-Turquet and Sir Kenelm Digby, who belonged to the court, where behaviour at mealtimes and banquets was inclined to be wild and uninhibited. 'Then was the banqueting Stuff flung about the room profusely,' writes Evelyn describing the Feast of the 'Companions of the Gartir' on St. George's Day 1667: 'The Cheere was extraordinary, each knight having 40 dishes to his messe: piled up 5 or 6 high.'

These books retain an almost mediaeval atmosphere, dishes are delicately spiced and scented with aromatic waters and perfumes; there are still the blancmanges like chicken mousses, the hippocras, the metheglin, the brouets, the leaches, the spring tarts, the prim-rose tarts, the almond broths, the piquant herb sauces for meat. Often Pepys would employ a special man to lay his cloth and fold his napkins into impressive fashionable shapes. Giles Rose in his *School for Officers of the Mouth* gives elaborate diagrams for pleating and pinching the napery into cockleshells, melons, partridges, tortoises and mitres. There are instructions for carve-peeling:[1] for adjusting the fruit, dignifying it into figures for decorating the table. From Rose's pages all the mediaeval personages emerge: the master butler, the master confectioner, the master cook and the master carver—'it is but reason that all common people should cut their own meat, so it is but just that all Kings, Princes and great lords and persons of quality should be exempted from this small pain . . . a carver . . . ought to be a very handsome, comely person, of a good behaviour and well clad . . .'

Even from these aristocratic pages the ghost of a comfortable peasant cooking is emerging mixed up with shades from France. There are Misson's wonderfully light and delicious suet puddings made to boil with the meat, from breadcrumbs, eggs, almonds, raisins, eggs and cream; there are recipes for pickled and preserved vegetables and fruit: cucumber, cauliflower, mushrooms, elder-flowers, thistle stalks, artichokes, samphire and ashkeys; apple omelettes, green cream tarts, spinach, oyster and herring pies, mutton stuffed with oysters, partridges cooked in cream, veal

---

[1] This means literally carving the fruit, as one peels it, into exotic shapes with which to decorate the table.

strewn with strawberry and violet leaves, roasted daffodil bulbs. In May, alexanders, fennel and thistle stalks were eaten tender and succulent, like asparagus, with melted butter or mayonnaise.

Such was the low standing of women that noble households like the Duke of Bedford's retained none for work in the kitchens. It is also interesting to see from his accounts that in the country there was no opposition to vegetables. The gardens at Woburn were furnished with pease, carrots, purslane, radish, endive, asparagus, parsnip, leeks, lettuce, beans, onions, cucumber, celery and all manner of fruit: cherries, peaches, nectarines, plums, pears, raspberries, strawberries. No longer were the seeds carefully conserved from year to year, now gardening had become a commercial concern and seeds, plants and fruit trees were purchased from nursery gardens surrounding London. It is interesting also to see that spices in some quantity entered the Duke's provision cupboards along with the dried raisins, currants and prunes, while in spring scurvy grass was mixed with the children's ale. Abroad the Duke dined plainly and solidly. From his dinner on October 16, 1689 at the Red Lion, Cambridge—as from many of Pepys's—it can be seen that fish and meat were now eaten together at the same meal, fast- and fishdays having lost their force.

For a brace of carp stewed with some perches ranged about them.	I 9	0
For a chine of mutton and a large chine of veal.	I 0	0
For making a pasty.	13	0
For a dish of tongues, udders and marrow-bones, with cauliflowers and spinach.	11	6
For a couple of geese.	8	0
For a hash of calf's head with sweetbreads.	11	6
For a dish of turkeys in a dish.	12	0
For a dish of collared pig.	0	0
For a dish of stewed oysters.	6	0
For a couple of pullets with oysters.	6	0
For a grand salad.	1	0
Second Course		
For 2 dishes of wild fowl.	I 4	0
For a jowl of sturgeon.	0	0
For a dish of fat chickens and rabbits.	8	0
For a stand of pickles with oysters, anchovies and tongue.	4	0
For a dish of snipes and larks.	6	6

For a large Westphalia ham and tongues.	1	5	0
For recruiting a dish of tarts.		3	0
For a dish of partridges.		4	6
For a dish of whipped sillabubs.		7	6
For a dish of artichokes.		3	6
For a 'solamagundy'.		2	0
For a dish of fruit.		3	6
For lemons and double refined sugar.		3	6
For oil and vinegar.		2	6
For my lord's table for butter.			4
For cheese for the servants.		1	0
For bread and beer.	6	19	8
For firing.		13	6
For porterage.		1	0

The second half of the seventeenth century witnesses a turning point in the history of cookery books. Two women writers appear, writing for other women: Shirley John and Hannah Wolley. Hannah Wolley is especially delightful. To her pages she introduces a certain rusticity. 'Fill not your mouth so full that your cheeks shall swell like a pair of *Scotch-bag-pipes*,' she cautions the ladies. She herself has attended many dinner parties where she has been disgusted with her hostess who, not being among Rose's Kings, Princes and great lords, has been obliged to cut her own meat, sweating, said Hannah Wolley, in cutting the joint as profusely as had the cook-maid in roasting it; so greasy was she after the performance she would clap her hands into her mouth, lick them and suck her knuckles; afterwards she would rub her teeth—most uncivil in company.

Ladies in the country were on the whole dedicated housewives. Foreign trade during the seventeenth century had established itself. During the last half of the sixteenth century the sweet potato had been discovered, suspected for holding aphrodisiacal qualities, and gradually introduced, as had tobacco. Now coffee, chocolate and tea—drunk green and weak—were coming from the East in ever larger quantities, conveyed by shipping companies such as the East India. Coffee houses were opening all over London and large sums of money had been made in the trading ventures. Those that had made their fortunes established great country estates, investing a good deal of their money in land, spending it lavishly on houses, farms and gardens. Men like Evelyn were inspired by architecture and gardens they had seen abroad. Great care and thought went into taming the shaggy country, turning it into delicious elm walks, water gardens, glades and grottoes; the aromatic lime walks jump out of Evelyn's diaries, hot cypresses and myrtles. The new white statues shine in the dusk, extravagant stones overgrow with moss. Out from the windows of the red chamber where Evelyn was born, one can look over the rising woods, the delicious streams, to the hills of Dorking; from the leads there are lovely prospects of variegated verdure; in the shadowy fragrant dining room one hundred and sixteen servants in green satin livery wait; and out in the garden two figures— ghosts of his parents—walk between the fountains and groves, beneath the pleached hornbeams, one of 'sanguine complexion mixed with a dash of choler', his hair hoary, curling, inclining to light, his beard brownish, the other well-timbered, eyes a lovely black, her disposition inclined to a religious melancholy.

Efficiently run country houses such as this were the centre of domestic industry, supervised by the lady of the house. She must see to the planting of new vegetables, the potting, curing, distilling and preserving, so that in autumn the great larder door clanged shut on marble and slate shelves packed with jars filled against the winter. She must see the fragrant spices were bought for the linen bags, the leaves and petals gathered for the pot pourri. She must candy sweetmeats, preserve wines, distil perfumes, prepare syrups, cordials, restoratives, fragrant oils, violet powders for her woollen cloths and delicious pomanders, she must make spiced pellets to burn on the fire. So that each house had its own personal flavour and fragrance, a mixture of the herbs and flowers that grew in the garden and the delicious warm thick smells of gums and resins, spices, rosewaters, musk and ambergris, scented woods and barks. All the work and expense that went towards making these agreeable aromas was not of course entertainment with which to fill the hours. Sanitary arrangements were still elementary, the Pepyses' latrine, for example, was situated in the cellar, a dreadful place which often overflowed with deposits from their neighbours'.

But improvements were on the way. Herbs and rushes were largely replaced with carpets, thus reducing the vermin, but the fight against dirt and noisome odours was still a constant drudgery and irritation.

Improvements were on the way. Thought was turning away from superstition and making new scientific discoveries. Previously all medical teaching had been based on the Greek humoral system: a mixture of philosophy, observation, experience and superstition. There were four primary qualities, the hot, the cold, the wet and the dry. These combined to make four elements, earth, air, fire and water, which entered in varying proportions to all matter. This doctrine merged with the Hippocratic theory that the body was composed of four liquids, blood, phlegm, yellow bile and black bile formulating the four different humours of man: sanguine, phlegmatic, choleric or melancholy. Thus were a lady to be alloyed with a surfeit of black bile she would be melancholy; but were the main ingredient to be yellow bile, then her constitution would be choleric, and so on. This formula applied also to food, and the digestive and nutritive value to its consumer was determined by each related quality and substance. Muffet in *Health's Improvement* writes:

> Touching the difference of meats in substance: some are of thin and light substance, engendring thin and fine blood, fit for fine complexions, idle citizens, tender persons, and such as are upon recovery out of some great sickness: as chiken peepers, rabbet suckers, young pheasants, partridge, heath-poulse, godwits, all small birds being young, all little fishes of the river, the wings and livers of hens, cockchickens and partridges, eggs warm out of the hens belly, etc. Others are more gross, tough, and hard, agreeing chiefly to country persons and hard labourers: but secondarily to all that be strong of nature, given by trade or use to much exercise, and accustomed to feed upon them: as poudred beife, bacon, goose, swan, saltfish, ling, tunnis, salt salmon, cucumbers, turneps, beans, hard peaze, hard cheese, brown and rye bread, etc. But meats of a middle substance are generally the best, and most properly to be called meats; engendring neither too fine nor too gross bloud.

From Burton's *Anatomy of Melancholy* it seemed everyone was in for a thin time. According to him there was nothing that did not cause a black thick melancholy, apart from a little whey, lettuce and bugloss. Milk and all that came of it increased sadness, as did spices; fruit was utterly forbidden, being windy to boot; beef, being a strong hearty meat, bred gross melancholy blood, also venison and hare, all fowl, ducks, geese, swan, hen, cranes and coots; all fish were unwholesome; all pulses and herbs were naught, while standing waters 'thick and ill coloured' such as pools and moats 'where hemp hath been steeped or shiny fishes live', full of mites, creepers and slime, could not be recommended either.

Illness in general was considered as something toxic inside to be evacuated. Treatments were either folk-lorish, herbal or purgative—consisting of enemas, emetics and bleedings.[1] Every orifice, natural or artificial, was employed. Boorde's remedy for itching, which he said came from the corruption of evil blood, was to prepare a good pair of nails, 'to crache and clawe and to rent, tear the skin and flesh that the corrupt blood may run out'. Against a pregnant woman's unnatural appetite he had known such lusts put away 'by smelling to the savour of their own shoes', while for 'the erection of the yerde to synne' the remedy was to leap into a great vessel of cold water, or to put nettles in the codpiece. Other medicines were often revolting: not only did they taste disgusting, they *were* disgusting. Usnea—the moss from skulls of criminals that had been hanged and exposed in chains— was declared a sovereign remedy for many diseases, and following the Crusades, Mumia—literally powdered up mummies—was a favourite pharmacon. Many diseases and disorders were put down to poor arrangement of the stomach. An air of mystery surrounded the whole area. The colour of the urine, it was supposed, was a guide to the state the previous meal had reached in decomposition. Were the water to be fiery red like the sunset, or a vanishing

[1] This was a remedy commended for nearly everything—vertigo, nausea, head-ache, acne, colds, gout or haemorrhoids. Pain was presumed to be caused by bad blood which must be let out. This was by no means a simple process. Not only must the right vein be selected from thirty-two sites on the body, including two under the the tongue, two on the genitals and two at the external angles of the eye, but so must the right date in the calendar. There were thirty-two dangerous days in the year which must be studiously avoided, particularly the first Monday in January and the second in October when whosoever was bled then 'shall die by the fifteenth or seventh day'.

flame, this indicated food and drink had left the stomach that digestion might be completed; if of the hue of blushing cheeks, racked wine, or greenish, it indicated food and drink were properly digested; greenish blue meant less food and drink should be consumed; greenish like an unripe apple that food was only half digested; of a leaden hue, or black like ink meant death; white indicated a boil.

Theories relating to the timing of sleep, sexual intercourse and dining were many. One was to beware of venereous acts before the first sleep, and especially to beware after dinner 'it doth engender the cramp, the gout and other displeasures'. After meat 'let hym make a pause. And then let hym stand and lene and sleep against a cupboard.' Much distress was caused by 'reptiles in the stomach'. Boorde believed there to be many kinds of worms, 'long white ones in a man's body, square ones in a man's hands and feet'. There were probably, he thought, worms in a man's tooth and definitely some in a man's ear.[1]

In the middle of the seventeenth century the Royal Society for Promotion of Natural Knowledge was formed, for discourse on all manner of subjects: the nature of comets, the circulation of the blood—for which experiments with live animals were carried out —and sundry curiosities, the observation for example of a corpse that in the grave grew over an inch of reddish hair. Improvements were made in preserving food and refrigeration. Lord Bacon had fatally contracted pneumonia in a blizzard gathering snow with which to stuff a fowl to experiment how long it would stay sweet; Pepys had been interested to learn, from coffee house chatter, the experiences of Canadian trappers who kept their fish frozen and sweet beneath their sledges for many months; now, against the summer, ice and snow were cropped in winter and stored below ground in cool dark ice-houses.

[1] An entry in Evelyn's diary dated August 9, 1682 illustrates how really frightful it could be to harbour a worm. On that day Dr. Tyson brought before a gathering of the Royal Society a *Lumbricus Latus* which a patient of his had voided: 'of 24 foote in length, it had severall joynts, at lesse than one inch asunder, which on examination prov'd so many mouthes and stomachs in number 400 by which it adhered to & sucked the nutrition & juice of the Gutts, & . . . The Person who voided it, indured such torment in his bowels, that he thought of killing himselfe,'

Instruments were constructed to aid the digestion. In 1659 Walter Rumsey contributed a stomach brush 'to take away distempers by rummaging and scouring the stomach'. It was two foot in length, made after the form of a long goose's feather 'with a small button of fine linen or silk, to the bigness of a cherry stone, fastened at one end, which goeth into the body, and with a string fastened at the other end, that a man may use it and draw it out at pleasure . . . It must be stirred gently and always used after some meat and drink as any man . . . findeth occasion for it.' In 1682 Denys Papin devised an engine for softening bones: the first pressure cooker. On April 12, 1682, Evelyn writes:

> I went this Afternoon to a Supper, with severall of the R. Society, which was all dressed (both fish and flesh) in Monsieur *Papins Digestorie*; by which the hardest bones of Biefe itselfe, & Mutton, were without water, or other liquor, & . . . made as soft as Cheeze, produc'd an incredible quantity of Gravie, & for close, a Gellie, made of the bones of biefe . . . the most delicious that I had ever seene or tasted . . . We eat Pick and other fish with bones & all without any impediment: but nothing exceeded the Pigeons, which tasted just as if baked in a *pie*, all these being stewed in their owne juice . . .

Much has been written of the improvements in husbandry at this time. Of the introduction of clover and turnips—a magic root, sovereign for cattle, swine, poultry and hunting dogs, producing 'very good syder', exceeding 'good oyl'. Some progressive and interested men did plant them, and write agricultural tracts on their findings, but in the main the new crops were not generally known until the last part of the next century. They had little impact on the quality of meat until then. The English country people were slow and lethargic, not quick in adopting new methods. Aubrey, in an unpublished, unfinished comedy, shows them more interested in rude and rustic junketings than in agrestic improvement. A mixed company of sow-gelders, dairy maids and gypsies were to give evidence in dialogue and song of the coarse ideas and disreputable behaviour of the squires, who were shown having left their wives and taken up with cook-maids, while several heiresses had made off with grooms. In one scene during supper the gentlemen stuff the food and drink into their mouths and—for reasons of their own—the marmalade into their pockets, then hurry out to hoop, halloo and jubilee, sleeping between while with the wenches and servants. At daybreak there comes a general vote to unhinge the cellar door and throw it from a cliff top into the River Dee. Blowing horns and clarions, which sets all the dogs in the neighbourhood a-barking, everyone rushes to play the jolly prank; and are seen later in the drama bursting into a tavern intending to drink a thousand cups of 'revell ale'.

England was still largely a shaggy untamed land. The state of the highroads was precarious. Venturing abroad for visits *en famille* it was the custom to proceed by closed carriage; according to Evelyn often the host's servants had an inconvenient habit of making the visiting coachman so cheerful a welcome that on their way home, the worse for it, they fell from their boxes unable to drive. Added to this hazard there was always the possibility that highwaymen and thieves would leap from the hedge to rob the traveller.[1]

Up near the border country it was especially wild. There were dark and secret valleys where, cut off by trackless wastes of grass, bent heather, sloughs and wet moss-hag, robbers lived, in much the same way as the Celts had done, by cattle raiding and thieving; their strongholds covered with turf, approachable only by secret paths through the treacherous mosses. Here were the remnants of a savage past, upholding the worst traditions.

> Of the mountain is the sweeter
> But the valley is the fatter;
> And so we deem it meeter
> To carry off the latter

chants the old border ballad, telling of cattle raids. But there was worse. Story relates that under the reign of James I a fearsome pirate, called Sawney Beane, lived with his ferocious wife near the

---

[1] On June 11, 1652, there is an entry in Evelyn's diary describing how, because of the heat, he was riding along the hedge in the shade. Three miles from Bromley two cut-throats leapt upon him, hauled him into a deep thicket and relieved him of his boots and the jewellery he was carrying. Then they tied his hands, bound him to a tree and left him tormented by flies, ants and the sun with only his grazing horse and a few sheep in sight. It was only after several hours that he managed to break himself free and return down the steep bank to the dusty highway.

shores of Galloway, in an enormous cave, stretching one mile backwards into the cliff. Here they stayed, without visiting any city, town, or village, for twenty-five years. During this time they conceived eight sons and six daughters, who in their turn pro-duced eighteen grandsons and fourteen grand-daughters. They supported themselves by robbing travellers and passers-by whom they slaughtered, and, in the best domestic manner, put their carcasses down to salt or pickle. So great was their supply that one version of the story has it they were able to throw unchoice arms and legs out to sea. Gradually the country became depopulated. One day however the family were caught at the hunt; some were dismembering a woman, some hacking her still living husband, when a party of horsemen hove into view. His Majesty himself, it is reported, was sent for. He, accompanied by blood-hounds and a body of four hundred men, set out to find the hellish crew. The blood-hounds entered the cave and set up such a yowling that His Majesty and his band joined them, penetrating back into the windings of the cave. A dismal sight met their eyes: a multitude of arms, legs and thighs hung up in rows, while a great many lay submerged in pickle. Sawney Beane and his hirsute family were conducted thence to Edinburgh. There justice was done, and without trial they were speedily dispatched. The men, says the report, were castrated, shorn of their hands and feet and left to bleed to death; the women were burnt in three fires. They all died, it was said, without the least sign of repentance, continuing to shout filthy curses to the last. [1]

[1] There is a rival story to this one, the manuscript account of which exists in the Bideford Public Library in Devon and was discovered there by Mr. John Lewington. This states that circa 1740 a certain John Gregg took up his abode in a cave near 'Clovaley' in Devonshire where, together with his family of Robbers and Murderers they lived for twenty-five years without so much as once going to visit any City or Town, robbing above one thousand Persons, whom they murdered and ate, until at last the hellish crew were happily discovered by a pack of Blood-hounds and were seized and executed. Apart from the difference in place and time the story is in most details the exact counterpart of Sawney Beane's.

CHAPTER SEVEN

CORPORATE GREED

Some people have a foolish way of not minding, or pretending not to mind what they eat. For my part, I mind my belly very studiously, and very carefully; for I look upon it that he who does not mind his belly, will hardly mind anything else.

DR. JOHNSON

I

The Misfortune of Fortunate People

ENGLAND LAY balanced on the brink of land enclosure. The sun rose and burned through the retreating mists, gilding the first mornings of the century, reddening the last mornings of silence and freedom. On the eve of the Industrial Revolution it lay, a leafy land, inhabited by five and a half million people, one and a half million dwelling in towns, four million in the country. It was a land mainly populated by peasant farmers, working land their grandfathers and fathers had worked before them; they were independent, equal to their neighbours. Their farming methods were in many cases poor, but their soil could produce a surplus. The rhythms remained unchanged. Winter was—and remained so during the most of the eighteenth century— a season against which one must prepare, stock up provisions: a white ice-siege. And when the thaw came in springtime, the sky and the barn doors would be opened, the swine would be released from winter, to wallow. Hens would leave their roosts, scratch and scuffle in the dust, cocks could fly up the mossy wall, clap their wings and crow. Larks nested in the old grass cart tracks.

More or less unhindered, one could still have steered over the hills and through the summer valley paths, through thick green grain, soaking trouser and skirt bottoms, through daisies and cowslips and poppies. In Chelsea there were hayfields, where on sultry afternoons one could lie in a calm of pleasure, hidden in private thickets, dozing over a book, away from people and noise, and the rose blossoms would wither and fall over the words, dragonflies would hum past. On the thick air the London churches would fling out the chimes of their bells; there would be the scent of bean-blossom;[1] the only sounds the ring of the mower sharpening his scythe, the soft breath of the cattle, the swishing of the grass, the raucous shouts of children and the voices of gossips rising and falling.

There, sheltered from the looming rush of commercialism, England lay, cut out as though a vineyard in terraces of class. There was no room for mediocracy—there was more genius per head of population in the eighteenth century than ever before and ever since. It was a century of freedom, brilliance, great wealth against poverty, reckless spending and self-indulgence; a century of paradox, of dawning compassion and violence, of brutality with elegance, debauchery with taste. It was as though an abyss had opened up, that undermined the safety of those well-secured terraces and revealed the subterranean roots of Puritan priglets twisting like strange slimy snakes, exuding black fumes of melancholy, foul stenches and stifling mists of hypocrisy; fore-casting the overcrowding, the taxes, the sanctimony that were to come. It was as though the aristocracy of England kicked up its high red heels, puffed on its blue face powder, whirled round its lace clothes, its curls and its muffs, determined to react, to have one last and brilliant fling. A peculiar wave of romantic sadness and yearning spread through the country; men were filled with a strange wild force which led on the imagination to seek the unobtainable. A new malaise struck England: a blackened ennui. Spleen. It was recognized as being particular to England. It was the result,

[1] This, the Horticultural Society writes, was the scent of the Horse, Small Field or Tuck Bean, which until this century was widely cultivated, filling the air at blossom time with its delicious scent.

said foreigners, of the water-laden climate and too much meat. It drove men desperate. Never had there been so much drunkenness, so many duels, such surfeit and brittle gaiety, sparkle and eccentricity. Spleen caused excess, excess caused spleen. One might argue that everything in the eighteenth century, the brilliance, the achievements, emanated from the energy set up to elude this spleen.

Boredom made society necessary. The brilliant companies and spectacles, the delicious dinners were diversion from melancholy. Often the least solitude was intolerable, producing instant ennui. Ennui was a luxury, as Horace Walpole told Madame du Deffand in a letter; it was the misfortune of fortunate people. As always, food and drink went to alleviate it, Roger North declaring: 'The profusion of the best provisions and wine was to the worst of purpose. Debauchery, disorder, tumult and waste.'

Drunkenness was an acknowledged vice, rising, with the marketing of cheap spirits, to its peak in 1740 to 1742. The unrestricted sale of cheap gin and other crude alcohol reached such excesses that people feared the whole social structure was being undermined. It affected all strata of society, not least the country squires, who, according to Lady Mary Wortley Montagu, were a rowdy lot: 'insensible to other pleasures than the bottle and the chase . . . their mornings are spent among the hounds, and their nights with as beastly companions with what liquor they can get.' Men drank, like Johnson, to be rid of themselves, to send themselves away. There were wild evening parties when the front door spun past so dizzily those returning home late found it almost impossible to effect an entry.

For young men with money it was fashionable to belong to a club or a gang. 'Our Modern celebrated Clubs are founded upon Eating and Drinking,'[1] said Addison, 'which are Points wherein most Men agree, and in which the Learned and the Illiterate, the Dull and the Airy, the Philosopher and the Buffoon, can all of them bear a part.' Unfortunately many of the club members did not restrict their activities to remaining on the premises eating and

---

[1] Members of the Golden Fleece Club were rechristened on the premises with such names as Sir Bumkin Guzzle and Sir Swigbelly Situp.

drinking. Having consumed as much liquor as possible they terrorized the nocturnal streets, intent upon causing as much nuisance as possible. The Hectors specialized in vandalism, the She-Romps Club dragged passing girls into the precincts and made them walk on their hands so that their skirts fell over their heads, and the Mohocks were so feared that their name was used as a bogeyman to frighten children into entering their small clothes faster, or finishing their groats. They lurked in dark streets waiting to tie their victims, crush their noses, gouge out their eyes, slit their ears and distend their mouths; some they rolled into the river, imprisoned in barrels.

Cruelty, too, was effective in alleviating the spleen. 'Ah tis the best lechery to see 'em suffer correction,' one of the characters in Aubrey's unfinished comedy had remarked. Now in the eighteenth century a wave of sadism blew across Europe, arousing a ghoulish passion in dungeons, cobwebs and corpses, in witch-craft, blasphemy and demonolatry—heresies that a hundred years ago would have been punishable by death.

Even gustatory gratification did not escape this macabre turn. To render meat more delicious and tempting all manner of dreadful tortures were devised for the living animals. Poultry, in order to put on flesh after its long journey from the farms, was sewn up by the gut—a practice which, according to Tobias Smollett, rendered the flesh rotten; turkeys were bled to death by hanging them upside down with a small incision in the vein of the mouth; geese were nailed to the floor; salmon and carp were hacked into collops while living to make their flesh firmer; eels were skinned alive, coiled round skewers and fixed through the eye so they could not move. 'I know nothing more shocking or horrid,' said Pope, 'than the prospect of kitchens covered with blood and filled with the cries of creatures expiring in tortures.' But expire in tortures they did. The flesh of the bull, it was believed, was indigestible and unwholesome if the animal was killed with-out being baited. Butchers were liable to prosecution if the brutal preliminaries were omitted. Calves and pigs were whipped to death with knotted ropes to make the meat more tender, rather than our modern practice of beating the flesh when dead. 'Take

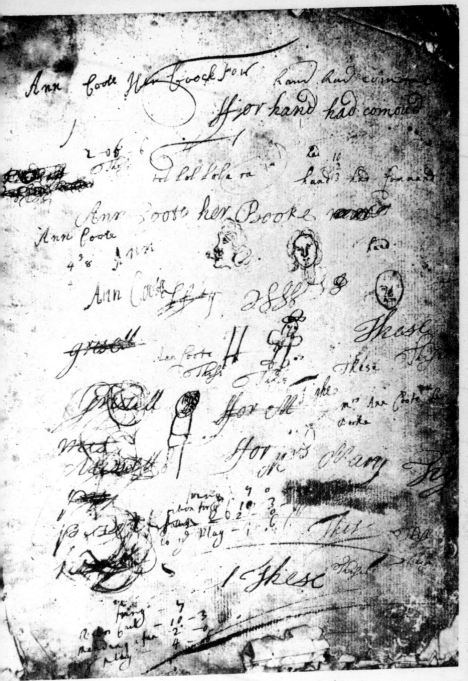

13. Front page of Ann Coote's Book of Medical Recipes

14A. The Guildhall, in 1761, at the beginning of the Lord Mayor's banquet

14B. 'The Brilliants'—Rowlandson's view of an evening in a Gentleman's Eating and Drinking Club

15A. George de Cari's 1816 caricature: 'Un Anglais attaqué du spleen vient se faire traiter en France.'

15B. Le Départ. 'Guéri du spleen par La Cuisine Française l'Anglais retourne à Londres en embonpoint.'

16A. Society was necessary to alleviate ennui. 'Conversazione' by Dickinson

16B. Doctor Johnson at dinner in a subterranean chop-house. By Dickinson

a red cock that is not too old and beat him to death,' begins one of Doctor William Kitchiner's recipes. Or to make a pig taste like wild boar 'take a living pig, and let him swallow the following drink: boil together in vinegar and water some rosemary, thyme, sweet basil, bayleaves and sage. When you have let him swallow this, immediately whip him to death and roast him forthwith.' On this subject Charles Lamb debated the vexed question: 'whether supposing that the flavour of a pig who obtained death by whipping superadded a pleasure upon the palate of a man more intense than any possible suffering we can conceive in the animal, is man justified in using that method of putting the animal to death?' His conclusions are unrecorded.

Perhaps the most elaborate and horrible recipe of all is the one repeated by Kitchiner, which is reputed to have originated from someone called Mizald; on how to roast and eat a goose alive.

> Take a Goose, or a Duck, or some such lively creature pull off all her feathers, only the head and neck must be spared: then make a fire round about her, not too close to her, that the smoke do not choke her, and that the fire may not burn her too soon; not too far off, that she may not escape free: within the circle of the fire let there be set small cups and pots of water, wherein salt and honey are mingled; and let there be set also chargers full of sodden Apples, cut into small pieces in the dish. The Goose must be all larded, and basted over with butter: put then fire about her, but do not make too much haste, when as you see her begin to roast; for by walking about and flying here and there, being cooped in by the fire that stops her way out the unwearied Goose is kept in; she will fall to drink the water to quench her thirst, and cool her heart, and all her body, and the Apple sauce will make her dung and cleanse and empty her. And when she roasteth, and consumes inwardly, always wet her head and heart with a wet sponge; and when you see her giddy with running, and begin to stumble, her heart wants moisture, and she is roasted enough. Take her up and set her before your guests and she will cry as you cut off any part from her and will be almost eaten up before she be dead: it is mighty pleasant to behold!!!

The Puritan disapproval of foreign food was now being gradually improved and shaped into substance for the mind. The type of food one ate, it was believed, affected your character, thus a diet of plain robust roast beef produced plain robust men, while

the French and Italian ragouts made gaudy nincompoops. It
was a theme worked on by many of the satirists:[1]

> When Mighty Roast Beef was the Englishman's Food,
> It ennobled our veins and enriched our Blood,
> Our Soldiers were brave, and our Courtiers were good,
> On the Roast Beef of Old England,
> And Old English Roast Beef!
>
> But since we have learnd from all-conquering France
> To eat their Ragouts as well as to dance,
> We are fed up with nothing but vain complaisance.
> Oh the Roast Beef, etc.
>
> Our Fathers of old were robust, stout, and strong,
> And kept open House with good Cheer all Day long,
> Which made their plump Tenants rejoice in this song.
> Oh the Roast Beef, etc.
>
> But now we are dwindled, to what shall I name?
> A sneaking poor Race, half begotten—and tame,
> Who sully those Honours that once shone in Fame,
> Oh the Roast Beef, etc.
>
> When good Queen Elizabeth was on the Throne,
> E'er Coffee, or Tea and such Slip Slops were known,
> The World was in Terror, if e'er she did frown.
> Oh the Roast Beef, etc.
>
> .   .   .
>
> Oh then they had Stomachs to eat and to fight,
> And when Wrongs were a-cooking to do themselves right!
> But now we're a—I cou'd—but good Night.
> Oh the Roast Beef of Old England,
> And Old English Roast Beef!

It is interesting to see how this supposition is borne out in the
menus of two well-known men of the eighteenth century. On
the one hand there is proper solid old Parson Woodforde serving
a proper solid dinner to his no doubt proper solid guests on April
20, 1774—not for them any frenchified stuff:

> The first course was, part of a large Cod, a Chine of Mutton, some Soup,
> a Chicken Pye, Puddings and Roots, etc. Second *Course*, Pidgeons and

[1] One of the favourite weapons of the satirists of this time was the satirical recipe.
It was an elastic device, interesting and agreeable to a public peculiarly attentive to
cuisine and satire. There were recipes of all kinds, ones to make drama, cuckolds,
sceptics, love-songs, and satirists.

Asparagus. A fillet of Veal with Mushrooms and high Sauce with it, rosted Sweetbreads, hot Lobster, Apricot Tart and in the Middle a Pyramid of Syllabubs and Jellies. We had Dessert of Fruit after Dinner, and Madeira, White Port and red to drink as Wine.

On the other hand there is Sir Francis Dashwood, who was anything but proper and solid. His menu, served at a dinner of the Hell Fire Club, is for voluptuaries, comprising seductive rich French dishes, which followed special restorative cocktails, christened with special restorative names like 'Strip me Naked' and 'Lay me down Softly':

Soupe[1] de Santé; Soup au Bourgeoise; Carp au Court Bouillon; Pupton of Partridge; Cullets à la Maine;[2] Beef à la Tremblade; Fricassé of Salamanders; Huffle of Chicken; a Stewed Lyon; Pain Perdu; Oysters à la Daube; Blanckmanger.

Everything at the Hell Fire Club was conducted on the grandest scale. No expense was spared. Everything was arranged, among carefully ruined towers, to give the greatest pleasure and comfort. Venereal disease, it was whispered, was so prevalent among its members that they were known to address one another as *Signor Gonorrhea* and *Monsieur de Croix de Vénus*. Among the brethren who were gathered together to enjoy pretty women and good food, incorporated with the new thrill of black magic and blasphemy, were the First Lord of the Admiralty, the Chancellor of the Exchequer and the most famous satirist of his day. Sir Francis himself was not without distinction, holding the office of Postmaster General and being the reputed author of a paper entitled 'The Technique of Farting'. To his villagers at High Wycombe he seemed a kind man. They had not forgotten his opening of a new formal garden when he had had the pleasant notion of inviting the minister to picnic in the grounds with his Sunday School. Together the minister and he had watched amiably

[1] See Appendix II, page 261.
[2] This is printed in Ivan Bloch's *Sexual Life in England Past and Present*. Presumably the original menu was inscribed in an elaborate eighteenth-century hand, difficult to decipher and interpret if one was not familiar with contemporary dishes. Cullets à la Maine would probably be Cutlets à la Maintenon, while Huffle of Chicken may have been Souffle—a flowery S and O having been confused for an H, and a Stewed Lyon is likely to be stewed loin.

as the children had played and squabbled round the curious curving lawns; running now to a triangular dense shrubbery, now up to race round two small mounds each surmounted with a bed of bright flowers. Would the minister care to climb the tower, Sir Francis wondered, to see to advantage the delightful prospect? They mounted and then to the minister's astonishment a stream of water shot suddenly from the shrubbery and, from the two red-mounted beds, fountains sprayed out white chalky rivers. They were looking down on the naked body of a woman, contrived from the contours of the lawn and plants. The minister's astonishment turned to horror. He fainted.

The gardens at Medmenham were a special feature of the place, filled with writhing Venuses, inscribed with bawdy Latin puns. All in white the 'monks' would file into the chapel, which would be suitably filled with foul stenches from smouldering rue and henbane, to celebrate Black Mass. This was generally enjoyed upon the body of a naked woman laid out on the altar, from whose navel the sacrificial wine would be imbibed. The scene was illuminated by inverted black candles and lamps supported by bats from which protruded enormous erect penises. While the fumes from the reeking herbs permeated the cracks in the ceilings and the white robes, the brethren chanted ribald rhymes, especially composed, in tune to well-known hymns. Outside 'nuns'—i.e. prostitutes sent down from London brothels —waited in the Roman Room. To raise themselves to a proper state of expectancy they were encouraged to ride a special toy; contrived like a hobby horse it had the head of a rooster, its neck turned round so that the beak (in the shape of a phallus) lay along its back. The brethren had resort to a small dispensary for aphrodisiacs; doctors and nurses were ready to revive anyone in case they passed out. The rarest and most amazing contortions were approved, some of the permutations requiring three or four people working as a team, some, stage props such as musical bells.

The brave English nature was not helped, the reactionaries believed, by the advent of 'slip slops'—tea and coffee—and their establishment as the main beverage. Tea especially was thought to be a pernicious drug: 'deleterious produce' of China. 'Your very *chambermaids* have lost their bloom,' thundered Jonas Hanaway, 'I suppose by *sipping tea*.' The infusion was, in his view, no less a horror than gin. 'What an army had *gin* and *tea* destroyed,' he roared. Beer had been a healthy drink with a definite food value. Small beer, Drummond and Wilbraham calculate, in *The English man's Food*, had a probable calorific value of 150 to 200 calories a pint. This would have meant that a daily ration of seven pints would have provided 1,050 to 1,450 calories together with the vitamins in the B group, and ascorbic acid. Now, since tea was drunk without the addition of milk, it meant it was little more than hot scented water. Nevertheless replace beer it did. By early in the reign of George II, all classes in town and country were drinking it in their own homes. At first some ladies had no knowledge how the strange foliage should be absorbed. Southey has a story of a country lady who, on receiving the present of a pound from a fashionable town friend, boiled the lot in a kettle and served up the leaves with salt and butter to her expectant tea party whose members unanimously voted it detestable and were astonished that even fashion could make such a dish palatable.

Nothing was expected to affect the character of a person more than his wet nurse. It was unfashionable to feed one's own children. Water was impure, and children who were weaned had always drunk very small beer. Apart from whey, cow's milk, especially in towns, was considered most unhealthy. Cows were kept in dark hovels and milk was often sold watered down, in filthy buckets, frothed up with bruised snails. Householders preferred to buy it straight from the udder, the cows being driven through the streets and milked at the doors. Human milk was recommended not only for young children but also for invalids and elderly people. The founder of Caius College, Cambridge, existed during the last years of his life only upon human milk—his case was only remarkable to Thomas Muffett because of the ill nature of the woman who gave him suck.

What made Dr. *Cajus* in his last sickness so peevish and so full of frets at Cambridge, when he suckt one woman (whom I spare to name) froward of conditions and of bad diet; and contrariwise so quiet and well, when he suckt another of contrary disposition? verily the diversity of their milks and conditions, which being contrary one to the other, wrought also in him that sucked them contrary effects.

Dr. Johnson was supposed to have received the bad eyesight and scrofula that scarred and distressed him all his life from his unsoaped wet-nurse.

It was recommended in such manuals as Bull's *Rules for Choice of Wet Nurses* that all candidates be perused like cows: the soundness of their teeth and gums, the clarity of their tongues and complexions, the firmness of their breasts and above all the goodness of their characters were each to be carefully examined. It was a career that very likely provided a useful source of income, and gin, to many a careless prostitute.[1] Particularly when the Foundling Hospital was opened, because of 'Frequent Murders committed on poor Miserable Infant Children at their Birth by their Cruel Parents to hide their Shame, and for the Inhuman Custom of Exposing Newborn Children to Perish in the Streets or the putting out such unhappy Foundlings to wicked and barbarous Nurses who undertaking to bring them up for a Small and Trifling Sum of Money do often suffer them to Starve.' This wish to halt the exposing of infants was not quite so much a matter of compassion as practicality on the part of Thomas Coram. Such infant death was a waste of British life, which could be better saved to work and fight for the British Empire. A new career was opened up in wet-nursing, and other things besides. 'Nothing is so common as the *rent breasts* for children to suck,' Cobbett recorded some years later, and what was worse 'a *man actually advertised* in the London papers about two months *to supply childless husbands with heirs*'.

[1] Havelock Ellis explains that the processes of sexual intercourse and breast feeding are very similar: 'In both cases we may observe the phenomenon of detumescence in an organ which has momentarily swelled and which, through the expulsion of a precious liquid, leads to the complete, physical and psychic satisfaction of the persons involved. The swollen breast corresponds to the erect penis, the avid, humid mouth of the child to the palpitating, humid vagina.'

2

Culinary Erections

All over the country beautiful houses sprang up. Moons of architecture, shining with a borrowed light from antiquity. Colonnades rose and porticoes curved against the soft green trees. The large parks contained looking-glass lakes, the hills rising from the edge in 'a various manner', in some places steep and bold, in others waving lawns, crowned and spread with wood; majestic oaks and beeches, opening out sometimes in large breaks to let in the views of others.

As the country grew more tame, its forests chopped, its thickets cleared, there came a reaction, an attraction towards the wild, towards nature. People ventured for pleasure to the mountains and the sea; no longer were they viewed as dangerous heaving expanses, but refreshing challenges. Houses, instead of sheltering in nests between valleys, now commanded the prospect. The statues, glades and grottoes were replaced by romantic wild effects, winding paths meandered past clumps of trees to the folly, or the hermitage complete with hermit. Unmown grass swept up to the door.

For the rich these were leisurely days. The rising of a morning; the observing from panelled window seats the early mists over the new park; the walking before breakfast picking flowers; the letter writing and the housekeeper interviewing; the music practice, the business of the day. At ten, perhaps, the sound of the gong, that delightful reassuring boom directing one punctually, like strong arms, to meals; into the breakfast room with its small table, bouquets of flowers, the smell of toast and the optimistic morning sun lying in long gold squares over the floor, its cream, its dark brown of coffee and tea. 'And then,' Maria Josepha Holroyd wrote to Gibbon, 'about 11 I play on the harpsichord, or I draw, 1, I translate and 2 walk out again, 3 I generally read, and 4 we go to dine, after dinner we play at backgammon, we drink tea at 7, and I work or play on the piano till 10, when we have our little bit of supper and 11, we go to bed.'

Dinner divided the day. Through the century it was a moveable feast. 'In my own Memory the Dinner has crept by Degrees from Twelve a Clock to Three,' wrote a contributor to the *Tatler*, 'and where it will fix no Body knows.'

An invitation to dine meant that one could be asked to spend seven or eight hours in the company of the host. Often no places were allotted, the guests, as Arnold Palmer said, entered in a polite mob to seat themselves promiscuously. But often there was a great to-do about the Place and Ceremony. 'I have known,' said Addison, 'my friend Sir Roger's Dinner almost Cold before the Company could adjust the Ceremonial.' Sometimes the guests might sit themselves down before as many as twenty or thirty covers. Smelling to the meat whilst on the fork was not recommended. 'I have seen an ill-bred fellow do this,' said the Reverend Mr. Trusler, 'and have been so angry that I could have kicked him from the table.' When dinner was finished the ladies left the table. Then there was freedom. The conversation might take a ribald turn. The sideboard could be opened to reveal a number of chamberpots which were passed round with the port. 'Nothing is hidden,' complained François de la Rochefoucauld-Liancourt, 'I think it is most indecent.' Or the company might comfortably and peacefully drop off to sleep, nodding and lolling and snoring agreeably together round the dinner table.[1]

Rich landowners in the country ate excellently, from their own produce: meat fresh from the aromatic pastures, fish straight from the streams and ponds, game from the moors, vegetables from the garden, milk-fed veal, and barrels of oysters sent from the beds.

The ladies kept scrap-books. Many were beautiful, with white crisp-ribbed leaves, bound with leather thongs; some held with a gold clasp, some made in emerald green leather and brown. Some belonged to the house and were handed down from wife to wife. Some belonged to the one woman; delightful fragments caught in an eternal sunbeam; mirrors of their tastes and interests.

---

[1] Hesketh Pearson writes, in *The Smith of Smiths*: 'It is many years since the nodding and lolling and snoring of a company of gentlemen at the dinner table was considered the appropriate conclusion of a hearty meal.'

The writing on the pages is sometimes immaculate, brown and round, sometimes spidery and illegible. Some pressed fernleaves between the pages, so that they emerge now from the shelves fragrant, slightly redolent of hay, only a little dusty and buffeted with time. To touch them is to smell the beeswaxed furniture on which they once lay; hear the rustle of the woman's dress, her steps falling down the long creaking floors as she approaches to take the book, add another recipe, remedy, or observation. Some were orderly and methodical with their additions, scholarly even, making clear indexes; others scatterbrained. A receipt for 'Cutlets Alderman Ready's Taste' appearing between 'Helps for Memory' and 'Direction for preventing or correcting the causes of injury in the shapes of young ladies'. Memoranda are scribbled hastily on the page: 'Molly owes me money lent in England.'

These are personal collections, made after visits with the neighbours. One can imagine them travelling out to dine in the closed carriage, or the sedan chair; see the savoury steam rising from Meryell Williams's—of Ystumcolwyn—special game pie; hear the congratulations afterwards in the privacy of the with-drawing room where the careful instructions are noted down. There they all are, the forgotten fragments of people's lives: Owen Glendower's lemon pudding, Mrs. Morris's sweet bag. Perhaps, while the men were exchanging jokes, passing round the port and the chamberpots, nodding off to sleep, the ladies would make an expedition to the kitchen to admire the ceiling stored with pro-visions—the hams, the black puddings, the sugar loaves, the sausages, the flitches of bacon—or step into the larder where the jars made a cold crack on the marbled shelves as the potted meats, the confections and the pickles were taken up to admire and set down again. Then, returned again to the security of the drawing room, more exchanges against the mysteries of illness: the pro-perties of a certain snail water in consumption, the excellence of hot pickled herrings when applied to the feet before a fit of ague, the virtue of frogspawn, or of churchyard worms distilled in rain-water and powdered for the case of falling sickness.[1]

recipes for meds.

[1] Ann Coote's remedy against Falling Sickness: 'Take churchyard worms which at the break of day are to be found for two houres together take very manny—the

It is charming to imagine these ladies enjoying the sociability of the season. Those who could not afford the expense of London, built tall delightful houses in the county towns. Here far away from London they met, exchanged news, jokes and recipes, and made matches for their daughters. Places like Haverfordwest, isolated, golden in the candlelight of their seasons, where the strain of waltzes floated down the cobbled streets to the river, over the sea of masts and the soft green; over the new crescents of Bath curving out to the hills, the long lines of houses looking down. And the new walls would echo with all the paraphernalia of etiquette and good manners. All the Handing In and the Hand-ing Out, the Allowing and the Permitting, the fluttering of fans and the rustling of dresses.

And what an epidemic of recipes and new dishes there was to match this splendour and elegance of entertaining. The women in this century—apart from the society hostesses—were, as we have seen, domestic beings, who took a real pride in their tables. 'It is certain,' wrote Charlotte Mason in *The Ladies Assistant*, 'that a woman never appears to greater advantage than at the head of a well regulated table, which should be always so supplied that the unexpected visit of a friend, or even a stranger should occasion no inconvenience and confusion.'

In the kitchens of the rich there was an abundance of every-thing: thick yellow cream, fresh butter, meaty succulent joints, vegetables shining and tender. The cookery books of the century were not stingy with the ingredients. 'I have heard of a Cook that used six Pounds of Butter,' wrote Hannah Glasse, 'to fry twelve Eggs, when every Body knows that understands cookery that Half a Pound is full enough or more, than need be used.' Quantities like this speak ominously of the general standard of cooking, for it is the *bad* cook who needs lashings of rich ingredients to make his

---

more the better, wash them in raine water three or foure times put them into an iron pot and with an iron helmit if it can be had and distill them, haveing put so much raine water upon them as will cover them two fingers breadth, distill them let all cook gently and turn over the worms and let them drye and make a powder thereof and powder it the dose is half a . . . [the word is illegible] of ye powder and nine spoonfulls of the distilled water every day in the morning fasting, continue this for a month for young folks and three months for ould or longer, the longer the better.'

dishes palatable. But the women cookery writers had an eye towards economy. For them it was a hard fight. The tradition still rested that the kitchen was the man's place. No doubt, as Johnson said, women could spin very well, but write a book of cookery they could not. Yet, in spite of roars from this great lion, women persisted and in the eighteenth century published well over a dozen cookery books.

To achieve a really clear picture of the English position it is necessary to draw a brief résumé of the progress made up till then in French cuisine. The seventeenth century had seen the opening of the *Grand Siècle,* the replacement of the culinary weapons of the Middle Ages by a *batterie de cuisine,* and the famous suicide of poor Vatel, Fouquet's *maître d'hôtel,* on account of his delivery of fish not arriving. This event shows the extreme importance that food played in French life. The *grands seigneurs* took an unparalleled interest in cooking; to them delicious food was an essential to life. Equally essential were their *maîtres d'hôtel* and master cooks, who were vital to the serving of a perfect dinner; these were conscientious men for whom competence and smooth arrangements were literally a matter of life and death. Master cooks, in gratitude for the interest and patronage of the *grands seigneurs,* christened many dishes in their honour. Thus the famous béchamel sauce is called after the Marquis de Béchamel, not, as many people might believe, invented by him, likewise the *Côtelettes d'agneau Maintenon* are in praise of Madame de Maintenon. In the well endowed kitchens many techniques were perfected, so that by the eighteenth century great cooks, like the skilled Carême, were able to blossom on all the assembled knowledge.

One sees from the pages of the English works a constant wrestle between the moral attitude and the French knowledge. It is obvious that most of the writers have consulted the French volumes. The exotic puddings, with names like Moonshine, Fishponds and Floating Islands, are all to be seen in the seven-teenth-century French books. A good sound common sense settles over the pages, especially those written by women, and one glimpses a peasant ingenuity of adaption and economy. There are substantial batter puddings baked under the joint so that the juices mingle as they cook, and lobster loaves, the bread-crust used as pie-cases; there are puddings within a suet crust, boiled in a cloth, containing pigeons, steak, or more economically liver, kidney and oysters—or combinations of them all. There is a new kind of pie, a pupton, from the French *poupeton*, the ingredients of partridge or pheasant, artichokes, sweetbreads, sweet potatoes and mushrooms are enclosed in a delicious veal forcemeat. Local ingredients are used in a practical way. Apples are mixed with horseradish for a delicious hot-fruity sauce to be eaten with boiled meat; by the sea, mutton is stuffed with cockles and herrings. Cakes are made with yeast left over from the ale-tub. There are triumphant voluminous pies: turkey pies, swan pies, Batallion pies, fish pies. And pies more Roman than English when under the same crust everything but the kitchen sink appears: chickens, partridges, rumps of mutton, squabs, pork, veal, beef, rabbits, chestnuts, coxcombs, bacon, sweetbreads, forcemeat, celery, asparagus and artichokes. Nasturtium, broom and elder buds are pickled for sauces. And another concoction, also Roman, appears—salamagundy,[1] a delicious salad of anchovies, chicken, lettuce and eggs, served with a salad dressing and garnished with grapes or flowers. But particularly English is the solid and practical country custom of serving a substantial pudding in front of the meat, that everyone might take the edge off their appetites and fill up on the cheaper food before moving on to the expensive. Mrs. Gaskell, in *Cranford*, deliciously refers back to this habit:

> We had pudding before meat, and I thought Mr. Holbrook was going to make some apology for his old-fashioned ways, for he began—'I don't know whether you like new-fangled ways.'
> 'Oh, not at all!' said Miss Matty.
> 'No more do I,' said he. 'My housekeeper *will* have these in her new fashion; or else I tell her that, when I was a young man, we used to keep strictly to my father's rule, "No broth, no ball; no ball, no beef"; and always began dinner with broth. Then we had sweet puddings, boiled in the broth with the beef; and then the meat itself. If we did not sup our broth, we had no ball, which we liked a deal better; and the beef came last of all, and only those had it who had done justice to the broth and the ball.'

[1] See Appendix II, page 245.

The gentlemen's works are decidedly academic. One can see they work extensively from paper. Traces of mediaeval language linger in the cookery terms. Of course many old-fashioned practices did linger. William Hickey relates a delightful story of a joke-pie being served to a rather disagreeable captain. The meat had been removed, the pastry had succeeded. Would Mrs. Grant be allowed to help Captain Mordaunt to a bit of tart? 'No Ma'am,' he had gruffly answered, to which 'she with a broad grin replied "Dear! now that's very ill-natured of you for you like cherry tart and these are I understand the first of the season". He then said he could help himself, pulling the dish from before her and began to cut it. The moment he took a piece out of the upper crust, out jumped an immense large frog followed by two or three of lesser size in succession, as fast as could be. Mordaunt instantly fell back in his chair as if he had been shot. His face was of a livid hue, and countenance horrible.' He brandished the carving knife so terrifyingly that both women screeched and ran out of the room.

But the old practices were largely adapting and changing. In 1746 the Earl of Warwick gave a banquet for more than six thousand persons. A wonderful collation was served on four tables, so enormous that they occupied the whole of four orange and lemon tree avenues. These radiated outwards, like the spokes of a wheel, from a great marble basin which was filled with a punch concoction flavoured with twenty-five thousand citrons, eighty pints of lemon juice, four large barrels of water, one thousand three hundredweight of sugar, three hundred biscuits and five pounds of nutmeg, and protected from the rain by an awn-ing. A charming little rose-wood boat moved over the beverage, propelled by a cabin-boy, who stood ready to serve the joyous crowd. Table decorations, though still exceedingly elaborate, were not always made of food. 'Jellies, biscuits, sugar, plums and cream have long since given way to harlequins, gondoliers, Turks, Chinese and shepherdesses of Saxon china,' wrote Horace Walpole. All these wandered about in front of the guests, among paper groves and silk flowers; meadows with cattle spread all over the table, sugar cottages rose beside barley-sugar temples;

Neptunes in cockle shells sailed over looking-glass seas. Sometimes the dinner table was so filled with impenetrable thickets, wells and leafy covets, mossy banks and fish-filled rivers that the guests were unable to see one another let alone communicate. Confectioners worked overtime to produce more exotic, more spectacular dishes. Lord Albemarle's produced a magnificent tower of gods and goddesses aspiring upwards to the ceiling, attaining the exalted height of eighteen feet. But when it was time to dress the table it was discovered the erection was too large to fit into the room. '*Imaginez-vous*,' complained the confectioner, '*que milord n'a pas voulu faire ôter le plafond*.' At a dinner given in honour of the birth of the Duke of Burgundy the dessert concluded with an impressive representation: wax figures proceeded by clockwork through the entire labour of the Dauphiness including the jubilant expulsion of the infant.

3

Buttock of Beef

> The universe itself is but a pudding of elements. Empires, kingdoms, states and republics are but puddings of people differently made up.
>
> A Learned Dissertation on a Dumpling

Food, the academics argue, had never been so good. The eighteenth century was the wondrous climax of English cooking and it was possible because of the improved methods of agriculture. The meat was now good, they say, the beasts were bred especially for the plate and not the plough; they were larger and more succulent and they were stored through the winter in the new fertile enclosures, fattened on juicy turnips and clover and served up steaming with new potatoes. This is not strictly true. No doubt a great deal of the food was excellent but it was not until the end of the century that the old leisurely pace of the country changed, that there was a new rushing of commercialism, that the new methods and improvements began to be felt. They came very slowly—

especially in the north—the new ways of drilling, draining, sowing, and manuring; the new methods of breeding and feeding cattle. Their influence on the excellence of the eighteenth-century diet has been over-emphasized. It is the same process of over-emphasis that labelled the mediaeval diet as poor, and attributed its low quality to unsophisticated agricultural methods. And there is a hole in the eighteenth-century agricultural argument: during a large part of it *the improvements did not exist*. It was men like Turnip Townshend and Bakewell who introduced the changes, who made their fortunes and retired to their estates to work over their theories. The great open spaces whose plough ruts had curved over the hills for a thousand years, rushing with water in rain-time like silver snakes, were gradually closed into fields, where the stock could be fed through the winter and a strict rotation of crops carried out. But Townshend did not devote himself to his estates, his theories and his turnips until 1730 and Bakewell did not begin his experiments with the shape of cattle until 1760. The country farmers, as we have seen, were slow to adopt newfangled ways. It was the amateurs, the gentlemen farmers who took them up. But roads were appalling, communications dreadful, and by 1768 turnips and clover were still generally unknown, while potatoes were not extensively used until fifty years later. It was not until the foundation of the Smithfield Club in 1794 that much advance was made with Bakewell's attributions. Sheep, during the most of the eighteenth century, were still small animals, producing very sweet mutton, animals capable of subsisting on the scantiest fare, while cattle were still lean and muscular. By the end of the century great stretches of land still lay uncultivated, covered with broom, in the north, in Westmorland and Northumberland; huge wastes lay over Devon, Cornwall and Wales.

As the century drew on, the whole structure and nature of England changed. From a fabric where the threads of town and country life wove harmoniously and closely together it wore to a loose pattern, rubbed in certain places into holes; industry removed from cottages and villages to urban factories, village life was left like a piece of knitting with the stitches dropped where the arts and crafts had been. Where the village tailor, carpenter, brewer, miller and harness-maker had been there was nothing, no occupation. No longer did the housewife spin; her spindle was silent. New industrialists set up factories, mills and businesses, on money derived from farming. There was a double flow of capital, from agriculture into industry, from industry into agriculture. No longer was each shire to be left in isolation, each hamlet with its own tradition, interests and character, its ghosts and its gossip. Each separate, self-sufficient unit was to be swallowed: to be ingested and hang as flesh on a smoking urban monster. The poet John Clare saw the agricultural 'improvements', the enclosure of land as a dreadful invasion and devastation of privacy and countryside.

> Inclosure like a bounaparte let not a thing remain
> It levelled every bush and tree and levelled every hill
> And hung the moles for traitors – though the brook is running still. . . .

But eighteenth-century London was a stimulating place to visit. Such an assemblage of people, of taverns, coffee houses and brothels, of friendships, that it was a different place for every person. It was the perfect place for the commercialist to exploit. There were men of expensive pleasure abroad with money to spend. Manufacturers were not slow to see there was money to be made by adulterating food: tea, beer and bread were the most obvious targets. They were helped with this by the snobbish attitude of these new urban inhabitants. They would eat only the finest white bread, the nutritious coarse ground rye-meal of the peasants was not for them. Soon, all kinds of nasty rumours circulated. Alum, lime and chalk, it was said, were added to make bulk, and, more dreadful still, a physician asserted with 'very credible authority, that sacks of unground bones are not infrequently used by some of the bakers amongst their other impurities, to increase the quantity, and injure the quality of flour and bread. The charnel houses of the dead are raked to add filthiness to the food of the living.'

A nice business was conducted by selling oranges at the theatres for sixpence each, whereas, elsewhere in the markets, the price was generally one or two for half a penny; these were purchased especially to pelt the actors: 'often and often,' complained Pastor Moritz, on his visit from Switzerland, 'whilst I sat there did a rotten orange or a piece of peel fly past one, or past some of my neighbours and once one of them actually hit my hat without my daring to look round in fear another might then hit me on my face.'

Now there is a paradox. Just at the very time that English food, according to the academics, was supposed to have reached untold deliciousness, the standard in London and the large industrial towns actually fell, while the instances of deficiency diseases rose. No longer were the towns self-supporting rural communities. Food had to be produced and conveyed from the distant corners of the country. Grain creaked in laboriously in heavy carts; meat came slowly and wearily on the hoof from Yorkshire and Wales; poultry and geese waddled down, no less exhausted from Norfolk and Suffolk; fast-trotting horses brought consignments of fish from the coast, which often arrived stinking. By the time many of these viands arrived on the plate they must have been thin, tough and gristly; inferior, one would have thought, to the mediaeval meat which had spent the summer quietly fattening, before being locally slaughtered around Michaelmastide. Fruit, it was whispered, was cleaned of its dust with spittle; vegetables travelled in barges that returned by night to the surrounding country, carrying the contents of London's latrines for the market gardens. Persons, said Trusler, used to the country would not relish the vegetables and fruit; they did not taste good. For while they were reasonable in price and abundant, to arrive fresh they must grow within easy travelling distance of London, and, according to Grosky, everything was impregnated with the smoke of sea-coal.[1]

[1] About a hundred years before this Evelyn had written a treatise against the pollution caused by the use of sea-coal: *Fumifugium or the Inconvenience of the aer and Smoake of London Dissipated.* To counteract the noxious smoke and smells he had the delightful suggestion of planting thirty or forty acres of fragrant flowers, trees, shrubs and herbs to the windward 'to tinge the air upon every gentle emission'. There were to be lavenders, violets, cowslips, jasmines, pinks, thymes, rosemaries, lilacs, narcissi, limetrees, plots of beans and peas, but on no account any cabbages 'whose persisting stalks have a very noisome smell'.

By the end of the eighteenth century, wood for fuel was extremely scarce, especially surrounding the towns, as acre after acre became enclosed. Sea-coal, producing its smelly penetrating smoke, had largely been substituted. Many of the urban poor could seldom afford to buy fuel to cook by. Consequently they were not a domestic race. On Sundays their joints were roasted in the bake-house oven; on other days many had to make do at the cheap ordinaries. An English dinner to impoverished lodgers like Pastor Moritz was not imposing: a piece of half-boiled, half-roasted meat and a few cabbage leaves boiled in plain water on which was poured a sauce of flour and butter.

In the *London Adviser and Guide* of 1786, Trusler gives a price list so that country people coming up to London might budget accordingly. From this it may be seen that while butcher's meat was cheap, poultry and game were comparatively expensive, rising probably from the landowners' policies of preserving game for their sport (and gain), guarding it with expensive game-keepers and mantraps.

> Average price of beef 4d—5d per pound.
> Rumpsteaks 7d per pound without bone.
> Mutton 4½d per pound.
> Veal 6d.
> Lamb 6d; pork chops 7d-8d; fat crammed chickens 10 weeks old 3s 10d; fat goose (10 lb) 5s; duck 3s; couple wild ducks 2s 6d; hare 4s 6d; pheasant 5s; brace of partridge 3s 6d.

In the fashionable squares fish was expensive, mackerel could fetch as much as 2s 6d, while it was half the price from criers, and at Billingsgate could be had for 4d or 5d. Thames salmon was double the price because it could be crimped. Women cooks cost twelve pounds a year, butlers thirty. They were by no means honest, all of them, and, according to Trusler, were up to all kinds of tricks, stripping the meat of its fat, melting more butter than was necessary and conveying the ends of candles into the greasepot.

For the mind there was plenty of first-class sustenance. London was the perfect place. It hummed with life. It was the perfect place for men like Boswell and Johnson to store their minds, to attend dinner parties and converse. A new sociability and ease surrounded mealtimes. Mediaeval meals had been massive affairs, a large and unselected gathering, servants and all, had sat down together in the same hall; later the Elizabethans had excluded the servants but meals were still massive impersonal affairs; during the seventeenth century the dining room had come into vogue, dinners had been family affairs, or state-occasions to which one could invite one's patron, or persons of similar consequence, to show off possessions and potential. Now court life had declined and mealtimes were seen as nice opportunities to assemble persons of wit and interest.

There is the agreeable occasion when the surliness of Doctor Johnson towards Wilkes was quite won over by the latter's assiduous attention in helping Johnson to the most succulent pieces of veal:

> 'Pray give me leave, Sir;—It is better here—A little of the brown—Some fat, Sir;—A little of the stuffing—Some gravy—Let me have the pleasure of giving you some butter—Allow me to recommend a squeeze of this orange;—or the lemon, perhaps, may have more zest.'—'Sir, Sir, I am obliged to you Sir,' cried Johnson, bowing, and turning his head to him with a look for some time of 'surly virtue', but, in a short while, of complacency.

Johnson was a man of appetite, and a complicated one. Because of his appearance, which he believed to be intolerably ugly, he was cut off from sex and directed his energies instead towards saporific exercise. So that he might not be hurt, and feel no envy, he used Puritanism as a protection, expressing outrage at wanton women—indeed, expressing a low opinion of women in general. Early in his life he was exceedingly poor, dining—and thinking he dined well—on a sixpennyworth of meat and a pennyworth of bread at an alehouse in Drury Lane. His manners, said Macaulay, were almost savage.

> Being often very hungry when he sate down to his meals he contracted a habit of eating with ravenous greediness. Even to the end of his life, and even at the tables of the great, the sight of food affected him as it affects wild beasts and birds of prey. His taste in cookery, formed in the subterranean ordinaries and *Alamode* beef-shops, was far from being delicate. Whenever he was so fortunate to have near him a hare that had been kept too long, or a meat pie made of rancid butter, he gorged himself with such violence that his veins swelled, and the moisture broke out on his forehead.

According to the disloyal Mrs. Piozzi his 'favourite dainties were a leg of pork boiled till it dropped from the bone, a veal pie with plums and sugar and the outside cut of a salt buttock of beef'. He had even been known to call for the butterboat containing the lobster sauce, during the second course, and pour the whole of its contents over his plum pudding. His demeanour provoked some caustic remarks from his landladies. What, his Scottish one wondered, did he think of his hotch potch? 'Good enough for hogs,' Johnson is supposed to have replied. 'Shall I help you to a little more of it?' retorted she. Dinner parties were events to which he looked forward enormously, but at the table you could not have said he was a polished guest. Beside his vigorous manner he had an absentminded way of grimacing, gesturing and muttering that sometimes terrified the other guests. Suddenly he might stoop down and abstractedly jerk off a lady's shoe. He was most disappointed if the food were not impressive. 'A good dinner enough to be sure,' he said sadly once, after such an occasion, 'but it was not a dinner to *ask* a man to.'

With its clubs, coffee houses and steak houses London was the perfect place also to be solitary, because you knew you never *need* be alone. It was a Mecca for eating and meeting. Boswell particularly recommended the steak houses, which were, according to him, most excellent places to dine. 'You come in there to a warm, comfortable, large room, where a number of people are sitting at table. You take whatever place you find empty; call for what you like, which you get well and cleverly dressed. You may either chat or not as you like. Nobody minds you and you pay very reasonably. My dinner (beef, bread and beer and water) was only a shilling.'

And it was the perfect place for companionship, for strolling comfortable friendship—like being well-filled with roast beef. You could saunter, dull perhaps, or animated, down Fleet Street. Oh! there was nowhere in the world like Fleet Street for Samuel Johnson, with its tall houses leaning over the street, its shops, its shining plate-glass windows lighted of an evening with candles gilding the silverware, the engravings, the books, cloths and paintings; with its druggists' shops whose great jars of spirits

gleamed like jewels, red, yellow, green and blue liquids catching
the small flames glittering and dancing; with its bustle, its gaiety,
its churchbells, its organs, its fiddles, its hurdy-gurdies; its street
criers selling meats, oysters and gilt gingerbread. You could
saunter down past the slender towers of St. Martin's-in-the-fields,
the tall columns of Charing Cross, or the Temple, where the
rooks cawed and the Thames moved silver, where Boswell walked
with Johnson. Boswell, lips pursed, savouring, tasting new ideas;
Johnson, eyes narrowed a little against the fading light, pondering,
playing his tongue backwards from the roof of his mouth as though
clucking like a hen, following them perhaps to St. James's where
you could drink a dish of tea, coffee or chocolate. Your pockets
filled—as was the method—with gingerbread and apples, you
strolled over the green of St. James's Park among the grazing cows.
Perhaps you would cross the river, see the long skyline and Wren's
new pale spires poking up from a sea of leaves, and enter Vauxhall
or Cremorne Gardens, where everything was built for pleasure.
The wide lawns and silent foliage, the exotic Turkish minarets,
the Arabian columned ways, the splashing waterfalls, wooded
valleys, dark ravines, crumbling ruins and shell grottoes. Everywhere there were arches and pillars hung with coloured lamps
and illuminated garlands of flowers; everywhere there was music,
brightly coloured clothes, lace and powdered hair. Here there
was a glimpse of a bare shoulder, there, hair piled up, threaded
with pearls or pink muslin. And under the groves, the high trees,
the orchestra played, and in the small dark places people were at
supper.

And in the evenings what a hubbub there was in the streets;
what lights, stars, eyes and scarves twirling and eddying below
the pale stone houses, the majestic ghostly façades, the moon
reflecting in the windows of the highest buildings; the bright
oyster houses, the wide foot-paths of the Haymarket shining under
the lamps, reflected in the mirrors of the restaurants. All doors
open, all windows illuminated to show soft velvet cushions,
red and gold rooms, and everywhere women laughing, whispering,
disappearing through brown mahogany doors: satin whispering
on stone, floating scarves, fluttering coloured ribbons. And at

every ten paces a prostitute, from the age of twelve upwards, was likely to approach you.

No city in the world had so many prostitutes, according to Schutz: 'no place in the world can be compared with London for wantonness'.[1] They rode in phaetons, loitered outside theatres, stood naked at their windows executing all manner of indecent postures, or rushed out in their underclothes to drag in gentle-men. There were, calculated Colquhoun, towards the end of the century more than fifty thousand prostitutes, of which twenty thousand were factory workers. Factories during the second half of the century became more and more a source for prostitution. Of this there were different grades. At the bottom of the scale came the street whores, available to be carnally and uncomfortably occupied in any dark alley; next came the girls who lived under the protection of a proprietor, to whom they paid all their wages and in return received food and clothing; on different scales came the brothels and bagnios, and highest of all were the fashionable courtesans, many of whom lived in very grand style, with delight-ful houses and liveried servants, adopting every extravagant whim and entertainment with which to titillate their lovers: appearing undressed at fancy dress balls, or upon the dinner table, in a tureen, dressed only with a sauce.

The bagnios were for the most part situated round the piazza at Covent Garden; apparently baths, their real purpose was to provide persons of both sexes with pleasure—expensive pleasure, especially when required by ladies. All noise and uproar was banned, every corner was carpeted, every taste accounted for; old people and degenerates might receive flagellation, for those with defloration mania special virgins were prepared. A humorous client list exists for one of the most notorious establishments, administered under the person of Mrs. Charlotte Haynes. Price list Sunday the 9th January:

A young girl for Alderman Drybones. Nelly Blossom, about 19 years old, who has had no one for four days and who is a virgin   20gns

---

[1] According to Pastor Moritz, London had such a reputation for being under-mined with syphilis that foreigners were nervous of travelling thither, lest they themselves should contract it.

A girl of 19 years, not older, for Baron Harry Flagellum. Nell Hardy from Bow Street, Bat Flourish from Berners Street, or Miss Birch from Chapel Street 10gns

A beautiful lively girl for Lord Spaan. Black Moll from Hedge Lane, who is very strong 5gns

For Colonel Tearall a gentlewoman. Mrs. Mitchell's servant, who has just come from the country and has not yet been out in the world 10gns

For Dr. Frettext, after consultation hours, a young agreeable person, sociable with a white skin and a soft hand. Polly Nimble-wrist from Oxford, or Jenny Speedyhand from Mayfair 2gns

Lady Loveit, who has come from the baths at Bath, and who is disappointed in her love affair with Lord Alto, wants to have something better, and to be well served this evening. Capt. O'Thunder or Sawney Rawbone 50gns

For His Excellency Count Alto, a fashionable woman for an hour only. Mrs O'Smirk who came from Dunkirk, or Miss Graceful from Paddington 10gns

For Lord Pyebald, to play a game of piquet, for *titillations mammarum* and so on, with no other object. Mrs. Tredille from Chelsea 5gns

Mrs. Haynes did her best to provide her customers with variety. She arranged special orgies and representations of fertility cults. Invitations would be sent out respectfully taking the liberty of advising Lord So and So that twelve beautiful nymphs (spotless virgins) would be carrying out the Famous Feast of Venus as celebrated in Tahiti under the leadership of Queen Oberea (whose role Mrs. Haynes herself would be taking). Twelve athletic youths would be engaged and the ritual would be practised before Lord So and So and his friends who enjoyed simultaneously a sumptuous banquet. Mrs. Haynes, it is recorded, retired with a profit of twenty thousand pounds.

While Mrs. Haynes was Queen of the Orgies, Mary Wilson reigned in her palace, equipped solely for the delight of ladies. This she describes in the *Voluptarian Cabinet*. Agreeable temples were erected and illuminated like shopping arcades. In the centre, from darkened bedrooms, the customers inspected the display goods, who were of all types, expert in all pleasures and designed to suit all tastes. For the genteel, elegantly dressed men-of-the-world sat in their windows, at cards, or absorbed in music; while for those more inclined towards muscle, rustic fellows set out straw, and athletes wrestled, naked, or swam. Unseen, the ladies could ponder, eyeing the flesh of this one, discarding the muscles of that, in the way of hats: too small, too large, too pale, too red. And when their minds were resolved they rang for the chambermaid and the gentleman of their desire was led in and introduced to them.

Important occasions were still marked by splendid feasting: whirls of too much wine and heat: mixtures of magnificence and terrible boredom. 'We were soon tired of the heat and stink,' wrote Mrs. Creevey, after an evening party at Brighton Pavilion. No less inferior was the Lord Mayor's Banquet which often fell into an orgy of gluttony and bad manners—for which councillors were especially renowned. They settled down to the meal, according to Edward Ward in the *City Feast*, tucking their napkins under their chins, pinning their sleeves to their elbows:

> Then all went to work, with such a rending and tearing,
> Like a Kennel of Hounds on a Quarter of Carrin.
> When done with the Flesh, they claw'd off the Fish,
> With one Hand at Mouth, and th'other in th'Dish.

When their stomachs were 'cloy'd', like Ameliaranne Stiggins[1] they stuffed all the goodies they had been unable to eat into their pockets—all the cheese cakes and custards—and carried them home for their families.

Creevey relates with relish his experience of a Lord Mayor's Banquet. As he entered, the first thing that caught his eye was the Princess Olivia of Cumberland. She stood out among a company of nine hundred: 'diamonds in profusion hung from every part of her head but her nose, and the whole was covered with feathers that would have done credit to any hearse'. She was a most tiresome lady and caused a halt in the procession of diners for more than ten minutes, while explaining why she must sit

[1] Ameliaranne Stiggins was the heroine, in 1920, of Constance Heward's famous book for children, *Ameliaranne and the Green Umbrella*. She lived with her mother, who took in washing, and her five little brothers and sisters, and they were very poor. On the day of the grand Christmas tea-party, that each year was given by the squire for all the village children, the five little Stigginses had such bad colds they were unable to go. So Ameliaranne took her green umbrella and filled it with goodies from the tea-table for her hungry and bedridden brothers and sisters.

at the right hand of the Lord Mayor. At last Creevey was seated, without sight of her. Above his table were three niches where were seated 'three men in complete armour from top to toe, with immense plumes of feathers upon their helmets . . . It was their duty to rise and wave their truncheons when the Lord Mayor rose and gave his toasts; which they did with great effect, till one of them fainted away with the heat and fell out of his hole upon the heads of the people below . . .'

Banquets given for royal occasions, such as the Coronation, were held at the Palace of Westminster, in the Great Hall. Often they seemed more like circuses than dignified meals. Above the tables that seated the most distinguished guests were galleries, from which the public was permitted to watch the grand spectacle. 'I was seated behind several ladies and gentlemen who were acquainted with some of the peers and peeresses seated at the table beneath us,' recorded de Saussure, a foreigner who had gone along to sight-see. 'When we saw they had finished eating we let down a small rope, which, to tell the truth, we had made up by knotting our garters together. The peers beneath were kind enough to attach a napkin filled with food to our rope, which we then hauled up, and in this way got plenty of good things to eat and drink. This napkin took several journeys up and down, and we were not the only people who had this idea, for from all the galleries round the same sight could be seen.' After the principal guests had risen, together with the King and Queen, it was the custom to throw open the doors for the crowd to enter, and grab the remains: linen, plates, dishes, even the boards from which the table and seats had been fashioned vanished, much to de Saussure's astonishment.

CHAPTER EIGHT

A NEW DESIRE ENCLOSED

Fate cannot harm me, I have dined today.
                            Recipe for a Salad—SYDNEY SMITH

I

A Business Lubrication

THE LAST Coronation Banquet to be held in Westminster Hall was in 1821, for George IV. It was a sweltering hot day. All nerves were frayed. People were anxious about the entrance of the food. They hoped there was not to be a repetition of the disaster that had occurred at the coronation of George III. The Lord Steward, Lord Talbot, had been ready to lead the procession, and gallop in grand style up to the throne when, in spite of all his frantic efforts, his horse had astonished everyone by proceeding in briskly, backwards. Now the trumpets sounded, the doors were thrown open and everyone heaved a sigh of relief: the horses were all facing the right way round. Three hundred and thirty-six silver plates heaped with poultry, tongues, pies and conserves were delivered safely. But, then it was discovered, the Dean of the Chapel Royal who was to say grace had vanished, and when at last he did appear he was so out of breath that no one could overhear his words. Two thousand candles flickered, the sun glared down through the high windows and, in the heat, complexions melted, dresses were ruined and hair-sets slowly unravelled. A small hitch added further to the discomfort; by some oversight only spoons had been provided to convey the food into the guest's mouths, and they made slow progress. Exasperated by the heat, the King adjourned to rest; at which

point a corporation of spectators departed the galleries to promenade, while others were busy tying together their handkerchiefs
with which to draw up chickens and bottles of wine. At this
Lord Gwydor—already in an irritable mood, having torn his
robe while assisting the King into his—was inspired to quarrel
with the Earl Marshal about their respective duties regarding
control of the ceremonies and struck him with his staff of office.
Chaos reigned. The day ended by the King being bled profusely.

The dissipations and extravagances of the court had whirled
giddily to a vortex, and at its centre, no less giddily, had spun the
Prince Regent himself. The new stones of Brighton Pavilion and
of Carlton House echoed to the strains of the waltz, the pop of
champagne corks, the chink of gold money passing hands, the
threatening boom of bankruptcy. The Prince Regent was an
exceptionally greedy man. His figure was remarkable. He loved
good food and his skin stretched obediently in order to receive
huge amounts. 'Prinney has let loose his belly,' wrote Lord
Folkestone on February 23, 1818, 'which now reaches his knees.'
He must have lived in a perpetual liverish fog. 'Give me some
money to buy a loaf of bread,' a street beggar is supposed to
have implored him, 'for I am very hungry.' 'Lucky fellow,'
returned the Prince, 'how many years have passed since I had the
delight of a good appetite?'

To delight his addled palate and prepare for him the most subtle
dishes of the French cuisine, the famous cook Carême came to
Brighton, where, it was said, he was very unhappy. Immense
prices were paid by the porcine aldermen for his second-hand
pâtés,[1] which they purchased hot from the Regent's table.

This was soon meat for the satirists to be turned to doggerel:

> A napkin let my temples bind
> In nightgown free and unconfined
> And undisturbed by women
> All boons of one, I ask of pâté
> At city feasts, to eat my weight,
> And drink enough to swim in.

[1] Pâtés were enormous pies which could be made from all manner of rich meats
like foie gras, pheasant, truffles, veal and lamprey. See Appendix II, pages 261-2.

During the French Revolution[1] and the Napoleonic wars there was a mass exodus of great private cooks from France. No longer were there the *grands seigneurs* to employ them. Men like Carême, Ude and Soyer came to England and worked in London clubs —like the Reform—and made their kitchens famous; others worked privately for certain rich men, or stayed behind in France and opened restaurants.[2] The French cuisine saved its country from financial disaster. By a treaty, made in November 1815, France was bound to pay a sum of five million francs within three years. Thanks to the gourmandise of German and British eaters, who flocked into France to relieve their spleen and fill stomachs of no ordinary calibre, they managed it. French cuisine had become a national asset. The paraphernalia surrounding it developed into the famous philosophy: 'Tell me what you eat,' Brillat-Savarin said, 'and I will tell you what you are.' It also led to a great deal of stupidity and enabled articles, such as the one published in the *Almanach des Gourmands*, to be written, explaining and excusing the methods of rearing geese for foie gras:

> Crammed with food, deprived of drink, and fixed near a great fire before which she is nailed by her feet upon a plank, this goose passes it must be owned an uncomfortable life. The torment would be altogether intolerable if the idea of the lot which awaits her did not serve as a consolation. But this perspective makes her endure her sufferings with courage. And when she reflects that her liver bigger than herself, larded with truffles and clothed in a scientific pâté, will diffuse all over Europe the glory of her name she resigns herself to her destiny and suffers not a tear to flow.

[1] Hesketh Pearson writes: 'The amount of food consumed by English gentlemen in honour of certain events in the French Revolution if distributed to the Parisian mob at a jucidious moment would have prevented the fall of the Bastille.'

[2] In the eighteenth century one could only eat at special cookshops or inns. But in France, in 1765, a man called Boulanger, a soup-seller, called his soups by the special name of *restaurant*—restorative. Their sale was so successful that he wanted to enlarge his menu, but since he was not a member of the *traiteurs* corporation—eating-house keepers—he was not permitted to serve ragoûts. Instead he offered to his customers sheep's feet in white sauce. The *traiteurs* brought a law suit. An Act of Parliament decreed that sheep's feet in white sauce was not a ragoût. Boulanger's sheep's feet in white sauce became famous all over Paris. From 1786 onwards the great cuisiniers opened restaurants nearly all of which were famous for a particular speciality. Salt fish with garlic was served at *Les Frères Provençaux*, while *Henneveux* offered private boudoirs.

The *hautes* English kitchens received a booster injection of French techniques, stimulating the heavy English tastes. The great joints were beaten into *quenelles*, raised to turbans, *timbales* and *vol au vents*, the puddings were puffed to *soufflés*, the fruit erected to *croquantes*, the sugar cakes manufactured into complicated pinnacles, spires and fairy tale castles. Between the lines of books such as Francatelli's *The Modern Cook* the classical, mediaeval roots are visible. Richard II, if he had sat down to one of Francatelli's dinners, would not have been ill at ease. There are the calves-foot jellies, the civets, the white puddings, the boudins, the black butter sauces, the cheese-cakes, the stuffed capons, the gauffres, the boar's head, the creams, the almond pastes; the umbles are there too, although they incline to be of the calf, rather than deer: ears, feet, liver, udders, tongue and brains. There are developments and innovations, it is true, which he would have found interesting. The charlotte has turned to a fruit pudding; the farina is removed and hedged around with 'tomata', the meat surprised and enclosed in potato pastes; the collops of meat, game and fish are served braised in clever sauces, inspired by nobody Richard had ever known, à la Richelieu, la Windsor, la Dauphinoise, la Régence, la Financière, la Prince Albert ... But in the main he would have settled down quite at home.

The cooks were again craftsmen—Ben Jonson's 'men of men'. Food was a material to carve, mould into shapes, colour, turn to different textures. Cuisine was an art for which enjoyment the epicure must employ all his senses: the eye to delight in the appearance, the nose to savour the aroma, the palate to experience the textures and juicy succulence, the ear to attend internally to the crispness of pastry, the crunchiness of nuts, the smooth frothiness of soufflés.

Ironically, at the very time that the most excellent cooking techniques were within the grasp of the new rich, the glossy leaves of the tea-drinking *Sanctimonia Britannica* matured, smothering any middle-class promise of earthy enjoyment. The bending stalks of Evangelicism reached over the wall and distorted the majority of bankers, merchants and tradesmen into a goodness that was quite ghastly. Here was a Puritanism: a revival of neurosis and hate of the body that would have gladdened any Jerome. It was true he might not have approved of their appurtenances and comforts:[1] the lazy tongs[2] to fight the distance, the cosy well-wrapped world of aspidistras and tablecloths—nice thick ones to cover up those rude legs. But he would have approved of their code: no sensation, no pleasure: a code of obedience. God and the Bible were undisputedly right. Provided you did your duty, were obedient to your sovereign and your country, they would reward you. 'The industrial age had begun,' Hugh Kingsmill wrote, 'and a life of duty not of happiness, a life, that is, devoted to money-getting, with the family sanctified as the money-getting unit . . .'

To be rich and successful was your God and your country's reward for services. Your worldly possessions not only pointed to your abilities—in the Roman way—but also they pointed out how *good* you were.

'A dinner lubricates business' is a well-known saying of Lord Stowell. The nineteenth century shows a great rise in entertaining. The houses and dining rooms were stages on which to display abilities and possessions. Dinner parties were convenient means of showing to friends, neighbours and competitors, the china, pretty wife and quantity of food one could afford.[3] The pretension and grossness was remarkably similar to any Trimalchio, but it was

---

[1] For those that could afford it England offered a standard of comfort that was unexampled. Prince Pückler-Muskall described arriving at an inn in Cheltenham during the last half of the nineteenth century. 'As I entered the inn which I might almost call magnificent and ascended the snow-white stair-case ornamented with a gilt bronze railing and trod in fresh and brilliant carpets, lighted by two servants to my room I gave myself up, *con amore*, to the feeling of comfort which can be found in perfection nowhere but England . . . all that a man can promote *with money* is excellent and perfect in its kind.'

[2] 'It is difficult,' E. F. Benson writes, 'to describe that anciently familiar weapon. There were two looped handles to it, like those of a pair of scissors, then a criss-cross of silver-plated bars, at the end of which was a pair of metal claws. As you pressed the handles together with thumb and forefinger inserted, the criss-cross of bars elongated itself, the claws approached each other, fixed themselves on the desired object, picked it up and brought it within reach.'

[3] A dinner served by the famous Francatelli consisted of *first course*, four soups, four fish, four hors d'oeuvres, four relevés, sixteen entrées, three joints on the side-board including a haunch of venison; *second course* comprised of six roasts, six relevés, two flancs, four contreflancs, sixteen entremets. Seventy dishes in all.

more material, for there is an absence of sensation and enjoyment, only anxiety to ape, and be as good as, the class above. Above all there was an anxiety over bankruptcy. This would be bad: God's punishment. It was bad manners—worse, it was *ill-bred*—to observe or know about anything that was ugly or gross.[1] It was exceedingly bad manners to know about the poor—these were wicked people, who deserved their punishment. God was seeing to that. There were, it is true, two kinds of poor. The good poor, with nice clean aprons, brushed frocks and swept rooms, who deserved a visit and perhaps a basket of cakes. But those that drank alcohol and lived in nasty rooms, brown with sewerage, those were not nice to know about. They were not for innocent ladies to worry their heads over: no, ladies should turn their backs, bury their pale noses into their bouquets and watch the pretty kittens playing on the lawn.[2]

It would have been considered most impolite to notice and remove any stains that might accidentally be bestowed upon a lady during a meal. Sydney Smith was very much taken with a certain Miss Markham who remained quite composed in spite of an unfortunate mishap: 'In carving a partridge I splashed her with gravy from head to foot; and though I saw three distinct brown

[1] The 1875 edition of the *Dictionary of General Biography* says about Juvenal: 'Good as are his intentions, however forcible as are his denunciations, the moral indelicacy of the age in which he lived renders these powerful satires too gross in their details for readers of the present day.' All mention of sex in public was indecent. In 1889 the Independent Advertising Act made 'any advertisement relating to syphilis, gonorrhoea, nervous debility, or other complaint and infirmity arising from or relating to sexual intercourse' an indecent publication.

[2] The following incident described by E. S. Turner in *All Heaven in a Rage* illustrates the curious Victorian mixture of commercialism, uncompassion and sentimentality. A member of parliament watching a procession of horses bound for the slaughter houses of Belgium noticed among them a pony with an identifying tape on a fetlock. The animal, he was told, was a family favourite on which all the children had learnt to ride and which had spent its last days pulling a mowing machine on the lawn. The hoof identification was to notify the slaughterer that the pony's hoof was to be returned to the family as a memento of its fidelity. Shipments of horses began to multiply in late Victorian years. Most animals went for human food. Some were made into sausages which were exported, and when matured were highly prized in England, selling for high prices. Thus it was possible, as E. S. Turner tells us, that the family who had requested the pony's fetlock might also have enjoyed eating some of the actual pony.

rills of animal juice trickling down her cheek, she had the com-plaisance to swear that not a drop had reached her. Such circum-stances are the triumphs of civilized life.'

Sydney Smith was quite untouched by any blight of appetite. He was a deliciously funny clergyman, with piercing eyes, prominent nose, a dazzling wit, and, as Hesketh Pearson said, was mentally of giant breed. He entered the Church because there was no alternative intellectual exercise available that could offer a career to a man of his means. He was often impoverished, loved by his parish and mingled a practical religion with a real enjoy-ment of life. Not for him any quibbling over the saying of grace such as Charles Lamb experienced: 'When I have sat at rich men's tables, with the savoury soup and messes steaming up the nostrils, and moistening the lips of the guests with desire and a distracted choice, I have felt the introduction of that ceremony to be unreasonable. With the ravenous orgasm upon you, it seems impertinent to interpose a religious sentiment. It is a confusion of purpose to mutter out praises from a mouth that waters.'

He was in his element before a well-furnished dining table, surrounded by good company. He once calculated he 'had eaten and drunk forty-four horse wagon-loads of meat and drink more than would have preserved me in life and health!' The value of the cart contents he put down to seven thousand pounds sterling. Like Miss Markham, one of the civilized circumstances of life, he believed, was a good host, such as Agar Ellis, who could mix up his guests at the table to a sparkling brew. 'That's the great use of a good conversational cook, who says to his company "I'll make a good pudding of you; it's no matter what you came into the bowl, you must come out a pudding".' Smith employed the food idiom freely when discussing matters of the day and his friends. Of Henry Luttrell, a companion-wit who could make 'all the country smell like Piccadilly' and who came for a day to test Mrs. Sydney's side dishes and stayed for a week, he wrote: 'He had not his usual soup-and-pattie look; there was a forced smile on his countenance which seemed to indicate plain roast and boiled, and a sort of apple-pudding depression as if he had been staying with a clergy-man . . . He was very agreeable, but spoke

17A. Frontispiece from *Memoirs of a Stomach* showing a rather choleric Victorian stomach and some of its ingredients

17B. An electric alarum for arresting nocturnal emissions

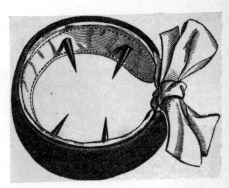

17C. Urethral ring for the same purpose

18A. Doré's view of the nineteenth-century London slums

18B. Seymour's view of a nineteenth-century Christmas dinner

too lightly, I thought, of veal soup. I took him aside, and reasoned the matter with him, but in vain; to speak the truth Luttrell is not steady in his judgements on dishes. Individual failures with him soon degenerate into generic objections, till, by some fortunate accident, he eats himself into better opinions. A person of more calm reflection thinks not only of what he is consuming at that moment, but of the soups of the same kind he had met with in a long course of dining, and which have gradually and justly elevated the species. I am perhaps making too much of this, but the failures of a man of sense are always painful.'

Sydney Smith's idea of life after death was both sensual and commonsense. Hell was to him a thousand years of tough mutton, or a little eternity of family dinners, while heaven was eating pâtés de foie gras to the sound of trumpets.

While he was king of the dining room, the dining table his throne, Frank Harris reigned in the bedroom, from the bed—and sometimes from the floor as well. He rated with the poor; he was not for nice ladies to know about. There was very little that Frank Harris could not do better than anyone else. He had only to read a verse and he knew it by heart, sing two notes and they were lower than any ever written, look at a woman and she would be consumed with passion and fall hysterical into his embrace. His *My Life and Loves* was written, as Steven Marcus has described a pornographer's Grand Tour of Europe, through the eyes of his penis.

There are two essential desires in man, Harris assured his readers: 'the one is for food, the other for reproduction. While both are imperious, the one is absolutely necessary; the other, to some extent, adventitious. But while the desire for food is necessary and dominant, it has very little to do with the higher nature, with the mind or the soul; whereas the sex-urge is connected with everything sweet and noble in the personality . . . It is so intimately one with the love of the beautiful that it cannot be separated from it.'

In most of his contemporaries' view the sex-urge was, however, anything but beautiful; it was unpleasant and it was bad for the health. Men of means, it was known, kept mistresses. Courtesans were sexy women: that way led only to disaster. Because it was not the method to seduce ladies of one's own rank, those less fortunate had resort to prostitutes. It was not at all nice. Nobody mentioned it. Wives were expected to do their duty, succumb to the animal spirits of their husbands, and that was that. 'I should say that the majority of women are not very much troubled with sexual feeling of any kind,' announced a learned nineteenth-century sexologist, William Acton. Syphilis was a blessing, it was the penalty of sin. Could the disease be terminated, which many men hoped it could not, fornication would ride rampant through the world. Masturbation led to madness and nocturnal emissions probably would as well.[1] Spermatorrhoea was recognized as a disease, causing complete lack of energy and exhaustion. Even Frank Harris found himself victim once or twice, but cured himself by securing his penis with a piece of whipchord. Special devices were marketed to cure the unfortunate sufferers: electric alarums—expanded by the erection—roused the sleeper by ringing a bell beneath his pillow; or a leather ring was attached, with sharp points turned inwards, so that at the erection the patient was roused by the pricking and could leap out of bed and arrest the impending emission.

Steven Marcus has pointed out the close interaction in Victorian thinking about sex expenditure and loss of money. The word for the dispensation of both was the same: to spend. Unwise and extravagant spending led to bankruptcy. Against these neuroses pornography bloomed together with all the expensive titillations for the impotent—or the nearly impotent: defloration, whipping, it could all be had for a price. Literature had been castrated, but below the surface the obscene books flourished. It was as though under the stern sepia faces of the family photographs there was a strong aversion to orthodox sexual exercise: an anti-

---

[1] Apparently, in Edinburgh, masturbation was so common a practice among young girls and their mothers, who operated not only digitally but with vegetables, that John Moodie, M.D., was, in 1839, concerned enough to devise a girdle of chastity. This was made from a rubber cushion covered with silk, linen or other soft material which formed a base into which a kind of grating was fixed to shield the genitals from manipulation. The apparatus was, in the best style, secured by a padlock.

reproduction wave, a leaning towards activities that displaced procreative processes: sadism, sodomy, fellatio, cunnilingus, lesbianism, coprophilia. The narrators see themselves, as Steven Marcus says, as rain and fertility gods, sprinkling supplies of semen from a never-failing reservoir; enjoying orgies of eating and drinking and never-failing sexual intercourse: a replica of the Celtic Otherworld. The food is always sexually stimulating, an aphrodisiac outside agent acting automatically to restore virility, potency and energy. A never-failing magic wand. A fairy land with the landscape of hot mounds, lush dark thickets, hot and warm, where there was no anxiety, where everything was all right. A primitive haven to which they could retire from the pressures of the urban respectable world; a party with bright red jellies and presents; a sweet land.

Children were not exempted from this severe knowledge of guilt. It was believed they were so steeped in original sin that it was most inexpedient to indulge them. Severity and deprivation were character-building. It was a parent's duty to see the child did not pay too much attention to sensual delights. Carnal indulgences such as lollipops were punished by doses of rhubarb and salt. It was often thought wise to allow children to go hungry. When the Brontës pleaded for more to eat, they were lectured on the sin of caring for carnal things and of pampering greedy appetites. The food at boarding schools was generally appalling; the boys at Radley College were obliged to grub for bulbs in the garden to supple-ment their diet.[1] 'Cowslip roots were a delicacy,' writes A. K. Boyd, in the *History of Radley College*, 'nasturtium, crocuses and hyacinth did not long remain in the gardens . . . Acorns were collected in great numbers and stored away in holes dug in the park. These were secretly cooked in the flames of candles.'

As a child, Augustus Hare was vilely treated, mainly at the instigation of his religious crazed Aunt Esther, whom he des-cribes as the inquisition herself, always fasting, denying herself everything, probing and analysing herself. She shut Augustus to sleep in two dismal uncarpeted rooms, looking out into the

[1] No sweets or fruit were provided and no tuck box allowed, but beer was served at meals—two glasses at dinner.

ocurtyard of a howling dog. He had no hot water, no heating; his chilblains worsened and his beloved cat Selina was hanged by the potty Aunt Esther in the name of some religious moral or other. A good deal of ingenuity went into devising one particular torture:

> I was not six years old before my mother [under the influence of the frightful Aunt Esther Maurice] . . . began to follow out a code of penance with regard to me which was worthy of the ascetics of the desert. Hitherto I had never been allowed anything but roast mutton and rice pudding for dinner. Now all was changed. The most delicious puddings were talked of—and *dilated* on—until I became not greedy, but exceedingly curious about them. At length *le grand moment* arrived. They were put on the table before me, and then, just as I was about to eat some of them, they were snatched away, and I was told to get up and carry them off to some poor person in the village.

2

Stomachs

> 'When a good fellow has been sacrificing rather too liberally at the shrine of the Jolly God, the best remedy to help the Stomach to get rid of its burden is to take for Supper some Gruel with $\frac{1}{2}$ oz of Butter and a tea-spoon of Epsom salts in it . . .'
>
> WILLIAM KITCHINER

Since the desire for food was a necessary function and could not be ignored, many people tried to disguise it with different breeches. Some—ladies especially—recognized eating as being a beastly, but necessary, function of the body, like visiting the lavatory; a business to be endured as little as possible in public, and never discussed. Others tried to raise it, in the French way, to a philosophy. There were speculations on the different sensations one feels when one is hungry; on the different qualities of hunger. A new character entered England and joined the learned cookery experts: the Stomach. 'Some Psychologists will have it that the Stomach is a Mill: others that it is a fermenting vat; others, again that it is a stew-pan; but in my view, it is neither a Mill, a fermenting vat, nor a stew-pan but a Stomach, gentlemen a

STOMACH,' one learned gentleman pronounced wittily. Often it was a severe dour creature, sometimes well-connected. The author of *Memoirs of a Stomach*, for example, is a Stomach with *Saxon* ancestors. A large round person, he lived together with Mr. Brain, Mr. Lungs, a footman called Smell and an officer called Palate, sometimes causing their owners severe pain as penalty for their irresponsible excesses.

> The stomach . . . is a very hospitable gentleman [read an extract in a newspaper, 1833], who is unfashionable enough to live in a sunk storey, as his ancestors have always done before him since the memory of man. The palate is the footman, whose duty it is to receive all strangers at the top of the stairs, and to announce their rank and quality before they are suffered to descend to the apartments of his master. The latter is occasionally rather irritable and choleric, and, in such humours, scruples not to kick out his guests, when their company is disagreeable, who rush past the astonished footman at the landing-place and make their exit with far less ceremony than precipitation.

Cookery books set themselves out to be more than cookery books. Their authors pictured themselves as benevolent, rosy-cheeked gentlemen, more guides and friends than cooks, whose purpose it was to steer their sheep through the black and greasy ways of the cooking pots. Each one claimed that *his* was the only book to be compiled through the skill and experience of the author. 'What I have published,' wrote the debunker of Roman cookery, Doctor Hunter of York, under the guise of Ignotus, 'is almost the only book, one or two excepted, which of late years has come into the world, that has been the result of the author's own practice and experience.' 'This,' announced Doctor William Kitchiner, when *The Cook's Oracle* was published, 'is the only English Cookery book which has been written from the real experience of a Housekeeper, for the benefit of Housekeepers.' 'The receipts,' he adds, 'have been written down by the fireside with a spit in one hand and a pen in the other . . .' *The Cook's Oracle* received great success. 'But,' said A. V. Kirwan, about forty years later in *Host and Guest*, 'never did a book less deserve renown. Totally desolate of arrangement, originality, it is an odd confused *olla podrida* of receipts, observations, maxims and remarks written to boot in a vain-glorious style, and filled with gasconading

vulgarisms and obsolete pendantry.' Some books took on the air
of comic works. 'You may curry anything,' instructed Mr. Arnot
of Greenwich, 'old shoes should even be delicious, some old oil
cloth or staircarpet not to be found fault with (gloves if much
worn are too rich)'. Questions were raised and deliberated upon.
Ought one to marry or not? it was asked. On the one hand yes,
because at the ceremony there would be a feast; on the other, no,
because you then took a woman who, for the remainder of her
life, ate half of the dinner. Doctor Hunter of York entered like a
comedian into an extraordinary partnership with Archaeus, the
inspiration of the seventeenth-century Jean Baptiste Van Helmont,
who believed the body and the organs were regulated by a spirit
—Archaeus—whose chief post was at the upper orifice of the
stomach, where he acted the part of a custom's official allowing
nothing with the air of contraband to pass. Now, by the whimsical
Ignotus, he was resuscitated. His pages are all repartee and
badinage. There is a vegetable soup which both Archaeus and
Ignotus are agreed is only proper for those who do not stand in
fear of gouty shoes and a pair of crutches; a macaroni pie sent
straight from the Pope's kitchen; an omelette which was the invention of a lady who had it regularly served up at her table three
days a week, who died at the age of ninety-seven with a piece of
it in her mouth; and a Mock Turtle soup which is 'a most
diabolical dish and only fit for the Sunday dinner of a rustic,
who is to work the six following days in a ditch-bottom'. Some
dishes not only contain gout, but also scurvy and rheumat-
ism. They find occasion to fall out over lobster pie which is in
Ignotus's view very whole, but Archaeus contends that it contains too many gouty particles. On several occasions they come
almost to blows, and it is only with the greatest difficulty that
Ignotus obtains the permission of Archaeus to insert such recipes
as the Cheshire Cheese Sandwich into his *Culina*.

The digestion was a subject of constant speculation through
the nineteenth century. Sydney Smith maintained it was 'the
great secret of life, and that character, talents, virtues and qualities
are powerfully affected by beef, mutton, pie-crust and rich soups'.
Friendships, he believed, were destroyed by toasted cheese;

lobster followed by tart brought on bad depression and suicides had been caused by hard salted meats. Towards the end of his life, learning that promotion was not to come his way, he confined himself to digestion, and, though often bed-ridden, lived merrily to an old age, with his wife: 'Mrs. Sydney has eight distinct illnesses and I have nine. We take something every hour and pass the mixture from one to the other.'

By the end of the century, all conjecture on the subject was over. Beaumont had cleared up the matter and explained it through his studies. These consisted of peering through a hole, made by gun-shot, into the inside of a French-Canadian trapper and observing all the peptic glands at work.

Although one may discover the standard of cookery *technique* from the culinary books, they by no means demonstrate the standard of individual *practice*. Because one can read of rich game pies, sucking pigs stuffed with truffles, timbale cases garnished with leaves, stalks and drooping feathers of angelica, it does not prove that such fare steamed on the dishes of every well-endowed household. Contemporary reports indicate it was otherwise and that on the whole the quality of cooking was extraordinarily low. Fragments from a green rustic past still linger. It was widely believed among women—both rich and poor—that they should not cure hams while menstruating. In 1878 a correspondence struck up in the *British Medical Journal* describing incidents when meat being rubbed with brine by ladies during these seasons had not taken the salt and turned bad. But on the whole, ladies were now too genteel to be domestic. Eating was associated too closely with the body, and its unfortunate excretory functions, to be polite. Consequently their kitchens and their dining tables suffered. Mrs. Rundell, writing anonymously in her *Cookery* at the beginning of the century, had some acid remarks to make:

Young ladies of our time pride themselves upon knowing nothing whatever concerning an art which most assuredly ought to be deemed essential in the mistress of a family. Generally speaking, there is a universal distaste amongst the educated classes of the female community of England to the details of housekeeping. We hear upon all sides complaints of the trouble of ordering a dinner; and the consequence is, that dinners are seldom well arranged, or the most made of the materials provided. There are comparatively few persons among the merely respectable classes of society who can afford to keep professed cooks—their wages being too high, and their methods too extravagant. It follows, therefore, that a plain cook, plain enough in most cases, is alone attainable, who can put a dinner on the table in a very slovenly manner . . . the mistress of the house, dependent upon her domestic, must be content to put up with an inferior and distasteful mode of living.

The dinner was sometimes not helped by cooks being employed, not on their qualifications of coction, but churchmanship: 'Engaged a cook, after a long talk on religious affairs . . .' Mrs. Battiscombe quotes in *Mrs. Gladstone*. Kitchiner recommends that a cook's palate, on becoming sluggish, be purged—like the bowels —by the apothecary; he suggests a potion comprising manna, senna and salts, to be regulated according to the dullness of the organ.

Even the great cooks had some nasty habits. Carême reports, with disgust, on their stinginess: presenting time and again the same elaborate set-piece at dinners, dusting it carefully and storing it away after the meal, until the next time.

'The English ideal of cooking is the best in the world,' Frank Harris said, but he went on to say: 'The drawback of English cooking is that England has scarcely any cooks, and so it is seldom you find their ideal carried out.'

'Nothing but joints, joints, joints,' complained Nathaniel Hawkins, 'sometimes, perhaps, a meat-pie, which, if you eat it, weighs upon your conscience, with the idea that you have eaten the scraps of other people's dinners.'

'Roast beef and mutton are all they have which is good,' agreed Heine. 'Heaven keep every Christian from their gravies . . . And Heaven guard everyone from their naïve vegetables which, boiled away in water, are brought to the table just as God made them.'

A glutton in gluttony was how Joaquim Pedro de Oliveira-Martins described the Englishman. Even the newly opened Simpson's met with his criticism. 'Certainly the climate requires hot and strong nourishment. These are traditional, as I went to see them in the classic tavern of Simpson, the real one, in the Strand. They gave me a slice of meat swimming in fat, a piece fit for Pantagruel, cut out on the spot from a sanguinary heap carried about among the tables.'

'The English system of cookery it would be impertinent for me to describe,' adds the Stomach '. . . when I think of that huge round of parboiled ox-flesh, with sodden dumplings floating in a saline greasy mixture surrounded by carrots looking red with disgust and turnips pale with dismay, I cannot help a sort of inward shudder.'

There was no doubt that the French system was far superior. The English dishes, in comparison with the excellent continental ones, Sydney Smith described as 'barbarian Stonehenge masses of meat'. Guests that went to dine anticipating a talented dinner prepared by a great French chef were sadly put out when only an English spread appeared. '. . . never was there such a take in,' says Macaulay, after his dinner with Lord Essex. 'I had been given to understand that his Lordship's cuisine was superintended by the first French artists, and that I should find there all the luxuries of the *Almanach des Gourmands*. What a mistake! His Lordship is luxurious, indeed, but in quite a different way. He is a true Englishman . . . A huge haunch of venison on the side-board; a magnificent piece of beef at the bottom of the table; and before my Lord himself smoked, not a *dindon aux truffes*, but a fat roasted goose, stuffed with sage and onions. I was disappointed . . .'

Often meat was eaten so high that it exuded a dreadful odour, pervading the whole of the dining room. Kitchiner advised that meat should always be hung 'such a time . . . as will render it tender, which the finest meat cannot be, unless hung . . . till it had made some advance towards putrefaction'. 'You can get the best game in the world in England,' Frank Harris wrote in *My Life and Loves*, 'but alas, the English always keep it until it is "high", or if you prefer the truth, till it is almost rotten. I remember one Englishman of great position telling me that he always hung grouse till the bird fell of its own weight, drawing out its legs.' He adds that Professor Mahaffy, of Dublin, only cared for woodcock when it was represented by a green sauce upon his plate. Ladies, naturally, found Harris's lunches delightful—the best in

England they said, because the game he served was so delicious, 'not smelly' they said.

Harris was the exact obverse to Johnson. Like Pepys he was fundamentally a Puritan, but he revolted and kicked at its grip, and enthusiastically achieved, according to him, hundreds of sexual triumphs. It was not sex, but gluttony that met with his disapproval: 'Self-indulgence in eating and drinking is simply loathsome and disgusting to all higher natures,' he spluttered, 'and yet it is persisted in by the majority of mankind without let or hindrance. What preacher ever dares to hold the fat members of his congregation up to ridicule, or dreams of telling them that they are not only disgusting but stupidly immoral and bent on suicide? . . . And what I want to know is, why shouldn't one speak just as openly and freely of the pleasures and pains of sexual indulgence as of the pleasures and pains of eating and drinking.' He put the whole trouble down to the impotence of the Apostle Paul. Himself he saw as the great romantic hero and saviour of women, whom he was constantly rescuing from beneath the fumes of gross and malodorous trenchermen. At one party he recalls he had the agreeable duty of escorting his pale hostess from the dining room, so intolerable were the evacuations of the Lord Mayor of London, Sir Robert Fowler.

No sooner had Harris sat down, with the carnivorous Lord Mayor opposite him, and had 'just taken a spoonful of clear soup when my nostrils were assailed by a pungent unmistakable odour'. He looked around him but everyone seemed oblivious, his 'rubicund little' neighbour quaffing champagne as for a wager. Never had Harris seen men 'stuff with such avidity'. After the first mouthful Sir Robert Fowler cried out to his host upon the excellence of the Scotch beef. 'When I turned to eat,' Harris narrates, 'I found my huge vis-à-vis smacking his lips and hurrying again to his plate, intent on cutting and swallowing huge gobbets of meat while the veins of his forehead stood out like knotted cords and the beads of sweat poured down his great red face!' The 'huge vis-à-vis' consumed several helpings of beef and Yorkshire pudding and moved on to the game—partridges so high that they fell apart when touched. 'I had never cultivated a taste for rotting meat,' Frank Harris tells us, 'and so I trifled with my bread and watched the convives.' Meanwhile the hostess, Lady Marriott, had a shrinking in her face corresponding to the disgust Harris was feeling. 'I looked away to spare her when suddenly there came a loud unmistakable noise and then an overpowering odour . . .' But the 'big glutton' wiped his forehead and finished a third plateful of the 'exquisite Scotch beef'. 'Quiet little' Lady Marriott was as white as a ghost, her meat lay untouched on her plate. But still the atmosphere got worse and worse, the smells stronger and stronger. By the time the soft herring roes on toast came the orgy had degenerated to a frenzy. Another unmistakable explosion. The hostess was as pale as death. She turned to Harris, who takes up the story. ' "I'm not very well," she said in a low tone, "I don't think I can see it through." "Why should you?" I responded, getting up. "Come upstairs, we'll never be missed!" '

Harris attended several Lord Mayor's banquets, he said they threw a remarkable light on manners and customs. He was always astonished at the gluttony.[1] On his first occasion he believed himself to be surrounded by ogres. All round him aldermen smacked their lips, the veins on their foreheads stood out, sweat poured down their faces as they received helping after helping (having tipped the waiter beforehand), stuffed in coloured meat, reaching down between mouthfuls to swig from Jeroboams they kept on the floor. One found occasion to question Frank Harris:

' "Why do you leave that?" he exclaimed, pointing to the pieces of green meat on my plate, "that's the best part"—and he turned his fat flushed red face to his second plateful without awaiting

[1] On November 13, 1828, among others, the following number of dishes were consumed at the Lord Mayor's dinner at the Guildhall: 200 tureens of turtle, 60 dishes of fowls, 35 roasted capons, 35 roasted pullets, 30 pigeon pies, 10 sirloins of beef, 25 apple and damson tarts, 50 blancmanges, 20 ordinary salads, 4 prawn salads, 50 hams, 40 tongues, 2 barons of beef, 60 dishes of mincepies, 40 marrow puddings, 10 Chantilly baskets, 26 dishes shellfish, 4 lobster salads, 50 roasted turkeys, 30 leverets, 50 pheasants, 2 dishes peafowl, 24 geese, 30 dishes partridge. For dessert there were 300 pounds pineapples, 100 dishes hot-house grapes, 200 ice creams, 60 dishes apples, 60 dishes pears, 50 savoy cakes, 30 dishes walnuts, 75 dishes dried fruit and preserves, 55 dishes rout cakes, 20 dishes filberts, 20 dishes preserved ginger.

my answer. The gluttonous haste of the animal and the noise he made in swallowing each spoonful amused me; in a trice he had cleared the soup-plate and beckoned to the waiter for a third supply. "I'll remember you, my man," he said in a loud whisper to the waiter, "but see that you get me some green fat, I want some Calipash—"

"Is that what you call Calipash?" I asked pointing with a smile to the green gobbets on my plate.

"Of course," he said, "they used to give you Calipash and Calipee with every plateful. I'll bet you don't know the difference between them; well, Calipash comes from the upper shell and Calipee from the lower shell of the turtle . . .

"Eat that up," he said pointing to the green pieces on my plate, "eat that up: it'll go to your ribs and make a man of you: I gained three pounds at my first Banquet; I did; but then I'm six inches taller . . ." He was indeed a man of huge frame.' And he went on to fill it with a bellyful of finest Southdown mutton, '" . . . three or four years old, if it's a day, and fit for a prince to eat, fair melts in your mouth, it does".' He finished the evening by being sick before Harris could convey him to his brougham.

There was nothing that agreed with Harris more than what he called a good 'wash-out' with his stomach pump; employing this towards the end of his life as many as nine days in ten and 'finding it no more unpleasant to wash out my stomach than to wash my teeth . . .' He was fond of such abluent contraptions, introducing his famous syringe, helpfully and often, to his numerous and astonished 'loves' to save them any ill effects from his attentions.

One way and another there was an enormous amount of food wastage, both from private meals and public feasts. Tschumi, the royal chef, remembers that after any big banquet at Buckingham Palace there would be queues of people outside with baskets, but he recalls that if a dish were spoiled by the apprentices it was thrown away. 'Sometimes dozens of pheasants or soufflés in which four or five dozen eggs had been used found their way to the garbage pails,' he writes complacently. 'So did quantities of salmon, sturgeon, trout or foie gras, which had been spoilt at some stage of their preparation. No one can learn cuisine without making a good many mistakes in the process, and it is essential that those learning have the best materials at their disposal. The standard of cuisine was so high in Victorian days at Buckingham Palace simply because there was ample food with which they could demonstrate their skill.'

The Queen herself was not interested in food. She liked only plain meals. Nevertheless her position as head of a vast, and growing empire demanded that her dinner table should be as fine as any in Europe. In 1873 she lent the palace to the Shah of Persia. There was a certain amount of worry and speculation over the arrangements. Finally he forwarded several slaves from Constantinople, but left his three favourite wives behind. The Shah would condescend to sleep in a bed, the Queen's Household was told, but he must have his meals served on the carpet—a special one, four yards square, with a nice coloured leather top. All went reasonably well during his stop, apart from some disturbing rumours that spread through London. The Shah, it was said, was alarmingly spontaneous in performing his natural functions, about the palace. Not only this, it was whispered that he had had a certain member of his staff executed in his presence, and then had him buried by night somewhere in the Royal gardens.

Many countries besides Europe were now influencing the British diet. Back from the West Indies came the esteemed turtle, with its much relished green fat; from India came a fashionable revival for hot piquant foods: soy sauce, cayenne pepper, chilli vinegar. Quintessences, ketchups, zests and suchlike learned mixtures were made commercially and sold. Kitchiner himself marketed a preparation: 'This piquante and savoury quintessence of ragout,' he advertised, 'imparts to whatever it touches the most delicious and highly flavoured relish ever imagined, to awake the palate with delight, refresh the appetite and instantly excite the good humour of every man's master the Stomach.'

During the nineteenth century there came an essential difference in the method of serving dinner. Up until now dinner had consisted of two courses, each comprising a dozen or more dishes which were laid on the table altogether—literally covering it—

to a formal plan for people to look at, as well as eat. Soup was already in the plates as the guests entered. 'After the soup is removed,' explained a foreigner, Prince Pückler-Muskau, writing in the late 1820s, 'all the covers are taken off, every man helps the dish before him and offers some of it to his neighbours ... If he wishes for anything else, he must ask across the table; or send a servant for it—a very troublesome custom in place of which some of the most elegant travelled gents have adopted the more convenient German and French fashion of sending the servants round with the dishes.'

By the 1850s this manner of serving—dinner à la Russe—had been adopted, and many people in their turn found fault with it, complaining that the joints were frequently mangled, that the portions often arrived luke-warm or cold, and that dinner was unnecessarily prolonged to four hours instead of two and a half or three. 'The present system [of dinner giving] I consider thoroughly tainted with barbarism and vulgarity,' grumbled Thomas Walker, one who had an excellent opinion of his own taste in food and party giving, 'and far removed from real and refined enjoyment. As tables are now arranged, one is never at peace from an arm continually taking off and setting on a side dish, or reaching over to a wine-cooler in the centre. Then comes the more laborious changing of courses with leanings right and left, to admit a host of dishes, that are set on, only to be taken off again, after being declined in succession by each of the guests, to whom they are handed round.'

Now the simple halves of the day were divided into quarters by four meals. No longer was it orientated towards leisure and pleasure. Trade had become respectable. It had become a working office day. Breakfast was no longer the easy sociable meal described by 'Humelbergius' to which you must not take dogs: 'It is only the common people and *les dames à la mode* who take such liberties ... A dog, how well soever he may have been brought up, spoils the furniture and produces no small embarrassment should he think proper to do his "little jobs" before you.' Breakfast had acquired a seriousness of purpose, a new and anxious atmosphere, and was eaten around eight o'clock. There was no time for dogs. The father intoned prayers, the dishes on the hot plates hissed and popped; there was the smell of fresh furniture polish, the aromas of kedgeree, sausages, cold pheasant and buttered muffins; the red and blue design of the carpet was seen through slits between the fingers. At one there was nursery luncheon: a substantial meal for the children, with a small portion carefully arranged on a tray for the lady of the house, the gentlemen lunching at the clubs, or chop-houses. In the afternoon—that nineteenth-century gift to mankind, as Arnold Palmer says—there was carriage exercise for the ladies and visits to be paid with the accompanying refreshments of tea and cakes. Then came dinner—a feast whose hour, as de Quincey noted, had travelled, like the hands of a clock, through every hour between 10 a.m. and 10 p.m. E. F. Benson in *As We Were* recalls dinner parties at Wellington College. A child, he stares down between the banisters to the long dining-room glittering like an Aladdin's cave as it lay prepared for dinner. The tapestry curtains would have been drawn together with a clash, the rows of decanters would stand ready on the fine oak sideboard along with the Copeland dessert service, the candle-light would move. There would be the sound of the doorbell and the ladies, like magnificent butterflies, would float upon the arms of their escorts into the drawing-room. And then the galaxy would pass out again and into the glittering cave, where there would be grace and an incredible banquet.

There was thick soup and clear soup (a nimble gourmand had been known to secure both). Clear soup in those days had a good deal of sherry in it. There was a great boiled turbot with his head lolling over one end of the dish, and his tail over the other: then came a short pause, while at the four corners of the table were placed the four *entrées*. Two were brown *entrées*, made of beef, mutton, or venison, two were white *entrées* made of chicken, brains, rabbit, or sweetbreads, and these were handed around in pairs (Brown or White, Madam?). Then came a joint made of brown meat which had not figured in the brown *entrées*, or if only beef and mutton were in season, the joint might be a boiled ham. My mother always carved this herself instead of my father: this was rather daring, rather modern, but she carved with swift artistic skill and he did not, and she invariably refused the offer of her neighbouring gentlemen to relieve her of her task. Then came a dish of birds, duck or game, and a choice followed between substantial puddings and more airy confections covered with blobs of cream and jewels of angelica and ornamental sugarings. A Stilton cheese succeeded and then dessert. My mother collected the ladies' eyes, and the ladies collected their fans and scent-bottles and scarves, and left the gentlemen to their wine.

There is a delightful and amusing sketch composed by Mr. Albert Smith, which not only illustrates the ghastly evening parties, but also the appalling shyness and the nice lack of appetite. We endure with his hero and heroine several hours of intolerable boredom and gentility. Mr. Ledbury, his round spectacles stuck on his round face, eyes Miss Hamilton. In what style of conversation should he address her? Is she slow or fast? he wonders, dullish or clever? a flirt or a prude? does she like music or politics? He can find no words and instead tries to button up his gloves, then remains rigidly silent behind her chair until the quadrille. He offers her his arm. One movement—Le Pantalion—passes without speech, except when some gentleman begs the pardon of some young lady for treading on her flounce. Mr. Ledbury however has not been idle. He has concocted a sentence and is now ready to deliver it. Miss Hamilton is busy searching for something among the petals of her bouquet. Mr. Ledbury draws himself up. Has Miss Hamilton been to many parties this season? Miss Hamilton, it is discovered, has not. Mr. Ledbury continues with the important business of buttoning his glove, Miss Hamilton is engaged in the investigation of her bouquet. What does she think of Alfred Tennyson? She is sorry to say she has not heard his poetry. Has Mr. Ledbury? Mr. Ledbury has. Several times. They wonder who the new tenor at the Opera will be, move on to how Mr. Ledbury can play, a little, the flute—an instrument which Miss Hamilton admires very much—and discuss the Wiltons of Eaton Square of whom Mr. Ledbury has never heard, but confessing nevertheless to an acquaintance wonders whether they are related to the Wiltons of Camden Town, which Miss Hamilton assures him they are not. During the waltz Mr. Ledbury has a misfortune. He mistakes a gentleman in a white neck cloth for a waiter and requests him to be good enough to bring a glass of lemonade. A Miss Mitchell plays at the piano. Mr. Ledbury and Miss Hamilton glide down the stairs to supper, where Mr. Ledbury mistakes the waiter for one of the guests, inquiring if he had heard Miss Mitchell's charming song; a question which so confuses the waiter that on being asked for a glass of lemonade he pours some negus[1] into an ice plate and dips wafer cake into a jug of hot water reserved for forks. By now everyone is arranged with tolerable accommodation; the ladies sitting, the gentlemen standing behind them. What may Mr Ledbury have the pleasure of procuring for Miss Hamilton? She thinks a little chicken, whereupon Mr. Ledbury brings a slice of glazed tongue, which, in her best public manner, she cuts into small pieces the size of an oat, two or three of which she manages to swallow and then lays down her fork. Mr. Ledbury, not having observed Miss Hamilton that lunchtime eating heartily out of a dish she had met with on its way up to nursery dinner, thinks that such a small appetite is remarkably *comme il faut*. The supper table is laden, there are barley-sugar bird cages and an enormous quantity of cold fowl, collared eel and Miss Hamilton's glazed tongue. In the middle rises the *pièce de résistance*: a lighthouse made out of rout-cakes[2] standing in the midst of a tempestuous sea of trifle, which no one dares to attack, until a young man, made bold by the champagne, conveys a few of the billows to a young lady's plate, together with the distressed mariner—cleverly fashioned

---

[1] A beverage which derived its name from Colonel Negus, composed of either port or sherry and hot water, the quantity of water being double that of the wine. Sweeten with lump sugar and flavour with a little lemon-juice and grated nutmeg. It is an improvement, continues the Victorian recipe, to add one drop of essence of ambergris, or eight or ten drops of essence of vanilla to every twelve glasses or so of negus.

[2] This is a Victorian recipe for rout cakes: Take 1 lb of sweet almonds and 1 lb of loaf sugar; beat your almonds and sugar quite fine and make it into a moderate stiff paste with the yolk of an egg. Make them into any shape your fancy may dictate. Use finely-powdered loaf sugar to dust your boards or blocks. In making them, place them on clean tins that are slightly buttered, so as not to touch, or lay a sheet of whitey-brown paper on the tin to put them on. Let them remain in a warm place all night, or a day and a night, before they are baked. Put them in rather a brisk oven; when lightly coloured over they are done. Ornament them with nonpareils, candied peel, icing etc. to fancy; make a mucilage of gum arabic, and lay it, with a small brush, over the parts where you wish the nonpareils to adhere; this is done after they are baked. If you wish to cut your paste out of blocks, put it in a stewpan over the fire; keep stirring it with a spoon or spaddle; stir it well to the bottom. When you find the paste does not stick to the sides of the pan, and comes altogether, it is done. Let it get cold before you cut it out. When the cakes are made in this way the impressions show much better.

in coloured sugar—who is clinging to a rock of *meringues à la crème*.

The candles dance and make pools of gold light reflecting the barley-sugar bird cages, the ancient mariner and the polite faces. Behind them heavy curtains hang against the night-black glass, against the hubbub of London streets on a Saturday night, where, not far away, the inhabitants of a different, ruder world—the working classes—are buying their Sunday dinner, which late on a Saturday evening may be bought at bargain prices from stall-holders who auction off the remainder of the goods cheaply. The new white gas lights, the smoky flares of the grease lamps, the individual candles stuck in bundles of firewood illuminate the stalls: the yellow haddocks, the onions, the chestnuts, the new glittering saucepans, the blue and yellow crockery, the crimson and white of the meats, the purples of pickling cabbage. Above all there is noise, shouting and *scramble*. Each stall holder shouting to outdo his neighbour, each shopper struggling to buy his food, to subsist.

Never before had there been such opportunities, but never before had conditions been quite so bad for those without fortune. Without training, or a trade, some, with wives and children to support, were obliged to earn their livings as best they could selling ham sandwiches outside pubs, or dressed up—street clowns acting at street corners earned wages that could be anything between 1s 10d and 15s 5½d a week. For women and girls without training there was little alternative to becoming a servant to the rich— either as a drudge or a prostitute. Often the one led to the other. Treatment was sometimes so hard, so uncompassionate that the girls ran away and took their living as best they could on the streets.

Often as a result of low wages and expensive fuel the diet of poor families was really appalling. Girls prostituted themselves to buy sweets and pies. 'I buy things to eat,' a girl called Kitty told the anonymous author of *My Secret Life*. 'I can't eat what mother gives us. She is poor, and works very hard; she'd give us more, but she can't; so I buy foods and gives the others what mother gives me; they don't know better—if mother's there, I eat some;

sometimes we have only gruel and salt; if we have a fire we toast the bread, but I can't eat it if I'm not dreadful hungry.' 'What do you like?' 'Pies and sausage-rolls,' said the girl, smacking her lips and laughing. 'Oh! my eye, ain't they prime—oh!' 'That's what you went gay for?' 'I'm not gay,' said she sulkily. 'Well what you let men fuck you for?' 'Yes.' 'Sausage-rolls?' 'Yes, meat-pies and pastry too.'

Further on in the narrative another girl receives a shilling each time she will feel the author's genitals; two shillings and sixpence if she permits the author to feel hers. With the money she bought fruit, sugar candy and bullseyes and ate them while travelling round in omnibuses. This the narrator thought very humorous: 'A girl of fifteen riding in an omnibus by herself for pleasure and gorging herself with sweets, out of the money got by feeling a man's prick in the street, seems an amusing fact,' wrote he.

3

Mass Evacuation

During the century communications improved considerably. At the beginning conditions were no better than mediaeval; indeed they were often worse, for no longer did each village have the advantage of being self-contained and self-sufficient. In the small village of Netheravon, where Sydney Smith was vicar at the start of his career, the arrival of the butcher's cart, once a week, from Salisbury was the chief event of the week, but when inclement weather made the tracks impassable it was unable to penetrate and the villagers were obliged to live on vegetables. In 1813, having moved on to Foston-le-Clay in Yorkshire, Sydney Smith and his wife set themselves to build a parsonage. For the purpose of transporting the necessary thousands of bricks and tons of timber he bought four oxen, which he called Tug, Lug, Hawl and Crawl. But the roads were so poor, with a mile of deep sand near the village, that Tug and Lug fainted from the strain and had to be fed buckets of sal volatile, while Hawl and Crawl 'just lay down in the mud and roared'. Gradually the main roads were surfaced with Mr. Macadam's new method of road surfacing and in 1830 travelling was considerably eased by the building of the first railways.

The Napoleonic wars had a major effect on the food of the poor. During the fighting they brought high prices for the farmers, but, when Napoleon fell, wheat prices tumbled, and there was an agricultural depression. The labourer's lot was generally very bad, especially in the south and all areas where there was no factory work to compete and raise the agricultural wages. Cobbett reports a case of thirty men being set to dig a twelve-acre field near Warminster—at ninepence a day, their wages worked out at four shillings a week, which was cheaper than ploughing. The down-lands that had been cultivated for corn during the boom-years became rough patches of thistle, but they still belonged to the farmers. The labourers had no plot of land, no common, and were often, Cobbett observed, forced to inhabit buildings no better than pig-beds. With low wages and no land their diet was at subsistence level. In Devon, breakfast, supper and tea consisted of kettlebroth (bread, hot water, salt and a third pint of milk), bread and treacle. Dinner was pudding (flour, salt, suet and water) boiled and eaten before the vegetables and any fresh meat that could be had. The Game Laws made it dangerous to supplement the diet with a hare or a rabbit. Until 1857 a family could be transported for seven years if convicted for poaching. The Game Laws were, in the view of Sydney Smith, barbarous and absurd—'the privilege of shooting a set of wild poultry'. They remained unrepealed simply because the majority of felons were poor. 'There is a sort of horror in thinking of a whole land filled with lurking engines of death—machinations against human life under every green tree—traps and guns in every dusky dell and bosky bourn . . .'

The labourers' lot was worsened by the Speenhamland System which specified that a labourer's wage should be made up to a reasonable living level by the parish. This had the effect of reducing everyone to the level of a pauper, relying on charity.

However hard, or however little a man worked, however lazy or conscientious, however little a farmer paid, everyone was reduced to the same level. In the winter of 1830 the field labourers rioted and burnt ricks. Three of the rebels were hanged, four hundred and twenty were convicted to be transported to Australia. Cobbett was delighted with the revolting rick burners: 'It is unquestionable that their acts have produced good, and great good too.' He pointed out that by destroying produce these men were not depriving themselves or their families of food, since they could not afford to buy it in any case.

Meanwhile for many of the farmers themselves, their standard of living rose. Cobbett complained that their farmhouses were more like painted shells than farmhouses; the mistress within, stuck up in a place called the parlour, with showy chairs and a sofa, swinging bookshelves with novelettes, and to eat, two or three nicknacks instead of a piece of bacon and a pudding.

In Cobbett's view, the industrial towns, and especially London, grew like great wens upon England, sucking and draining her strength, turning the peasantry into half-starving paupers. The system had been turned upside down. The rural skills: the domestic brewing and baking, had disappeared. The villages had lost their local character. There was a mass evacuation to the factories and towns, where not only was fuel scarce, but women who had put in a hard day's work in the factory did not have the time, or the energy, to cook large meals. 'Nowadays,' complained Cobbett, 'all is looked for at shops. To buy the thing *ready made* is the taste of the day: thousands who are housekeepers buy their dinners ready cooked.' Many ate at cheap unsavoury eating and chop-houses, the effluvia of which steamed up through the iron gratings. 'Oh the 'orrible smell that greets you at the door,' wrote Surtees. 'Compound of cabbage, pickled salmon, boiled beef, sawdust and anchovy sauce. The cloth is filthy, mustardy and cabbagy . . . Flies settle on your face, swarm on your head, everything tastes flat, stale and unprofitable.'

This mass evacuation to the towns had an alarming effect on the population. In 1798, Malthus had caused an uproar by publishing the first edition of his essay *The Principle of Population.*

This stated that the population will always increase faster than means of subsistence, and went on to prove it arithmetically and geometrically. It seemed unquestionable, like multiplication tables. He was seen by men like Cobbett as a monster furnishing everyone with lies. 'A man that can suck that in will believe, literally believe that the moon is made of green cheese,' snorted Cobbett, after reading the census figures which showed a forty per cent increase in the number of people living between 1801 and 1821. But in spite of his disbelief the population continued to expand from 8,900,000 in 1801 to 18,000,000 in 1851.

England was able to support herself with her own produce until 1850—not only support herself, but produce a surplus, and export corn. During the '50s and '60s great progress was made in animal husbandry and manuring, but ironically they came to be appreciated only by the '70s, at which time Free Trade and 'demand' for cheap food had smashed to death an agricultural policy based on wheat. Within fifty years the greater part of the country's food came from abroad. An inevitable consequence of a diet depending on purchased food was that the food of most people tended to become uniform in both town and country.

With commercial production, food values fell. Rickets, scurvy, green sickness, to say nothing of syphilis and gonorrhoea, were rife. Unless one could afford to pay the best prices, tea, coffee, bread, beer, pepper and butter were all adulterated, containing trace elements of lead, copper, mercury and arsenic to build up in the system. In the very class that had taken upon itself the moral leadership of the country were men deliberately poisoning and cheating their neighbours for the sake of gain and accepting it as the normal state of commerce. Business morality had never been so low than at the time Christian observance was at its most ostentatious. 'The condition of meat sold to the poor people was equalled by that of fish,' wrote Drummond and Wilbraham, 'even the pickled herrings offered for sale in the poorer districts being often partly decomposed owing to faulty preparation.' Eggs were often fertile with the embryo quite well formed. Even 'Humelbergius', feeding at the tables of the fortunate, says that one of the miseries of dining abroad was eating poached eggs and feeling your bread meet with a certain resistance in the interior of the shell in consequence of its containing a little half-formed, half-cooked chicken.

In 1855 adulteration became news. In 1872 the Adulteration of Food, Drink and Drugs Act was passed whereby it became an offence to sell any mixture containing ingredients for the purpose of adding weight. Narcotics disappeared from beer. In 1875 a confectioner was fined for colouring his sweets yellow with surplus pigment left over from painting his cart. Food, helped by great leaps forward in scientific knowledge, began to be a serious commercial business. Margarine was first manufactured in the late '60s, accompanied by all kinds of nasty rumours that undesirable fats were being converted into spurious butter. Horse fat, it was said, was obtained from the knackers, and some sinister men had been observed in the Thames, salvaging lumps of fatty refuse near the Metropolitan sewers. There were jam, chocolate and biscuit factories. There was the first advertising. In 1870 Thomas Lipton had two of the fattest pigs he could find driven through the streets of Glasgow with I'M GOING TO LIPTON'S, THE BEST SHOP IN TOWN FOR IRISH BACON painted on their nicely scrubbed sides. Later he hired traction engines to draw enormous cheeses to his shops every Christmas. In 1874 Australian tinned meat began to arrive on the market—large lumps of coarse-grained meat, surrounded by an unpleasant looking lump of fat. It was known to the navy, who had the doubtful benefit of being served up with it in their messes, as Sweet Fanny Adams, after an unfortunate lady of that name who, in 1867, was murdered and hacked into steaks by her lover.

CHAPTER NINE

TARMAC WINTER

'There's cold chicken inside it,' replied Rat briefly;
'coldtonguecoldhamcoldbeefpickledgherkinssaladfrenchrolls
cresssandwidgespottedmeatgingerbeerlemonadesodawater—'
The Wind in the Willows—KENNETH GRAHAME

I

The Last of the Sows' Udders

AS THE last years of the nineteenth century passed into the
radiance of an Edwardian Indian-summer of leisure for the
rich, we can look back on them nostalgically with Leonard
Woolf: at the spring picnics which he remembers, in glades
carpeted—as they never are now—with flowers, the dappled
sunlight, the hundreds of velvety butterflies: at the sooty, sour
London soil sprouting little but spiders and cobwebs; the solid
safety of his nursery, the tall guard, the blazing fire, the singing
kettle, the comfortable fug; the *silence* broken only by the clopping
rhythm of horses' hooves drawing the broughams through the
night. Once this was shattered by the strange and terrifying
shrieks of a woman, passing under his window, then fading to
silence. From the almost rural peace of Holland Walk there led
strange narrow side-streets into dark unknown places. Slums—
foreign underworlds whose inhabitants were vague shadows
flitting across the security of one's life, like black frightening dreams.
A drunken man appearing in tatters as the luggage was being
loaded on to the omnibus to take everyone for a holiday, a
Frankenstein swearing and cursing, becoming violent and being
hurried away by the police. The police again, flinging a woman

down in the Earl's Court Road, her battered black hat rolling away into the gutter, while a small growling crowd gathered cringing and the *respectable* passers-by averted their gaze and hurried on into the twentieth century.

It opened on a series of opposites: great safety on the one hand, extreme poverty and precariousness on the other; malnutrition and surfeit; great comfort and discomfort. The dew of those first mornings fell on stained malodorous streets, on ripening nectarines and peaches, brown crackling leaves and great sweeping lawns dotted with flower beds where later in the day there would be garden parties, special satin tea gowns and silk parasols. For the rich was there ever such a time? the sumptuous dark drawing rooms, the elegant houses, the tremendous and solid comfort, the glittering parties: shooting parties, racing parties, betting parties; luncheon, garden and Friday to Monday parties. Arnold Palmer describes, in *Moveable Feasts*, the agreeable moment when there would be a knock at the door and there would be a tea tray and bread and butter, followed by all the paraphernalia of lighting fires, ashbins, firing wood, blacking brushes, candles and hot water—which would have been carried up from the basement. All so delightful when one was lying warm in bed with a day of pleasure stretching away in front: a day—depending on your taste —of leisurely conversation, eating and reading, or, more vigorous, of sport. While, J. B. Priestley tells us in *The Edwardians*, a good deal of the ladies' time was taken up in changing their clothes—to be properly equipped for a weekend in one of the great houses she must take with her several large trunks and would probably change half a dozen times a day—a good deal of everyone's time was taken up in eating; 'not since Imperial Rome can there have been so many signposts to gluttony'. First there would be breakfast. A breakfast perhaps like Edward VII's, of haddock, poached eggs, bacon, chicken and woodcock, or perhaps like the one Priestley describes: porridge and cream, pots of coffee, China and Indian tea and various cold drinks, the sideboards (so large that they fit no longer into our cramped modern dining-rooms) groaning with rows of savoury, silver, breakfast dishes bubbling over spirit lamps; the cold meats, pressed beef, ham and tongue and that Edwardian bird—ptarmigan; the fruits heaped up, the melons, peaches, nectarines and raspberries, the 'scones and toast and marmalades and honey and specially imported jams'. And then the lunches, eight and twelve courses, including pigeon pies, maybe, with the legs sticking out—like the ones Leonard Woolf liked. Teas, gossipy, easy teas—very confidential—the wasps humming over the jam, the thin slices of bread and butter, toast, brioche, Madeira and Dundee cake. And then there was dinner consisting of a dozen or so courses in the grandest houses. Then at midnight there would be sandwiches, devilled chickens or bones, brandy, whisky and soda.

'It is fairly common knowledge now,' Priestley tells us, 'that the Edwardian house-party, while severely determined to keep up appearances, discreetly provided opportunities for lovers, not necessarily young, to enjoy themselves, the males having been fortified by a final drink or two, a last ham sandwich, or a bit of devilled chicken.' Each bedroom door held a tiny brass frame into which was inserted a card with the name of each guest carefully inscribed. It was one of the hostess's duties to arrange the bedrooms carefully and conveniently. Priestley tells us that many of the sexual intrigues may have arisen from boredom. 'The talk through most of these luncheons and dinners was vapid. The women prattling, the men uttering pompous nothings.' Any subject worth discussing was generally barred. The 'lusty males, crammed with all that Edwardian food and inflamed by all its drink, were constantly tempted, were avidly longing to discover what the women were really like once the frippery and finery and social disguise were removed . . . the little tap on the bedroom door behind which the delicious creature, with heroic bared bosom and those great marmoreal thighs, was waiting— oh it was all irresistible!' Mr. Priestley remembers with nostalgic relish.

While the aristocracy were passing the nights in nocturnal adventure and the days in a procession of changing clothes and huge dishes, ordinary housewives were tailoring their meals which had inevitably lost some of their size. Meal habits, as Arnold Palmer has pointed out, were moving to our present situation:

'the disappearance of meals altogether: an undistinguishable population, indistinguishably nibbling like rabbits in a national
park'.

But for the time being the rich rabbits were fairly isolated and
distinguished. They nibbled elegantly on lovely terraces, surrounded by purple lilacs and scented pinks. Still uncrippled by
taxes, people had money with which to be eccentric and free,
money to spend selfishly in creating personal effects, which were
not always beautiful. Frank Crisp, for example, a solicitor of
Henley, worked hard, ate a great deal and erected in his garden
a range of Swiss mountains, complete with china chamois,
underground lakes, caves festooned with spiders, china hob-
goblins and other surprises. But there were not going to be many
more like him. Like him, or like the Duke of Portland, who at
the turn of the century undermined his place with underground
passages; driving tunnels lit by gaslight, walking tunnels that
His Grace might promenade in privacy and not meet anyone,
tunnels to convey His Grace's food in a heated railway truck and
tunnels leading to the kitchens where on a spit chickens perpetually
turned, one following another so that whenever His Grace should
call one was always ready roasted.

There was money for travelling. Ottoline Morrell could embark on long journeys abroad for her health, take drives by night
surrounded by fragrant odours and fireflies, eat purple figs and
ripe peaches. Leonard Woolf could go off with Lytton Strachey
on leisurely reading parties to secluded parts of the country, where
there would be dark remote pools and landladies who retained the
last of a peasant economy, serving ominous, but local dishes: 'For
breakfast the inside of a she-goat,' wrote Lytton Strachey, 'at
lunch sow's udder trimmed with tripe and parsley smothered in
thick white sauce.' There were still country inns famous for their
food, like the one at Holford, recalled by Leonard Woolf, where
the best of English food was served: the crusty bread, the fresh
butter, cream and eggs, the magnificent beef, mutton and lamb,
the wonderful bacon and the enormous cured hams hanging from
the kitchen rafters. The country districts still served their local
specialities, the foods the region grew best and had produced for

hundreds of years, making pies and cheeses, meat puddings and treacle roly-polies and wonderful joints.

'What distinguishes the lamb and mutton in this country,' wrote H. D. Renner in *The Origin of Food Habits* at the beginning of the century, 'is the same thing as distinguishes the beef, namely the English pasture grazing. The difference in flavour with that of other countries is even more striking than with beef.' The meat depended for its succulence and flavour on its *maturity* and proper hanging; not for the Edwardians any pale tasteless mass of wobbly flesh, rushed through farms for quick turnover. It was hearty meat, such as Harris's alderman had enjoyed, the finest Southdown mutton, fit for a prince and melting in the mouth, 'three or four years old if it's a day'. 'Cattle in England,' wrote Escoffier in 1907, 'are killed at an age varying from 3 to 4 years.'

1902 saw the arrival of the fish-and-chip shops which emanated from the hot pie and cook shops. There was a growth in eating out. In London hotels and restaurants there was a remarkably high standard of food. Simpson's was well to the front with its joints 'fit for Pantagruel', its turbots, delicious pies and puddings. Forty years later Arthur Moss was to become Master Cook there —one of the three English Master Cooks—which entitled him to wear the Black Cap of the Master Cooks, made for him in black velvet by his wife. But in those days his mother had to go out to work and he spent a good deal of time with his grandmother in Brixton. He remembers sitting in her kitchen, cross-legged on the floor in front of a great Dutch oven, basting the mutton as it cooked. In 1912 he began a job at a bakery in Wandsworth, working under the skill of a superb German pastry cook. Moss remembers the wonderful smell of muffins, crumpets and buns, which costing about a halfpenny each were sold with the bread in the morning; cakes and patisseries were displayed in the afternoon. Marvellous aromas emerged from the shop in the early mornings as the cottage loaves, big and round with a smaller loaf on top, brick loaves with notched tops, and coburgs, split open during baking, came out of the ovens.

The people in Wandsworth were poor; most of them cooked on open fires with a tiny oven at the side. On Sundays they queued up at the bakery to have their joints—bought cheap at the market the night before—cooked for them, for which they would be charged 4d to 6d. And then he remembers they ran home like the wind, their joints wrapped in a warm cloth. Next door the butcher sold boiled beef, salt pork and carrots, and faggots, which were made by Moss at two o'clock each morning. The butchers still had their own slaughter houses, the milkmen kept their cows tied up in sheds so that the milk was still warm when sold: a beverage which Moss remembers with disgust, ever since he drank a warm mug of milk frothing straight from the cow. Moss's dislike was upheld generally; the unpopularity of milk probably accounted for the general malnutrition of poor children. A survey made in Sheffield, in 1900, showed that sixty per cent of mothers in working class districts were feeding their young children on quite unsuitable foods—mainly bread and jam. As a result instruction in the Board Schools was being wasted, children were often so hungry they fell asleep during the lessons. J. B. Priestley remembers that what he calls the 'lower orders' were poverty stricken. He himself was a member of the lower middle classes, and although his family lived carefully, frugally even, he was certainly well-nourished, with the main meal in the middle of the day, a colossal Yorkshire high tea and uproarious parties at Christmas time when he laughed himself in a red haze at charades. It was a life when there was none of the common anxiety there is now, it was more secure. This Mr. Priestley puts down to the fact that there were very few clever people persuading everyone to buy what they could not afford to buy, and making them discontented that they were not buying so much as their neighbours.

Changes were on the way. It was as though all over the country the installation of electricity had switched on the illuminations behind people's eyes, showing up the dust lying thick over the old taboos and beliefs. It was a time of new thinking and reforms. Homosexuality, it was realized, could be a congenital condition rather than a vice, marriage could be a relationship rather than hordes of children and drudgery. Already in the field of medicine there had been vast improvements. The discovery of chloroform, antiseptics and anaesthetics made it possible to undergo operations with reasonable safety. The motor car was waiting just below the horizon ready to roar in and shatter all silence and peace, whirl people up on to its wheels, spin them dizzy from their own rhythms and fling them into new ways and neuroses. Women were waiting, scissors poised, to cut their hair, shorten their skirts, flatten their bosoms, rise from the horizontal helpless role of mother and advance vertically as a competitor of men. The leisurely, serene and protected lady was vanishing forever. 'Let us pay her tribute of a short pause,' wrote Arnold Palmer, 'watching her as she slowly mounts the stairs and disappears along the landing. Something is disappearing with her . . .'

2

Entre Deux Guerres

1913 dawned and never, as Lloyd George remarked, had the sky been more perfectly blue. It was a brilliant summer. London seemed the capital of the world. There were balloon races to Paris, crowds at Henley; the public whirled dizzily at fairground merry-go-rounds and everyone danced. There was the Turkey-trot, the Ragtime, the Bunny-hug and above all there was the Tango—and a most immodest dance it was considered too; nevertheless there were Tango Teas, Tango Lunches, and Tango At Homes. From Germany the Kaiser watched enviously. It was his jubilee year. State events must be more glittering than any in England. Everyone must improve his table-manners. Berlin must be made as fashionable as London. But it was difficult. To the Kaiser's irritation his splendid campaign was cluttered by peasants, looking for work. His envy and greed proved too much. In 1914 war was declared.

Between the years 1851 and 1911 the population had doubled from 17,900,000 to 36,000,000. The 1917-18 conscription involved a medical examination of two and a half million men.

It revealed a national level of health that was very poor. Of every nine men of military age in Great Britain, three, it was discovered, were fit and healthy, two were on a definitely inferior plane of health and strength, three were almost physical wrecks, and the remaining one was a chronic invalid with a precarious hold on life. For the rich, during the war, there was little change in the routine of their lives. Those at home were not affected physically by the war. Bad news would come from the front and to mask the sadness they whirled ever faster in a hard glittering gaiety. There is hardly a date in her diary for example which finds Lady Cynthia Asquith dining or lunching alone; between the sociable meals and visits she pauses only to pop along to Fortnum and Masons to dispatch comforts—chocolate, pheasants and cod cutlets[1]—to her husband at the front. Towards the end of the war the poor were possibly slightly better off. By 1918 the government had taken into control all the important foodstuffs, which had the effect of raising the general standard of diet, since the price was controlled and brought within reach of the people.

In spite of the politicians' wishes to design a Britain fit for heroes, the diet and condition of the poor after the war reverted and according to Drummond and Wilbraham became almost as bad as it had been in the worst years of the Victorian reign. Meat was seldom eaten more than once a week, fresh milk was seldom seen, thousands of families were affected by unemployment, with as little as one shilling and sevenpence to spend a week on food. The farmers were producing the food all right but the people could not afford to buy it. In 1931 the diets were so poor that an Advisory Committee on nutrition was called. The government was beginning to realize that the country could not be efficient unless people were fed adequately. It must work towards a revised Darwinian theory: the Survival of the Fattest. Food prices must be brought within people's reach. And so, in 1931 there were new marketing schemes for the farmers, and the Milk in Schools Scheme began, subsidizing milk, making it available to children at cheap prices. This was to have a double-edged effect, not only to enable the children to feed cheaply and well on

[1] In the days before deep-sea trawling cod cutlets were luxuries.

protein food but to supply a market for the farmers and overcome the prejudice that had always kept the consumption of milk low. The enormous development of canning and refrigeration caused the emergence of large scale concerns such as milling firms, tea blending firms and the United Dairies to control the market. Individual butchers and grocers simply became agents, buying their joints and goods from jobbers rather than fixing their own prices and mixing their own blends. Thus there was a swing in sales technique; instead of competition in price and quality, retailers concentrated on advertisements and modern shop fronts to seduce their customers. Quality became more or less uniform, and there appeared on the market many prepared powders for the convenience of making custards, caramels, blancmanges, and jellies. There was every kind of domestic and foreign fruit available in tins.

In eating out there was a tremendous growth, restaurants combined eating with dancing and the Licensing Laws of 1921 permitted drinks to be served after 11 p.m. provided food was also ordered. By now the motor car had snorted over the horizon into life, down the narrow dusty roads, had astonished the horses; the women had cut their hair short, shortened their skirts and flattened their breasts; they sipped cocktails and served at tennis. The years fox trotted and charlestoned by. And everyone in London, according to Horace de Vere Cole, over ate:

> The pangs of hunger are no guide,
> Since all in London over eat
> Her devil kitchen opens wide
> Thence calves, and flesh and roasted meat.
>
> Girls and waiters, artists, kings
> Are flung together in a pot
> In foetid restaurants, where rings
> Of blueish smoke obscure the lot.

Meals were still delicious: succulent joints, lobsters, yellow cream and treacle tart. But they were small and lighter, many people having to economize on domestic service, although they were inclined still to be extravagant. In 1937, Euphemia Lamb held a party at which every guest was served with his own pot of

19A. 'Picnic on the River'—twentieth-century style. By Sir Alfred Munnings

19B. 'Autumn Cannibalism' by Salvador Dali. Dali like many contemporary painters depicts the horror and sinister undertones of scientific 'progress' with its plastic foods and relegation of animals to machines

20A. A conveyor belt of turkeys passing in from the bleeding tanks in the last stage of their processing. They are loaded living at one end, are slaughtered, plucked and drawn in the middle, and emerge processed and packed at the other. Note the empty hooks travelling out again to collect their next assignment

20B. The main selling agents—sex and security. Providing ladies buy the nice advertised product the assumption is that a dark and handsome man will whirl them away to a palace of romance (fully equipped with the latest labour-saving appliances) where they will live happily, satisfied, ever after

caviar and a goose. There was still time to linger over good conversation and pen wonderful gossipy letters. It is significant that the
Bloomsbury group, who stood for everything that was civilized,
should serve the most excellent and carefully planned meals—as
those that remain still do: deliciously cooked breads and marmalades, succulent meats and hollandaise sauces, perfect vegetables—
from no tin or deep freeze. These were—and are—enjoyed in beautiful curving dining-rooms, warmed by log fires, scented by
pomanders, brightened—like Ottoline Morrell's—by the suns of
yellow taffeta on grey walls.

In 1939 war was again declared. Hitler moved into Poland
and finally the old ways were shattered forever. Rationing was
introduced. To this much thought was given. Professor Drummond was responsible for the foundations on which the programme was drawn. He saw that an even allocation of proteins,
fats and sugar must be distributed among the population at prices
that everyone could afford. Bread and margarine were fortified
with vitamins and minerals, the consumption of milk, potatoes,
oatmeal, cheese and green vegetables was increased. People dug
for victory, supplementing their diet with potatoes and green
vegetables from their allotments. There were widespread programmes of cookery instruction. Changes in food supplies made
it necessary to learn to use unfamiliar foods like dried eggs, and
dried skim milk. But although the rations allowed some people
for the first time to eat a balanced and wholesome diet, to the
people who had been well off before the war, they seemed appallingly frugal. In 1942 the *Wine and Food Quarterly* offered recipes
for roast potatoes 'so delicious and satisfying that one hardly
misses the beef or lamb of better days'. Restaurants were limited
to a maximum price of five shillings a meal, and a system of
apportioning the protein; thus one could have one main course
of fish or meat, one light hors d'oeuvre and a pudding. So at
Christmas 1946, at Simpson's when the treat of one dozen oysters,
costing four shillings, was offered, it meant that if one were to
choose them one must forgo the turkey, lamb, beef or hare, since
each of these cost four shillings also, and pass on either to Christmas pudding, or fruit cocktail, mincepie or ice-cream, all at one

shilling. At Lyons it was possible to buy a substantial hors d'oeuvre, a made dish and a pudding for one shilling and nine pence.

Rationing lasted for approximately fifteen years. It had the effect of changing the British diet in a major way. It reduced the overall standard to a uniform level. Everyone, whether rich or poor, whether in the town or country, was eating the same food. And when the terror, the flames and the bomb smoke had cleared, when the lights had gone up on London and the food controls were lifted early in the 1950s, a strange phenomenon was to be seen. Under cover of the black-out, science had reached in and made off with the seasons. The shops were filled, no matter whether it was spring, summer, autumn or winter, with the same millions of canned, frozen and dehydrated vegetables, soups, meats and ice-creams.

3

Fuel not Food

Show me the way to lose weight
I'm tired of dragging it around
I had a nice shape long long ago
But now I'm much too round.
Song from *Singalong with T.O.P.S. Songbook*

The 1945 peace was followed by major reforms. There was to be a marriage of mind, health and food. There should be no more hungry uneducable scholars, no more expensive food, available only to the rich. Education, Health and above all Agriculture were to be supported by the State. Benefits of this would be twofold: encouraging the farmers to produce more food would cut down the need for imports, conserve currency while providing the public with a reasonably priced, well-balanced diet. Guarantees and subsidies paid out each year to the farmers would enable them to assess their returns accurately and plan their policies on a sound business foundation.

The engines heaved themselves into position and creaked slowly round. It seemed they were functioning splendidly. The

farmers expanded and by 1953 all controls could be lifted, cheap
food was abundant for everyone. Now at last it was a Britain fit
for heroes. No longer were the diets of the rich and poor different.
Indeed with all the taxes levied by the government to finance
the free Education, Health and Agriculture systems, no longer
were the rich and poor so different either. At last the Whitehall
economists had everyone beneath them, like fussy hens with their
clutches of eggs; before, controlling the rich had been like controlling a stack of straw in a gale of wind, the money had blown
away out of hand. Now they manured the old Puritan commercial roots with a spirit of competition and envy so that the
middle classes exploded with a passion for profit that was
stronger than ever before, inflating like a huge balloon which
enveloped most of the country. Wage policies ensured that they
had never had so much money. Freed from the austerity of the
war-years they spent and they spent. For the next ten years
everything expanded, including the birthrate and the population.
Hire purchase schemes and door to door salesmen persuaded
housewives to buy hoovers and encyclopedias, new televisions,
new washing machines, new cars. Never, as Macmillan remarked,
had they had it so good. Money had replaced muscular power.
For a man to be potent he must have an income as fat as his penis.

The country became slashed with tarmac, contaminated by
the coughing exhaust fumes of motors cars; the horizon became
pierced with tall, mostly ugly, buildings that rose up into the
sky—tall blocks of flats with small restricting rooms in which
to hold and suspend the expanding population above the earth.
Everywhere there was less green and more noise. The land seemed
like one huge and ugly machine, its population small grey
undecorated cogs working anonymously to roll ribbons of grey
concrete over the old values, severing the soil from the land.
No longer, as H. J. Massingham said, was it an organic system
working as yeast; a pyramid built with the sound bottom of
humus and peasant tradition. Its foundations had been cut away
by land enclosure. The structure was precarious, perched above
holes which were patched with synthetic wisps. The old values
were buried under concrete. Progress and Profit, like two black

tanks, waited, expectant and expectorating, to demolish the past. To go against Them was the heresy of the time. All destruction, stupidity and narrowness was excused in Their Name. 'The ultimate aim of any activity must be to make profit for its owner,' announced C. B. Daniell, nicely summing up the modern credo.

The rise in birthrate began to cause alarm, not only in Britain and Europe, but the world. Behind laboratory walls, research in the new field of nutrition progressed. To improve the yields of crops, artificial fertilizers were compounded; to remove weeds— unnourishing marguerites, poppies, groundsel, daisies and butter/ cups—noxious poisons were bubbled and dehydrated into pow/ ders and dark concentrated liquids. More processes of canning, freezing and dehydrating were perfected. The food industry was swept up into the great creaking machinery, while agriculture was business—competitive business—the farmers were a political instrument. But the economists saw they must be pushed, they must become always more productive, always more streamlined. Their processes could not be competent if animals were fed on food humans could eat, or occupy land that could be employed for crops. Indoor systems were devised which reduced labour costs, raising efficiency. Animals were confined in a constant environ/ ment, controlled, fed and watered by electricity. The problem was, as the economists saw it, a mathematical one: how many pounds of foodstuff would be required to convert into protein— meat, milk or eggs? How could so many pounds of waste/matter and surplus be converted into foodstuff? There was, for example, a world surplus of fats. The National Renderer's Association spent millions of pounds on researching. At length it was triumph/ antly discovered that dairy cattle fed on concentrates of fat yielded improved quantities of milk. But unfortunately there was a world surplus of milk as well; Europe was drowning in it, Britain could not sell all hers, and underdeveloped countries refused to drink it. Undaunted, scientists discovered means to convert surplus from dustbins into swill; and condemned horsemeat, blood, offal, fish/flour and protein from petrol into nuts and cake. They also discovered a means of converting them into mock meat with which to fodder the humans: 'food analogues' which threatened the animals themselves. But for the moment the real meat remained unchallenged. The more animals that could be crammed into a small space, the more profitable it was. Provided lack of space did not effect the animal's efficiency rate of conversion, provided they still laid eggs and put on flesh in the proper manner it was unnecessary they should turn their heads, groom their flanks, stretch their wings. Gone were the days of the sheep called Molly and the cock called Chanticleer, which not only had provided Chaucer's widow with food, but also companionship and warmth. This was business: no sentimental stuff; animals and birds were mere digits on paper. These methods, said the economists, were the Modern World's Answer to farming; that, no Thinking Man could deny. It was the way to keep pace with The March of Time and the Immeasurable Strides of Science, agreed the Farmers' Union. It allowed farmers to compete with the Urbanized Industries, to answer Demands, to blow with the Wind of Change, to gather with the Nations of the World in working Towards the Goal of providing food for the Undernourished Underdeveloped Millions.

At this stage it is important to make one thing clear. Our farming systems have nothing whatsoever to do with food supplies in the underdeveloped countries. And any 'attempt to justify the system by reference to starving millions is arrant nonsense', wrote a recent contributor to *The Times* correspondence columns. Each year Britain sends millions of pounds to developing countries through the Ministry of Overseas Development, but no home-produced food. It would be unsuitable for practical reasons. To enable it to travel it would have to be processed, its preparation would require a certain knowledge and equipment. One load of dried eggs, it was whispered, was dispatched. It was fed to the developing nation's chickens. Animals, as nutritionists know, are a particularly inefficient source of protein, in spite of all those 'immeasurable strides of Science'. For the amount of food they consume their yield is strikingly low. They are a luxury-food that poverty-stricken nations can seldom afford. Beans and oats yield far more calories: far more protein, calcium and iron. Besides which intensive methods are highly unsuitable for developing countries, which need work-providing husbandry rather than labour-saving.

Meanwhile back in England there was plenty to exercise the scientists. It was necessary to devise methods to eradicate the pests and diseases for which intensive conditions made a fertile bed. Active pesticides were compounded, which sprayed a constant stream of poison into the air; antibiotics were automatically included in the animals' feed; it was discovered that a more efficient rate of conversion could be achieved if hormones were to be injected into the animals.

The farmers, encouraged by the government grants, expanded. They produced more and more food—particularly milk, pigs, chickens and eggs.[1] Everything seemed to be progressing splen-

[1] Behind the scenes promoters of the industries, those 'clever people' whose job it is to persuade people to buy more than they can afford and more than they need, work hard to 'educate' the public into buying their products. And they succeed. 'Thanks to the efforts of Britain's chicken farmers the population of Britain has become a nation of chicken eaters,' Mr. Ron Mayes, an executive officer of the British Chicken Association, announced in 1968, at ' A chicken for all occasions' event at the Waldorf Hotel. 'No branch of agriculture,' he went on to say, 'has shown such rapid expansion in twelve years.' 'Last year we produced 230 million chickens and, taking an average weight of $3\frac{1}{2}$ lb, this means the people of Britain ate 359,375 tons of chicken, representing about 12 lb per head of population. Compare this with twelve years ago when chicken consumption was 1 lb per head of population, or $39,062\frac{1}{2}$ tons. Now we have a weekly sale through the shops of $4\frac{1}{2}$ million. This means that there is not a second of any shopping day when someone is not buying chicken.' Turkey production, the *Meat Trades Journal* reported, has doubled during the past six years and could nearly double again during the next six, according to the Ministry of Agriculture's Turkey Adviser. He believed that the turkey population could reach 25 million in 1976. Another Ministry of Agriculture speaker gave a warning that the market might be approaching saturation. Mr. Derek Kelly, Managing Director, said he believed the future of the British turkey industry was assured. 'Although production ran ahead of the demand from time to time, the industry was still only scratching the surface of the potential market'. From the U.S.A. come reports that the turkeys are being bought up by manufacturers of 'pet' food and canned for 'pets'. To facilitate marketing the poultry meat, packing stations have been erected all over the country. They achieve the highest degree of automation. Birds are loaded alive and flapping on the hooks of conveyor belts, suspended upside down they travel to be slaughtered, drawn and plucked. But if only the birds had no feathers their meat might be cheaper. Over this problem a Professor of Bird Genetics has been exercising herself. After several years she has triumphantly produced the final horror: two hundred bald, walking, oven-ready chickens, which inconveniently suffer from the cold so that they lay

didly until in the 1958 Price Review it was revealed that the farmers' contribution to the Balance of Payments was, after all, doubtful, since instead of importing food to feed the people the country had had to import food to fatten the animals. A reduction in milk, pigs, eggs and wheat was advised.

Prices fell, wages rose. To carry the losses farmers were obliged to expand more and more—along scientific lines. Long low windowless houses were to be seen all over the country, more and more animals were crammed into less space.

In the shops there had never been so much food. So many shelves of canned vegetables, flesh, puddings; so many prepared meals; so many frozen and dehydrated birds, meats and fish. Food was now simply something that happened provided you had the money: milk waited in the bottle, sardines in the tin. For the marketing boards there was a disagreeable fact. Supply was increasing faster than demand. Worried Boards and Manu⁄ facturers asked one another: could Britain be made to drink more milk, eat more eggs? Could it also be made to eat more bread, more cheese, more breakfast cereals, more butter, more butter substitutes, more sweets and biscuits? Advertising schemes were launched, slipping, through the medium of television, into people's houses between the murder and cowboy films. Millions of pounds were spent each year on promotion. Ballerinas danced with glasses of milk, men floated down through the air suspended from parachutes, woolly farmers wandered through hedges searching for eggs. There were sunshine breakfasts and walks in wheatfields; people were urged to go to work on an egg. It was all very wholesome and rather exciting: exciting because the main selling agency was sex—sex and security—the assumption being, provided you bought and ate your nice dehydrated beef curry, you would automatically be rolling, scented and elegant, around in bed after it with your delicious dinner companion. Later on, providing you bought your sunshine breakfast, you would have a nice smiling wife, or husband, and a nice (small) smiling family, together with a nice house, cooker, refrigerator and saucepans.

fewer eggs, have more ulcers and need more food than feathery ones. Their future seems to be economically dubious.

Everyone responded very well, they did their best. But they simply could not eat their way through all the food. Each year there were thousands of tons of unconsumed cheese, chickens and eggs. Red/faced officials at the Egg Marketing Board were breaking out three million crates of eggs a year. Meanwhile imports continued to flow in.

As the years passed into the '60s an awkward fact was observed. There was malnutrition in the country, malnutrition and disease. But these were due to no shortage or failure of harvest. Obversely, this was malnutrition owed to surfeit. A new disease had entered the affluent society: obesity. One in two people was eating more food than he required. In November 1965, Mrs. Renée Short called in Parliament for a national campaign against obesity. 'Is the Parliamentary Secretary aware that about two thirds of the people in this country are overweight and that this leads to heart disease, arthritis, posterial backache and flat feet? Does he not think that it would pay dividends if Parliament were to undertake a campaign of this kind which would relieve the National Health Service of a good deal of the problems which are caused by over/weight? Was he also aware that large numbers of children are overweight and if so . . .' The Honourable Lady was advised acidly to 'slim her questions' by the Speaker. In 1967 the Obesity Association held its first meeting. Obesity caused more diseases than any other complaint. Slimming was business now, as well as food. Thousands were spent each year on special diets, massage, magazines and health farms. Cases were reported of people entering hospital for the purpose of starving. Humans are perverse creatures, food was plentiful so now it was no longer a sign of prestige to be plump.[1] It was fashionable to be as thin as possible. Teenagers, modelling themselves on the famous Twiggy, often lived at near starvation levels.

In 1967 there were special groups formed, whose members

---

[1] In primitive countries it is often a sign of opulence to be plump. In the nine/teenth century, the explorer Speke came upon the harem of the King of Karagwe, whose wives were so fat they could not stand upright but flopped like seals on the floors of their huts. Their diet was an uninterrupted flow of milk sucked through a straw, and if they resisted they were force/fed, like the foie gras geese of Strasbourg, while a man stood over them with a whip.

collectively clubbed together to lose spectacular tons of flesh. The Weight Watchers was introduced from America, where special clubs to help ladies Take Off Pounds Sensibly are well embedded. There, their organization is vigorous. There are special rituals and games to pass the fat weary hours. The Weight Recorder knocks at the door. 'Who pounds at our door?' the ladies cry. 'Not who pounds, what pounds,' the Weight Recorder corrects. 'Surplus pounds,' comes the chorus. Sometimes ladies who have failed to Take Off Pounds Sensibly must wear aprons with pig emblems. But to cheer them there are games: Scrambled Foods and Calorie Baseball—when the pitcher calls out the name of a food to the batter, who has to call back the calorie value. And there are songs like 'We are Plump Little Pigs, who eat too much Fat, Fat, Fat'. And humorous telephone calls when a disguised voice hisses darkly: 'Ah! Ha! Put down that ham sandwich,' then rings off. There are special diets: the Dormitory Diet, the Vilhjalmur Stefanson's Amazing Stone Age Meat Diet, the North Pole Slenderizing Diet, the Eat-All-You-Want Diet. During one diet, consisting of complete starvation, one lady developed a painful attack of gout, triggered off by the fats, proteins and acidities in her own flesh; several more died of heart failure.

Reasons for this epidemic of obesity are more complicated than greed and persuasion. Despite our urbanized affluence, our equality of women, there is evidence of increasing neuroses, anxieties and boredom. No longer is ennui the misfortune of the few fortunate rich, it is the misfortune of the majority, since the majority is fortunate. The instances of over-eating come, as they always have, as a direct result of empty leisure, but this in the '60s is reinforced by modern pressure. Food is being employed as a distraction from the inner emptiness of people's lives. Cases are also noted when food replaces sex. An American psychiatrist recorded the case of a patient who was impotent; whenever he had a strong sexual urge he went, not to his wife, but to his refrigerator.

If sex and food were forbidden subjects to the Victorians, manual labour is our modern taboo. Our tinned civilization, as

H. J. Massingham said, protects itself by every ingenuity of mechanical gadget and has come to look on labour as an undignified horror, unfit for man. 'Any invention which saves labour,' John Stewart Collis criticized, 'is, ipso facto, a good thing.' Everything about our society is tinned. Because of convenience foods, their manufacturers state, housewives are enjoying more leisure than ever before. 'They enable the housewife to put a meal on the table within minutes instead of hours,' wrote John Burnett, in *Plenty and Want*, 'they are part of emancipation, adapted to small kitchens and meals round the T.V. No one but an archaist would condemn them . . .' Often the housewives, instead of employing their leisure to satisfy and soothe their minds, hurry out to work in order to earn money. This means that even if they wanted to they would not have the time or the energy to prepare vegetables, stews and pies. To feed their families they must use prepared packets and tins. Accordingly they are suffering from feelings of guilt and inadequacy. They are cramming their husbands and children with too much food. They are raising families of Billy Bunters. Fat babies, plump children and husbands, it is believed, are automatically associated with loving mothers and attentive wives.

Manufacturers have been quick to recognize the commercial value of babies and children; so much the better if they can trade on a mother's guilt. Even such plastic devices as blobs of caviar are concocted—blobs of caviar, scampi, artichoke leaves and escargots—with their authentic taste and colouring incorporated, to be strung like beads and placed across the pram for the baby so suck. While mothers are encouraged to feed their babies themselves—more for value of the relationship than nutrition—increasing numbers do not. For them there is a useful Living Nipple Bottle Attachment, which may be purchased; when touched this emits a series of giggles and grunts, so that with his synthetic feed the baby should not feel isolated and unloved. For older children there is every kind of sweet, biscuit and drink for the mother to offer as a token of her love, or as a bribe for the child to behave well.

Together with the attitude towards sex, the attitude towards children has altered. In the interest of society there should not be too many children from any one partnership, no longer is it necessary to produce large numbers to ensure the survival of a few. With smaller families children have become idealized. In spite of emancipation they are still considered the fulfilment of a woman. But science, which with its 'strides', very largely makes the work of men and women redundant—reducing the once essential tasks like gardening and cooking to hobbies—may also tread childbirth into obsolescence. In the view of some, such as Peter Jeffrey writing in the *Guardian*, if women are to achieve real equality 'one of the things that would have to go is the woman's right to enjoy rearing her children to the exclusion of other work. To knock off work in order to bring up children would henceforward be a luxury that had to be paid for.'

It has been suggested that when families are smaller and generally planned the love for each child becomes more concentrated, whereas in larger families the parents' attentions are spread over a greater number and therefore diluted. As the numbers within families grow less, so does the discipline. The anxiety and guilt, on the other hand, grow more; parents are terrified of losing the esteem of their children who, as they grow up, are frustrated by the anxious attention, and restricted space, and fight to break free.

From reports we read in the newspapers it would seem that our post-war society is becoming one massive misbegotten combination of Doctor Johnson and Frank Harris, but combining their appetites without their wit, coupling Johnson's troughmanship and corpulence with Harris's priapism. Sex, as Patrick Goldring has pointed out in *The Broilerhouse Society*, is now encouraged as a pastime: an excellent exercise requiring the minimum of equipment. But often the husband is too exhausted earning the money that pays off instalments on the bed to use it for anything more than sleeping. Frustrated housewives, in desperation, are reported by *Suck* to be gathering in Surrey for morning coffee, but instead of cards they are holding masturbating parties. Others are enjoying gas, milk, coal and insurance salesmen. One paper reported the case of a coalman taking three days to deliver some coal to a certain address; another, of a gasman causing a housewife to sniff a bottle of cleaning fluid because he said it prolonged their sexual enjoyment—the housewife was overcome by its fumes and died.

Suck—the newspaper that 'focuses attention on the orgasm'—publishes recipes for 'orgy butter' and 'bold red warm body rubs for fun loving people'. It also offers some helpful hints to ladies who wish to retain their partners' attentions. 'By the way, ladies,' it asks, in a jolly nuncle-ish sort of manner, 'do you always have sex in the bedroom? Have you ever thought of going over to your husband some night in the living-room and running your hands over his body? When was the last time you felt him up under the table at supper?' It continues in a more marriage-guidance-counsel sort of tone: 'What is needed in sex is an element of suspense . . . next time he's on you, do something different. Have you ever tried slapping him on the ass? Try it. Caress him first with your finger tips and finger nails and then suddenly bring your hand down hard across his ass. The results are almost always rewarding.'

4

Death in the Pot

Let us eat flesh, but only for hunger not for wantonness. Let us kill an animal; but let us do it with sorrow and pity and not abusing it, or tormenting it, as many nowadays are wont to do.

PLUTARCH

Meanwhile back in the farmyard all is not well. Ruth Harrison, in her book *Animal Machines*, pointed out that intensively produced animals may provide dangerous meat, permeated with antibiotics[1] and pesticides; Rachel Carson, in *Silent Spring*, that

[1] On April 6, 1970, Paul Levy wrote in a letter to Michael Holroyd: 'I seem to have eaten something with penicillin in it on Saturday. I am violently allergic to this substance, and the world came close to losing an author of some promise. But a night in hospital restored me to health and humour. The sour cream garnish on

herbicides and D.D.T. are polluting the waterways and seeping through the land. In 1969 the Swann Committee was set up to examine these hazards. Antibiotics in food, D.D.T. and certain herbicides, it was decided, should be banned. Fleas, flies and lice, rats and mice show signs that they are building a resistance to pesticides; while we show signs that we are building a resistance to antibiotics—some infections, venereal and otherwise, no longer responding. Hormones used to fatten animals may lodge in the meat, possibly emasculating male adolescents and causing cancer. Thousands of cases of salmonellosis have been traced to infected broilers. Major diseases in the land come from too much food, not too little. Of these coronary thrombosis is one of the most prevalent. At the beginning of the century coronary disease was almost unknown. Like cancer its causes have not been pinpointed, but a sedentary life with too little exercise and too much food, too much nervous stimulation without the physical energy to follow, definitely does not help. Professor Yudkin believes that too much sugar in the diet may be the root of the cause, and a healthy safe regimen is one of fresh eggs, meat and milk. But 'Horizon' on January 24, 1970 showed that intensively-produced animals, on account of their own lack of exercise and scientific feeding, provide protein containing large amounts of saturated fat.[1] Natural meats, such as hare, venison and all beef, sheep and stock reared without benefit of modern scientific aid, contain only unsaturated fat. It has now been proved that a large consumption of saturated

---

my steak is the suspected source. I wish farmers would dose their cattle with nothing stronger than aspirin.'

[1] It is not so much the presence of saturated fats that is the danger, as the absence of unsaturated fats. Animals that select their own food produce three times as much protein as fat, intensively produced animals vice versa. Doctor Crawford at the Nuffield Institute of Comparative Medicine has proved chemically that there is a serious change in the quality of meat. In a letter to the *Lancet*, December 27, 1969, he points out: 'The high-saturated fat, low-quality product appears specific to the modern intensive system and does not apply to any other animal system.' Our modern fat content is fine for energy, fine if one wants to wage war or climb Anapurna, he says, but no good for rebuilding vital body cells which cannot be made in the body by anything else. We have solved the acute nutritional problems, how to supply proteins and vitamins, but now it looks as if they may supply the wrong kind of food.

fat causes high deposits of dangerous porridgy cholesterol in the blood. These rest in the arteries, blocking and clotting the blood supplies; or, more dangerously, fragments may break from the main body and travel to lodge in the lung or brain and cause fatal obstruction. The increase of saturated fatty protein from modern scientific feeding methods corresponds so closely with the increase in coronary disease that they must be directly related.

People are becoming more and more anxious and bewildered about the content of their food and its pollution. Increasing numbers are turning away to more expensive 'Health Foods' which are reared by old-fashioned organic methods.

Farmers, meanwhile, who wish for an old-fashioned way of life, away from the urban rat-race, are finding it impossible to escape from modern pressures and make a living. They cannot afford labour, new machinery or the expensive new scientific feeds, they cannot even afford tinned, dehydrated and frozen foods for themselves. They feel they are being squeezed out. There is no room for small individuals any more; directed by Whitehall economists, they must join collectively into factory groups, their 'unprofitable business' should be abandoned, they should 'unsentimentally cut their losses' and 'get into something more rewarding'. Everything should be mass-produced. The economists see the country as a paper-plan, a dormitory for the urban masses, with a crazy-paved back garden. Earth and rural life have gone out with the peasants and the land enclosures. A tarmac factory—farming remains, but even this is being threatened. Meat substitutes, it is reported, may challenge traditional cuts, while milk substitutes challenge milk and margarine challenges butter. Is farming really necessary? is a question currently resounding through the economists' chambers.

There is increasing concern over this mass commercialization. 'How big a step is it from the broilerhouse to Auschwitz?' asked an article in the *Guardian*. And on another occasion: 'the fact is that an increasing contempt for lower forms of life may be leading us, especially in an agnostic age, to a contempt for man himself.' Numbers of young people, both in America and England, are rebelling against this mass-produced car-crazy life. They yearn, not to stand out publicly upon the hard grey tarmac, or, in motor-cars, roar up and down it, but to burrow beneath, make a private contact with the earth, live a simple life from the soil once more; do their own thing. Some escape from the crowds into a private coloured world of drugs; some vanish to the remaining isolated pieces of land, to live. Through their hallucinations and their ritual killings they see themselves as religious as any Early Christian, and as persecuted, persecuted by their parents and the bank-clerk mind. And like the Early Christians they do not see themselves as fanatical and ill-equipped. Their parents are like the Romans; they find it hard to understand why they cannot *wash*.

Perhaps the most depressing thing of all about this affluent age is that overall standards of quality are reduced to a mean average. There is no excellence any more, or very little. This is especially salient in the field of cookery, where the quality—especially in catering establishments—is probably as low as it has ever been.

As Derek Cooper remarked in *The Bad Food Guide,* not only is it impossible to tell margarine from butter, but we are rapidly reaching the stage where it is impossible to experience any taste at all. Like gardening, cooking has become a hobby. Never has there been so little need to cook. One can simply open tins, unwrap polythene, thaw pies and prepare powdered potatoes—no need even to add milk, butter, salt or pepper—and hey presto! there's a meal. Paradoxically never has there been such an interest in cooking, so many articles in magazines and newspapers, so many books. They are best-sellers, along with books on how to get thin, and on sex. But a recent survey showed that the majority of women read them only from curiosity, in the same way as they would read a description of the landscape of Russia, or the moon; they have no intention of using the facts to any practical purpose.

What people eat in the privacy of their own homes naturally is as much their own business as how they eat it. But when it comes to eating out in a restaurant it is a different matter. The further from London one goes, the worse—with very few excep-tions—the standard becomes. The general situation has achieved farce. We have too many people in the country, wage policies ensure that there is no one to work in the kitchens, preparing vegetables and whipping eggs—just as wage policies ensure that it is almost impossible to buy and drink a Sunday cup of tea out of season in the country—so everything comes either from packets or tins and is served precisely the same as at home, only three times as expensive. The main appetite is the caterer's one for profit. 'If your appetite for profit is as good as your appetite for meat and poultry, WELCOME . . .' read a butcher's advertisement at Hotelympia 70, the international Hotel and Catering Exhibition. Here one observed a mass organ emerging. A popular palate, which dulled as it is by sweets, spirits and tobacco is far more flaccid than any mediaeval one. Before a product is marketed thousands of pounds are poured into market research to find out how the public likes it, a demonstrator of tinned curry told me. 'This way there's no risk. You might make some curry to an individual recipe and your customers might think it too salty, too spiced, too . . .'

She need not have worried. No matter the season, no matter the scenery one can generally expect to sit up to the same meal. Outside the rain may sweep across purple mountains, or the sea may pound against the cliffs, and there will be tinned or packet soup, prawn cocktails—made with factory made mayonnaise— meat cooked the day before, sliced on a bacon slicer and heated up in packet gravy, yellow brussels sprouts; there will be frozen rainbow trout, withdrawn moments before from polythene, usually a very inferior steak, and, perhaps, for a special treat, salmon served with *Sauce Duglère*—i.e. the same heated up factory made mayonnaise (and the whole lot, during some, or all, stages of its processing will have got lavishly sprinkled with sodium glutamate, so that the following day one experiences nasty sensations with the top of one's brain freezing cold and out of order). These will be followed by the dreary ice cream, which so long as it is not called *Dairy* may be made from any surplus fat, or a plate of tinned fruit served with 'today's way to whipped cream'— an aerated blob made with a device called the Spark Whip Cream Whipper, a miraculous invention which will froth up half a pint of cream and half a pint of milk to the volume, and price, of four pints.

In Mr. Moss the Master Cook's view, the standard of food to be had in the shop has generally deteriorated. The quality of meat in the ordinary shops he says is very low and vegetables are bland and tasteless. Brussels sprouts are no good until they get the frost on them, the same applies to celery. It never used to be possible to get either before the first frosts, now they are forced and marketed all the year round.

In the Western Isles, breathtakingly beautiful, the quays are knee-deep in herrings, haddock and cod; at luncheon frozen fish fingers are served. In 1967 four and a half thousand tons of mussels, three and a half million oysters, a thousand tons of lobsters and seven thousand tons of langoustines were gathered—and exported. In fishmongers by the sea, do we see heaps of black shining mussels, piles of oysters, lobsters, John Dory and grey mullet? Do we see lobster teas and mussel soups in the small seaside restaurants and cafés? It is remarkable if we do. It is generally baked beans, fried cod and chips. 'No demand' for anything else; as there's 'no demand' for venison or mutton. To mention mutton to a butcher is to see him react as though you had removed your knickers in his shop. 'People don't want it, they don't know how to cook it.' Which mostly means there is not enough profit in mutton. More money is to be made by calling it lamb, or shipping it abroad along with all the venison, mussels, lobsters and oysters.

Some restaurateurs who really do care and do their best to prepare careful and delicious meals blame the present low quality on the public. 'They're like a lot of arrogant sheep,' one told Derek Cooper. 'They don't come to enjoy a civilized meal, they come to stuff themselves and see how much they can spend. If I put asparagus on the menu at 30s a stick some fool, showing off to a client, would buy it. Women pick their way among the expensive dishes but usually have Steak Diane because they like all the drama and attention at the table. A certain type will deliberately pick the most expensive items on the menu.' This is an interesting parallel with a prostitute, a man must *pay* for her company.

Eating out has become an experience, but not one for the

palate. Interior decorators are employed to make eating a meal in a restaurant a dramatic experience. The atmosphere, it is believed, will seduce people in. When there are monsoons splash, ing into crocodile-infested lakes, one does not notice the crowd of waiters giggling in the tropical plants handing round the plate of whitebait that is about to be served to you; when there is a naked woman to watch, the wine waiter is a chimpanzee and the pudding comes in a bed-pan, you might not notice the disgusting salad of beetroot, hard boiled eggs, tired lettuce and dreadful dressing, the pale dead meat. At one well-known chain of restau, rants the pudding did not come at all; the factory, the waiter explained, that prepared the special *gâteau-maison à la surprise* had burnt down: there was no pudding.

Science has made it possible for us to eat fish fingers and peas instantly from the polythene, drink milk from a bottle; it has made it possible for us to illuminate and heat our rooms at the touch of a switch, to be transported with ease across the world in a matter of hours, instead of years, to swallow pills and medicaments that stop us conceiving, or dying from infection or fever. It has made it possible for the people of Britain to grow over nine hundred years, from one to fifty-eight million; for them to drug animals, degrade them, turn them to food machines; to turn England from a land of oak forests and silence into a land of tar and musak: a giant overcrowded supermarket with a mediaeval lack of privacy. Solitude is an expensive luxury. The nightingales have left Berkeley Square; aeroplanes whine through the night-dark bedrooms. The great gardens of Cogidumnus at Noviomagus, the forests where the wild bulls roamed, the village where the summoner strolled, the fields at Woolwich where Pepys gathered cowslips: all are beneath the tarmac. The soul of the country has gone with the peasants and enclosure. Progress and Profit are the new gods: sons of man, they are born of the Puritan, commercial urban movement. They have usurped—as did the Christian God—the fertility gods of nature: the animals, the birds, the sun and the rain, the trees, the wind and the mountains, these are tamed, mere irritants: the sun is too hot or too cold for sunbathers, the wind is too strong or too little for yachtsmen, the rain is too wet. The elements too are degraded: playthings for an affluent society which values that only which is new. No longer are plantains, dandelions, thistles, burdock and celandine valued for their properties, no longer are they gathered carefully, their roots and stalks preserved; they are weeds to be liquidated and poisoned along with the fleas, lice and flies.

Science has made all this possible. Already there are signs that it is turning nasty. The balance of nature is upset. There is death in the pot. The country and food is polluted and the pill, according to Malcolm Muggeridge, is 'going to provide one of those great human catastrophes like the Black Death.' Sterility, not fertility, is the great cry. 'Life is one animal,' Samuel Butler said. And slowly we are killing it.

As we waddle into the '70s we complete a historical circle. With National Assistance, subsidized food and violence on television and cinema, we are again within the Roman policy of Bread and Circuses to appease the boredom of a materialistic urban people. But there is a difference. The Romans did everything with a style and view to pleasure. We are still draped with the rags of Christian guilt. We are ashamed to enjoy ourselves, often we do not know how. We do most things with a view to financial or personal gain. From occasional periods of famine and mortality, owed to epidemics and inadequate harvests, we move to a regular malnutrition and departure, due to surfeit and epidemic of obesity. We continue to break out our eggs, store our unconsumed poultry and cheese; worry over our low milk consumption, our weight and our heart disease. The Boards continue to spend millions on promotion schemes; the large farmers continue to overproduce eggs, turkeys, chickens and pigs, the small ones continue to be squeezed out, and sink; the birth-rate continues to rise, the experiments continue to be conducted— experiments like producing battery cows, and providing mother substitutes for lambs to enable the ewes to spend their time pro-ducing, rather than rearing, their young.

There are still small pockets of England left, unchanged and unscarred. There is still a piece of coast-line, in crowded southeast Kent, that runs from Kingsdown to Dover and on to Folkestone; a path that follows the sea, high above the cliffs. In summer butterflies move over the wild flowers and herbs, over the sanfoin, mugwort, wild parsnips and carrots, marjoram, thyme and mint, harebells, the purples of knapweed and vetches. Inland the fields of barley stretch, swaying in the wind. The aeroplanes fly high there; there is only the occasional drone, the occasional throb of a boat. The gulls swoop and scream; there are larks, the moan of the sea. There is no sound from traffic or engines. It is still possible to breathe in a silence that is England. 'Let us pay her the tribute of a short pause . . .' Something is being swallowed in a corporate greed. Something is vanishing forever.

Deal, 1970

APPENDIX I

THE STUFF OF DREAMS

THE SUBJECT of aphrodisiacs is subtle and complicated, both psycho-logical and physiological—one about which very few people really know anything. They have heard of oysters and celery of course. But just why are they eaten? They contain nothing that is chemically stimulating.

Belief in aphrodisiacs is rooted in the past, when fertility was one with sexual potency; it emerges through a tangle of magic and folklore. Their use is tied in with the notion that sexuality does not come from within oneself, but depends upon some outside agent that can be taken at will and mechanically. Like all witchcraft and primary magic, they function through auto-suggestion. The preparation acts as a placebo. The patient knows he will automatically be restored to potency. He is. In the same way that bodies have been known to abandon their disabilities in the holy water at Lourdes they may be released from their hysterical inhibitions.

Erotic stimulants, as the American sexologist James Leslie McCary has pointed out in his article 'Aphrodisiacs and Anaphrodisiacs', have played a significant role in the majority of world cultures. Every sort of means has been contrived arti-ficially to stimulate sexual desire. His list is long. It includes baths, salves, smells, parts of animals, erotic cookbooks, household lamps and drinking cups manufactured into sexual forms, ether, blood (especially menstrual blood), contraceptives shaped like hands and little men, tattooing, the recorded sounds of heavy breathing, moans and gasps. To these urtication may be added and unguents made from unsavoury items such as lion's fat, the pounded livers and semen of young boys, lard and garlic. Harry E. Wedeck, in his *Dictionary of Aphrodisiacs*, offers us one love potion which requires a putrified human corpse, mixed together with animal and human testes and ovaries, pimento and alcohol. The more disgusting the potion, the more likely it was to work: a unique marriage between Puritanism and Epicurism.

Of all aphrodisiacs the best known and the most used is probably food. McCary points out that there is a closer and deeper connection between eating and sexual desire than is generally realized: '. . . a well-fed body naturally includes "well-nourished" sexual organs capable of vigorous and continuous expression,' he reassures us. By the same token 'hungry or undernourished persons cannot expect to have the rich, full sex life of people . . . who have no "oral longings".' 'When,' he goes on to say, 'one has eaten a carefully prepared, subtly seasoned meal, together with wine, in an *ambiance* enhanced by soft music and glowing candles, one experiences a delightful glow—not only of the senses, but also of the body—a feeling that can hardly be present after one has consumed a typical American meal of meat loaf, boiled potatoes, and watery beans in a boarding house or diner. Eating a meal of fine food is an exciting and rewarding experience for the different senses of seeing, smelling, and tasting.'

Women, it has been observed, are far more likely to be captivated and persuaded into bed after a delicious (and expensive) dinner. Professor McCary has a special pudding which he prepares and serves to his guests, 'made of slices of pears and strawberries soaked in Cointreau and drenched in a fragrant sauce of beaten egg yolks, confectioner's sugar, cloves and cinnamon'. More than half the persons, he tells us, who have eaten this dessert 'have commented that it was a very "sexy" dish . . . The dessert is smooth, rich and creamy in texture—qualities we subconsciously equate with sexuality. In addition, its redolence (cloves, cinnamon, liqueur) is "exotic", another word we tend, however vicariously, to identify with sexual concepts.' After concoctions such as these the body and mind realize such a condition of euphoria, that 'it is only natural . . . to be well prepared to the ultimate physical and emotional expression—love-making'. And the meal is satisfactorily terminated; a termination which the German nutritionist Dr. Hans Balzli seems also to have enjoyed: 'After a perfect meal we are more susceptible to the ecstasy of love than at any other time . . .' he divulges. This combination of eating and sexual desire was commercially recognized and exploited, particularly by the French at the turn of the century, when it was possible to hire a luxurious private dining-room with facilities for exercising the après-dîner ecstasy. One must not forget the part alcohol would play at such a perfect meal. Physiologically it dilates the blood vessels and psychologically lifts moral inhibitions, introducing a sexually responsive and light-hearted frame of mind.

But even without benefit of puddings, drinks and dinners there is a very close parallel in the way the nervous system functions towards hunger and sex, as the brain specialist Berry has pointed out. With regard to both there are hollow entrails capable of varying degrees of distension, though in the one case it is the full viscus which stimulates the system, in the other the empty; but in both the impulses travel to the brain-centre, where they are appropriately sorted. Biologically the sexual impulse is a development from the nutritive, the British anthropologist Crawley tells us, and 'one of the most obvious links between the two is the kiss . . .' To this Fielding, writing in 1929, adds: 'It is a significant physiological fact that one kind of nerve structures, called *Krause's end bulbs*, which are unusually large and sensitive, are found principally in the clitoris, penis and lips.' 'The sensual internal surface areas of the sex-organs,' Dr. Balzli agrees, 'correspond to the taste-buds of the mouth.' Thus, both sexual desire and a delicious aroma may make the mouth water. And Coriat (writing in 1921 on the region of the great unconscious) puns unconsciously: '. . . the pleasure derived from satisfying hunger is at the bottom sexual, possible because of the close interlocking or practical identity of the two cravings.'

On top of these nervous and physiological connections between eating and sexual expression, 'there also exists,' McCary tells us, 'a number of basic physical analogies between various forms of foods and both the male and female genitalia. In other words, not only does eating equal intercourse, but also food equals penis, vulva. Although little known even to specialists, the making and eating of phallic foods (the representation of certain foods, usually bread, cakes and other pastries, in the form of sexual organs) is a custom that has been practised for centuries in many civilisations throughout the world as a significant religious rite.' For example there were Greek cakes, *mylloi* mentioned by Athenaeus, the priapic and venerial breads, the *coliphia* and *siligone*, that were sold in Roman bakeries and by prostitutes, and 'the extraordinary species of ornament', pastry representations of the *'membra virilia, pundendaque muliebria'*, which had so shocked the Reverend Mr. Warner when he had discovered them described between Legrand d'Aussy's pages, *Histoire de la Vie Privée des François*. At dinner they were served, said Warner, 'doubtless for the purposes of causing jokes and conversations' among the dinner guests. In Legrand d'Aussy's view this obscene confectionery was an incredible excess and depravity, and, he was sorry to say, it had lasted for over two centuries.

Ideas concerning the erotic value of food spring from two sources: the rarity or newness of food—such as the potato when it was first introduced into England—and the Doctrine of Signatures. This states quite simply that like cures like. Thus scarlet fever should be cured with a red cloth, while sexual potency would be retrieved by eating food whose external characteristics either smelt vaguely reminiscent, or resembled the sexual organs. Thus oysters qualify, not for any chemical content, but because of their similarity to the female genitals; and aromatics such as sage, musk, carraway, ginger and origan because of the identity detected in their odour. Vanilla is an interesting example, McCary tells us; originally the word meant vagina, having been so christened 'because some ancient Roman shrewdly recognized the similarity of the vanilla root to the vaginal canal'. Bulbs, snails and eggs were supposed by the Greeks to produce semen, 'not because they are filling but because their very nature in the first instance has powers related in kind to semen'. Chestnuts, the Elizabethans believed, were flatulent and therefore stimulated lust: 'yea further,' writes Buttes in his *Dyets Dry Dinner,* 'this nut in his huske much resembleth *Testes*, the instrument of lust.' The Elizabethan vegetable garden sprouted the instruments of debauchery. Carrots were thought 'to be a great furtherer of Venus her pleasure, and of loves delights'; onions excited Venus, increased seed and milk; asparagus 'manifestly provoketh Venus'; while in Paris the street vendors cried the merits of artichokes:

Artichokes! artichokes
Heats the body and the spirit
Heats the genitals.

'Let the sky rain potatoes, let it thunder to the tune of Greensleeves, hail kissing comfits and stone eringoes: let there be a tempest of provocation, I will shelter me here,' says Falstaff, in *The Merry Wives of Windsor*, showing that the carrot-like roots of the sea-holly—the eringo—were also supposed to be venereal. These were often candied, or iced with sugar and eaten as sweetmeats. Perhaps the most curious of all roots was the mandrake, which with its forked tuber resembled the thighs and

legs of a man, and screamed when torn from the ground. 'This wort . . . is mickle
and illustrious of aspect,' note the Anglo-Saxon leech books, 'and it is beneficial.'
At night it was supposed to advertise its presence by shining 'altogether like a lamp.
When first thou seest its head, then inscribe thou it instantly with iron lest it fly
from thee; its virtue is so mickle and so famous, that it will immediately flee from an
unclean man, when he cometh to it; hence, as we before said, do thou inscribe it
with iron, and so shall thou delve about it . . . And when thou seest its hands and
its feet, then tie it up. Then take the other end and tie it to a dog's neck so that the
hound be hungry; next cast meat before him, so that he may not reach it, except he
jerk up the wort with him.' Traditionally the root enjoyed as its favourite habitat
the shadow of the gallows, where it was supposed to thrive on the fat and blood of
criminals. McCary points out that mandrakes are mentioned in *Genesis* XXX:
14-16, in the incident when Leah employs the root to lie with the promiscuous
Jacob. Sure enough the seed was sown and nine months later we find her adding
one more to his illegitimate tribe.

Satyrion also was a root much enjoyed by the Romans and the Greeks. With its
tuberous root and erect fleshy stem it resembled the mandrake in structure and was
said to possess erotic properties even when held in the hand; but generally it was
drunk in wine. There was also hippomane, a beverage so vigorous that when it was
placed on the genitalia of a brass mare, Pliny tells us, it excited extreme rut in all
approaching stallions. About its composition there seems to be divided opinion.
On the one hand it was believed to have been the fleshy protuberance evident on a
colt's head at birth; on the other it was those secretions and sediments obtained from
the reproductive organs of mares and colts. All in all, stimulants were so powerful
according to Theophrastus 'that they can affect as many as seventy connections,
blood being finally secreted'.

Many Classical aphrodisiacs relied on the powers of sorcery, and were surrounded
by all the mumbo-jumbo and incantation of witchcraft. With their crabbed hands
illuminated by moonlight, sorceresses concocted foul philtres at gravesides; they
wove spells to transform old men into youths of twenty, which necessitated the use
of human marrow and liver; they constructed sachets of seagull anodine which,
according to Xenophon, made gentlemen 'amiable companions with the ladies';
but usually the charms were revolting, containing generous quantities of menstrual
blood and human sperm. Saxon ladies also, according to the Reverend Mr. Cock-
hayne, who disapprovingly leaves that portion of the text respectably veiled in Latin,
were inclined to mix excrement with their menstrual blood in order to bewitch men
and seduce their lovers into adoring them. Mediaeval and Elizabethan belief in
aphrodisiacs consisted mainly of a hash of repeated Classical recommendations,
adapted to their own needs. One finds a faith in satyrion, mandrake, hippomane,
which 'will make Men mad with love' and cockle-bread, a magical cake made from
menstrual blood. Many of Wecker's hints to '*make one valiant in Venus Camp*' in
his *Secrets of Art and Nature* come from what he calls 'a written book'. 'If any man
desire to be a strong Soldier in the Camp of *Venus*; let him be armed with such
meat; chiefly with Bulbas roots, for they all provoke Venery,' he instructs. 'So

Rocket taken plentifully, Onions . . . peasons, parsnips, Anniseed, Coriander, Pine Kernals; amongst these *Satyrion* moves exceedingly and stands most forcible in this business, and provokes Womens desire. Nettles are belonging to *Venus* . . . Nor must we omit Sparrows brains . . . but if any man would provoke a woman, let him prinkle his Glans with Oyl, Musk or Civet, Castorem or Cubebs, or any one of these, for these so quickly provoke.' There are many other remarkable aids to mutual felicity. 'It is wonderful,' he notes, 'that the great toe of the right foot annointed with the ashes of a Weesil with Honey or Oyl, will suffice abundantly for those that by reason of age or otherwise are almost dead in this matter, and are very unfit to serve *Venus* in her Wars any longer'. That a woman may 'admit of her Husband . . . then let her Husband take some suet of the middle Goat, that is between the great and the small Goat, and let him annoint his yard with it and then lye with her; she will love him and not lye afterwards with any other'. For mutual good humour he suggests that 'if a man carry with him the heart of a male Rook and the woman the heart of a female Rook they shall always agree'; and to 'confine love once obtained that its attention might not wander', Wecker instructs that one should 'procure such a quantity of Hair of the party beloved as will make a Ring or a Bracelet and wear it either on your finger, or wrist, and it shall by secret exciting the Imagination produce its certain effects'.

Cantharides, infiltrating probably from the Orient, along with spices, at the time of the Crusades, was also employed. Better known as Spanish Fly, cantharides is probably the most notorious of all aphrodisiacs. It is a beautiful sheen-covered beetle, found in Southern Europe, which is dried and powdered. Its ingestion results in acute irritation of the gastro-intestinal system, with accompanying dilation of the blood vessels; all of which stimulates the genitals. In 1758, Sade is reputed to have given a ball at Marseilles. Into the pudding course he inserted chocolates so delicious that few could resist them: they contained Spanish Fly. The ball degenerated into a licentious brawl and even the most modest woman could not do enough to satisfy her priapism. Probably the most remarkable account comes from Cabrol, a pupil of the famous Ambroise Paré, who describes a visit to an unfortunate patient: 'In 1572 we went to see a poor Orgonian man in Provence, who was affected by the most horrible and frightful satyriasis one could ever see. The fact is this; he had quartan fever: to cure it he had consulted an old sorceress, who made him a potion composed of an ounce and a half of nettles and two drams of cantharides, which made him so ardent in the venereal act that his wife swore to us by her God that he had been astride her, during two nights, eighty-seven times, without thinking it more than ten . . . and even while we were interviewing him, the poor man ejaculated thrice in our presence, embracing the foot of the bed and moving against it as if it were his wife.'

Before modern drug and hormone treatment yohimbine was the most widely used stimulant for increasing sexual drive. This is obtained from the yohimbé tree, indigenous to Central Africa, and has been used for ages by the natives. It stimulates the nerves of the spinal column, which in turn excites the genitals.

There are other erotic assistants, which, like tickling stones and little bells, depend upon exterior manipulation. In primitive countries, these often involve operations. In the Philippines and Borneo, *ampullangs* are inserted into the penis just before intercourse; these consist of a match-like piece of copper, two inches long with little nail-like heads at each end. The Patagonians use a *guesguel*, a wreath made from the stiff hairs of a mule's mane, which embraces the male organ, apparently effecting such delight that the women foam at the mouth and, after intercourse, relapse into a stupefied exhaustion. Japanese women are supposed to employ the *Watama*—a device consisting of two metal balls, one light, the other heavy containing quick-silver. These are inserted, the lighter ball first, and at every moment the spheres vibrate, delightfully: actions which are particularly suited to the hammock or the rocking chair.

Once again we have a paradox: a well-fed population with 'well-nourished sexual organs capable of vigorous and continuous expression'. But it is a population which feeds on a factory-produced 'meat loaf, boiled potatoes, and watery beans' kind of meal, which, consumed in an *ambiance* enhanced by the television, engenders no 'delightful glow' either of the body or the senses, and is hardly an 'exciting' or 'rewarding' experience.

APPENDIX II

RECIPES

THE TECHNIQUE of Roman cooking was basically simple. Meat and game were roasted on a spit, basted with a spiced crust and glazed with honey; sometimes the joints were stuffed, often they were served with a peppery piquante sauce. For sophisticated tables the *pistor* pounded the flesh into a fine paste, when it was seasoned and peppered and either enclosed in the fine skins of intestines and cauls—becoming sausages and haggises—or rolled into dumplings and rissoles, simmered in broth or fried. Hams were salted and cured. Fish was either grilled, boiled or baked and served whole, or pounded by the *pistor* into kromeskies and croquettes. Liaisons were obtained by the use of breadcrumbs, ground hard-boiled eggs or ground pine-nuts—the Italian *pignolia*, the fruit of the umbrella or stone pine. Batters, omelettes and custards, both hot and cold, were made by stirring beaten eggs into the puréed basic ingredient; fish and small birds were cooked in the custard, like Toad in the Hole, either in a pan, or enclosed in a pastry case. Soups were basically farinaceous, cheap sustaining dishes which are parents of all ingenious peasant dishes such as the French cassoulets, the Spanish paellas, the English baked beans and pease puddings.

The only Classical Roman recipe book which is known to us is that compiled by Apicius. Many of the recipes are elaborate and sophisticated, with meat being scented with aromatic gums and rose-petals. To say these are representative is as true as saying that during the eighteenth and nineteenth centuries the French bourgeoisie fed on a diet of Carême and sugar temples. One knows from the numbers of published books that this was not so. One knows also from Pliny that dishes such as oysters, sea-urchins and sows'-bellies were considered excesses and were offered at dinners, along with sexy Cadiz dancers, to raise the appetites of liverish voluptuaries. They were a kind of food pornography designed for Heliogabali and Vitelli.

No examination of Roman food would be complete without some words on the popular and controversial *garum*. Its unsavoury reputation has been based on the description of Apicius who tells us that anchovies and other small fish were thickly salted and left to ferment in the sun—a process very similar to the preparation of soy sauce.[1] But Apicius also gives us an easier way, which consists mainly of boiling

[1] Here is a Victorian recipe for the Chinese preparation of Soy Sauce: Equal quantities of soy beans and wheat are boiled together, and then triturated between stones, water being added occasionally. The mass is cooked in a pan, and cut into

the fish in a strong brine. With the addition of tabasco sauce and sweet grape-juice the resulting substance is not at all unlike Worcester Sauce. Nepeta, rue and silphium, an unidentified root which it is thought might be related to asafoetida, were included in some of the more elaborate recipes. These, administered in small quantities, give a surprisingly fascinating and fragrant effect. Such scented dishes were probably believed to contain aphrodisiacal qualities and used at the most voluptuous feasts. It is interesting to note that many Eastern dishes still contain asafoetida.

Harvey Day, the expert on curries and spices, tells us in his introduction to *The Second Book of Curries* how Roman cuisine was influenced by that of the East. The finest cooks, he says, were inveigled westwards to Rome by fat rewards to prepare the fashionable Lucullan Banquets. He also points out the resemblance between the Roman and mediaeval schools of cookery. He explodes the fancy that spices were used to mask tainted food: 'The idea that tainted fish and meat can safely be used in curries because the power and pungency of spices will disguise the taste and odour is a mistaken one,' he writes. When one realizes the relationship of Roman and mediaeval food to the spiced peppery Eastern dishes, quite a different picture emerges. For instance, curry and pilaff do not meet readily with criticisms of being over-spiced and unpalatable. As Harvey Day points out, often the truth is the opposite. People do not realize the *subtlety* of Eastern dishes and are inclined to go along with the view of one of his acquaintances: the stuff is only real when it is so hot that it takes the skin off the tongue. Whether mild or peppery, to judge from the recent epidemic and popularity of Eastern restaurants all over Britain, it is a taste far from being obnoxious to the modern British palate.

With the following recipes I have tried to show how British cookery developed: its basic structure, its evolution from Roman techniques. By putting these recipes to a modern workable text, I aim to show also how many of them resemble prepara-tions, both foreign and familiar. In most recipes I have given no amounts, these are for the cooks themselves to decide and adjust according to their taste. For convenience I have substituted Worcester Sauce for garum. I have given the Latin and Middle English texts only for the first two recipes respectively. The sources may be consulted in Apicius's *De re coquinaria* and *Two fifteenth-century cookery-books* edited by Thomas Austin.

Alicam vel sucum tisanae sic facies[1]
Barley Soup with dried vegetables
Put a leg of pork, or more economically pig's trotters, and a cup of pearl barley into a saucepan and cover well with water. Bring to boil and add a tablespoon of oil,

---

thin slices, which are kept covered with straw for about twenty days. When com-pletely fermented, the separate slices having become mouldy, they are washed with water, placed in a vessel, and their weight of water and salt added. In this condition they are kept for a number of days, and are finally again triturated between stones.

[1] *Alicam vel sucum tisanae sic facies*
Tisanam vel alicam lavando fricas, quam ante diem infundis. Imponis supra ignem. cum bullierit, mittis olei satis et anethi modicum fasciculum, cepam siccam,

a bouquet of dill, onions, savoury, salt and coriander pounded together. When cooked purée barley, stir in a mixture of ground pepper, lovage, pennyroyal, cummin, vinegar, very sweet wine, honey and Worcester Sauce, and serve.

Patina de asparagis frigida
Cold Asparagus Patina (This is delicious served hot in small pots for a first course) Purée asparagus (a tin of asparagus tips is good), mix in four beaten eggs, arrange small birds (the Romans used figpeckers), slices of chicken or rolled up fillets of firm boneless fish in the bottom of a dish, pour over asparagus purée and bake in a low oven.

Compare this with Mrs. Glasse's eighteenth-century *Pigeons in the Hole*.
Take your Pigeons, season them with beaten Mace, Pepper and Salt; put a little Piece of Butter in the Belly, lay them in a Dish and pour over a light Batter all over them, made with a Quart of Milk and Eggs, and four or five Spoonfuls of Flour; bake it, and send it to Table. It is a good Dish.

Roman sauce for pigeons and small birds
Mix together, like a mayonnaise, honey, pounded dates, pepper, lovage, coriander, caraway, chopped onion, mint, yolk of egg, Worcester Sauce, vinegar, very sweet wine, or grape-juice, and oil.

Another
Pepper, chopped parsley, lovage, mint and fennel blossom are moistened with wine, to these add toasted hazel nuts, or almonds, honey wine, vinegar and Worcester Sauce. Put mixture into pan and heat. Stir in chopped green celery and nepeta. Makes incisions in birds and pour sauce over them.

Patina ex piscibus quibustibet
Fry in oil any cured fish (smoked haddock is good). Lay strips of cooked bacon over it and some spring onions. Pour over a dressing made from Worcester Sauce, honey and vinegar.

Lumbuli assi ita fiunt
Roast loin of pork stuffed
Rub a boned or a chined loin of pork, skinned and complete with kidneys, on both sides with a mixture of ground pepper, coriander, fennel seed, ground pine kernels (or ground almonds), and roast basting with a mixture of Worcester Sauce, oil and honey.

---

satureiam et coloefium, ut ibi coquantur. propter sucum mittis coriandrum viride et salem simul tritum et facies ut ferveat. cum bene ferbuerit, tollis fasciculum et transferes in alterum caccabum tisanam, sic ne fundum tangat propter com- busturam. lias bene et colas in caccabo super acronem coloefium. teres piper, ligusticum, pulei aridi modicum, cuminum silfi frictum, ut bene tegatur. suffundis mel, acetum, defritum, liquamen, refundis in caccabum super coloefium acronem. facies ut ferveat super ignem lentum.

Compare this to Creole *Cherry-Glazed Pork Roast*
A loin of pork is sprinkled with salt, pepper and ground cloves and roasted covered
with a layer of sliced onion. Half an hour before it is cooked the onion is removed
and the top is spread with cherry jam, when it is put back for the glaze to set.

Omentata
Sausages
Pound grilled pig's liver, add pepper and Worcester Sauce, enclose in skins, wrap
in bayleaves and smoke.

Isicia ex spondylis
Scallop sausages
Mix minced scallops with some cornflour and beaten eggs, season well with
pepper, wrap in caul and fry. Serve with *Ius in Pisce elixo*.

Ius in pisce elixo
Sauce for fish
Made like a mayonnaise from pounded hard-boiled egg yolks, dates, honey,
lovage, cummin, onion, origan, mustard, vinegar, Worcester Sauce and oil.

Patina ex soleis
Sole in white wine
Place sole in shallow pan, poach in a mixture of stock and wine, add pepper, lovage,
origan, bind sauce with raw eggs, sprinkle with pepper and serve.

Isicia plena
Pheasant dumplings
Take cooked pheasant (or any other cooked game), mince with the liver, mix to a
paste with suet, Worcester Sauce, a little concentrated stock, pepper, tabasco and
grape-juice and poach in water or stock flavoured with Worcester Sauce.
These are good served with a peppery, sweet-sour gravy made of tabasco, stock,
Worcester Sauce, quince-apple cider, honey or grape-juice, thickened with corn-
flour.

Leporem farsum
Stuffed hare
Stuff hare with nuts, peppercorns, breadcrumbs and giblets bound with a beaten egg.
Roast hare and serve with a sauce of onion, savory, pepper simmered in a little
concentrated stock and spiced wine, thickened with cornflour.

Compare this with Harvey Day's Turkish *Roast Chicken with Pine-nut Stuffing*.
Sauté ¼ cup of *pignolia* in butter until pink, remove and sauté chicken liver in same
butter. Return nuts to pan add ¼ cup of currants, 1 cup of rice, salt, ginger, cardamoms, garlic, coriander and chilli and 2 cups of boiling water. Cook slowly and
add 2 tablespoons of butter. Stuff chicken with mixture when rice is tender, and
roast as usual.

Tarentine minutal
A Fricassé of sausages and forcemeat balls
Fry chopped leeks in oil, add forcemeat balls and small spiced sausages, simmer in sauce of broth thickened with cornflour and flavoured with pepper, Worcester Sauce, lovage, origan and grape-juice.

Salacattabia Apiciana
Pound together celery seed, dried pennyroyal, mint, ginger, raisins, honey, vinegar, oil and grape-juice so that it makes a dressing. Next place in a bowl alternating layers of boned and cooked chicken, bread, sweetbreads, grated cheese (cheddar is good), cucumbers, fried *pignolia* or almonds, and chopped onions. If liked a little good jellied broth improves and moistens it. Pour over the whole the prepared dressing. Chill and serve.

Compare this to Sir Theodore Mayerne's seventeenth-century *Salamongundy*.
Fill a dish with alternating layers of minced chicken or veal, slices of hard boiled eggs, anchovies, lemons, every kind of pickle, sorrel, spinach and chives shred very very small. Over the whole pour oil and vinegar.

Compare again to Mrs. Glasse's eighteenth-century instructions for *Salamagundy* when a dish was lined with strips of lettuce, and cold chicken, anchovies, minced yolk of eggs, a few onions and chopped parsley were mixed together and heaped in the middle. A salad dressing was poured over the whole and the dish was garnished with grapes, french beans or flowers.

It is interesting also to compare the two recipes for Roman sausages with *An Entrayle* and *Sir Kenelm Digby's White Pudding*, page 249.

Roman Dulcia
Dates stuffed with ground almonds, rolled in salt and simmered in honey.

Garum
Make a very strong brine, and test its strength by throwing an egg into it to see if it floats. If it sinks the brine does not contain enough salt. Put fish—sprats, fresh anchovies, or, if these are not available, fresh herrings—into brine. Add origan. Put on a good fire until it begins to boil fast and reduce. Let it cool and strain two or three times until clear. Seal and store. Before use, tabasco and grape-juice may be added.

Mediaeval cookery is based on the same principles as the Roman. Baked meats were enclosed in pastry coffins, meat was roast and boiled or ground into meat balls, sausages and puddings. Liaisons were achieved with breadcrumbs, blood, eggs and ground nuts. Any preparation prepared and simmered with broth and vegetables in a pot was a pottage; nowadays casserole means the same thing. Many of the dishes are similar to curries and pilaffs. When the crusaders travelled eastwards to liberate Jerusalem they transported with them their households: their cooks, their kitchen equipment and wives. Like most people who travel abroad they developed a taste for foreign food. Their cooks learnt to make the spiced dishes. They returned with recipes and the spices to make them. We find then an English compromise: a mixture of commonsense, local ingredients and Eastern exotica, a mixture which lasted in *haute cuisine* until the advent of Putitanism some 400 years later. Mediaeval people loved comforting sweet dishes, made from egg custards, nuts and honey. They loved also jellies and brightly coloured foods. Dishes were reddened with sandalwood, gilded with saffron. Marrow was often added for richness and succulence. Venison, and, on fish days, porpoise, were served with furmenty. This was a famous dish, which lasted into the Victorian era, made from wheat, and especially new wheat.

Furmenty with venyson[1]

Husked wheat is boiled in water until it breaks, when it is strained and stirred into a custard of milk and egg yolks and heated gently over a low fire until it thickens. Sugar, salt and sugar are added and it is served with boiled venison and a little of its broth.

When one realizes the expense involved in the extra process of milling the wheat, one sees that this is a highly practical dish. It is interesting to compare this fourteenth-century recipe with two recipes: a Victorian preparation for *Frumenty*, a dish particular to Mothering Sunday (somewhere between the Middle Ages and Victorian the positions of the *u* and the *r* became reversed), noting that this is *more* spiced than the mediaeval; and the famous *Devonshire White Pot*, which one sees is simply a development of Furmenty, although instead of the whole husks it is made extravagantly from flour and in some cases even bread.

Frumenty

To one quart of ready boiled wheat allow two quarts of new milk; keep the whole stirred over a slow fire, and, from time to time, throw in well-washed currants or stoned raisins, allowing about a quarter of a pound of fruit to the above quantity of milk. When sufficiently boiled, remove from the fire, and stir in the beaten yolks of three eggs, previously mixed with a little milk. Flavour with nutmeg, cinnamon, and sweeten to taste. Do not boil again, but stir for a few minutes over the fire.

[1] *Furmenty with venyson* (There were few, if any, rules for spelling).
Take faire whete, and serve it in a morter, And vanne away clene the duste, and wassh it in faire watere and lete it boile till hit breke; then do awey the water clene, and caste thereto swete mylke, and sette it ouer the fire, And lete boile til it be thik ynogh, And caste thereto a goode quantite of tryed rawe youlkes of egges, and caste thereto Sapheron, sugur, and salt; but late it boile no more then, but sette it on fewe coles, lest the licoure waxe colde. And þen take fressh venyson, and water hit; seth hit and bawde hit; And if hit be salt, water hit, sethe hit, and leche hit as hit shall be serued forth, and put hit in a vessell with feyre water, and buille it ayen; and as hit boyleth, blowe awey the grece, and serue it forth with ffurmenty, And a litul of þe broth in the Dissh all hote with the flessh.

Sir Kenelm Digby's White Pot
Add 12 egg yolks and 4 whites to 3 quarts of cream. Mix in ¾ lb sugar, 2 grated nutmegs and a little salt. Add, if liked, ½ lb raisins. Lay some thinly sliced white bread over the top (this is improved if buttered as in Apple Charlotte). Bake slowly in the oven.

Lyode Soppes is a rich version of bread and milk. Its title comes from the French and means *allayed* soppes, i.e. mixed soppes. Thicken milk by stirring in egg yolks and heat slowly over fire, sweeten with sugar and sharpen with salt and pour over some fine white bread.

Salt was often used in conjunction with sugar in mediaeval and seventeenth-century dishes, as in the same way the Romans used brine with honey. Used carefully it is an excellent combination as may be seen from Creole *Banana Cream Whip*: Mix together one cup ripe bananas, one tablespoon lemon juice, ¼ cup sugar, ⅛ teaspoon salt. Fold in ½ cup of whipped cream. Chill. Serve within one hour garnished with sliced bananas.

Gelye de Chare (Meat Jelly, *Char* being Old French for meat)
Prepare a broth by simmering calves' feet and shins in white wine until they are soft. Strain the broth and pour over pork ribs and young chickens trussed with their legs and feet to give more gelatine (or use a good stock with gelatine). Simmer until the meat is firm but not disintegrating, skimming off the fat. Strain the liquor, adding pepper, saffron and vinegar, strain through a cloth until clarified. Cut the pork into chops, lay out in a dish with the carved skinned chicken, pour over the jelly. Allow to set and strew with almonds, a few curls of ginger and cloves and serve. Sometimes mediaeval people arranged the spices so that the jelly was decorated like a hedgehog.

Gelye de Fysshe (Fish Jelly)
(Made from fresh-water fish, but for convenience any suitable sea-water fish can be substituted.)
Cut fresh pike into pieces and simmer in good gelatinous stock (mediaeval cooks used calves' foot), add perch, tench and eels, together with plaice and any fish bones and sounds. Simmer slowly skimming all the while, taking care to keep the fish whole. Strain and clarify the jelly, colour and season, pour over the boned and skinned fish. Garnish with flowers and serve.

Stuffing for pork, geese, ducks, crane and capon
Steep slices of bread in vinegar, add garlic, grated cheese, creamed hard-boiled eggs (in season grapes, raisins or chopped apples can be added, some chopped marrow and almonds). Stuff the joint and baste with a mixture of vinegar, saffron, rosemary or sage with the addition of a little honey.

Stuffing for Chicken
Mix parsley, suet, mashed hard-boiled yolks of eggs, pepper, ginger, cinnamon, saffron, salt, grapes, a little pork and cloves.

Sauce Verte

Chop any good herbs (parsley, dittany, mint, pellitory, sage, etc.) fine with garlic, pepper and salt. Mix with bread that has been steeped in vinegar. Grapes may be added and a pinch of spices. This is especially delicious served with poached eggs, or underneath baked eggs.

Cokentrice

Cut a chicken and a small pig in half. Sew the front half of the pig to the hind half of the chicken and vice versa. Stuff, spit and gild by basting with egg yolks, ginger and saffron, spinkle with parsley juice, or finely chopped parsley and serve.

A goos in hogepotte (Jugged goose)

Cut goose in joints, simmer in water or stock until tender. Thicken the broth with pepper, breadcrumbs or boiled blood, season with ginger, cummin, galingale, beer, minced fried onions and a little wine. And serve.

Harys in Cyueye (Jugged hare)

Joint hares, simmer in salted water and when tender thicken the stock with pepper, saffron and breadcrumbs, sharpen with ale, simmer a little more, season with chopped onions, gently fried, parsley and a little vinegar.

Compare these last two to the Victorian *Civet of Hare*:

Divide the hare into joints and fry with half a pound of fat bacon and a little butter. Add a tablespoon of flour and a pint and a half of stock. This is simmered for an hour with small onions, mace, a bay leaf, a teaspoon salt, cayenne, a small lump of sugar, a few mushrooms. Strain, put back meat, the bruised liver, a cupful of blood and half a tumblerful of port. Simmer a little more, squeeze over the juice of half a lemon and serve.

Beef y-Stywyd (All meat was usually spit and roasted a little first, to seal it)

Cut ribs or quarters of beef into pieces, simmer in stock to which is added cinnamon, cloves, cubebs, coriander, grains of paradise, minced onions, sage and parsley. When beef is tender thicken the sauce with breadcrumbs steeped in broth and vinegar, taste, if necessary add more salt and vinegar; strew on saffron and serve.

Compare this to the preparation for *mutton pilau* given by Harvey Day in *Curries of India*.

12 cardamoms, 12 cloves, 12 black peppers, 3 one inch sticks of cinnamon are simmered with 2 lb of boney mutton and two onions. Boil till meat is tender and 'you have a tasty soup', Harvey Day writes.

Alows de Beef or de Moutoun (An English Shish Kebab. The title comes from the French *aloyau de boeuf*, which means the flesh end of rib of beef.)

Good beef 'cushions' and buttocks of mutton are cut up into steaks. Coat them in finely chopped onions, parsley, hard-boiled eggs, marrow, suet, powdered ginger and saffron, sprinkle with salt, spit and roast. Lay on a dish, dress with vinegar and verjuice, strew over a little ginger, cinnamon and hard boiled egg yolks and serve.

An Entrayle
Cut up roasted chickens and pork. Mix them with grated cheese, spicery and salt and beaten eggs. Stuff wombs (or bake in a buttered dish), boil and serve.

Sir Kenelm Digby's White Pudding (Black pudding is made in the same way, but contains blood.)
Capon and veal are minced with bacon, egg yolks, cream, salt, cloves, nutmeg, mace, pepper, ginger, stuffed into intestines and boiled.

Pome Dorres
Salt and pepper minced fillets of pork, bind them with egg white, make into balls, roast on a spit, basting with a batter made with egg yolk, flour, almond milk, a little sugar and green chopped herbs.

Poumes
Mix minced meat with pepper, cinnamon, ginger, cloves, dates, saffron, raisins and roll into balls, either simmering them in broth, or roasting them on a spit and basting them.

Compare these last two to Harvey Day's *Tick-Keeah Kebab*.
Pounded beef or mutton is mixed thoroughly with white of egg, tablespoon of yoghourt, tumeric, garlic, ground onion, chilli, peppercorns, ginger, ½ teaspoon of ground hot spices (coriander, cumin, cardamom) and salt. The meat is rolled into balls, rubbed with butter, skewered and grilled.

Brawune fryez
Coat thin slices of pork or chicken in a batter of beaten eggs, flour, saffron, salt and sugar. Fry in fresh fat, place on a dish and serve strewn with a very little sugar.

Froyse (the word fraize means a round pancake)
Cut beef or veal into very small pieces, mix with beaten eggs, salt, pepper and saffron. Fry in fresh fat and serve.

Compare this to *Patrick Lamb's Bacon Fraize*
Coat very thin slices of bacon in a thick batter and fry.

Brawn en peuerade (the word comes from the French poivrade)
Simmer slices of meat in a good beef or chicken stock, add small whole onions, vinegar, cinnamon, cloves, mace, plenty of pepper, and simmer until the meat and onions are cooked. Thicken sauce with breadcrumbs, sharpen with vinegar and wine, strew with saffron and salt and serve.

Compare this to *Victorian Pork Cheese*, eaten cold for breakfast:
Cut small 4 lb cold roast pork, one pound of which should be fat, the rest lean. Season highly with pepper and salt. Add 6 to 8 chopped sage leaves, 2 tablespoons

minced parsley, ½ tablespoon thyme, marjoram, mace, lemon rind and nutmeg. Put meat, spices and herbs into mould, cover with strong gravy. Bake in moderate oven. Let meat stand until cold. Turn out and eat with mustard and vinegar.

Blaunde sorre or blandissorye (this means literally white red, sorre being the old French for reddened; originally the dish must have been reddened with sandalwood) Ground almonds are simmered in either wine, or beef or chicken broth; if it were a fish day fish broth was used. Next they are drained and mixed with ground chicken meat, or, on fish days, ground codling or haddock, seasoned with almond milk, strewn with fried almonds and a little sugar and served.

Blamanger is precisely the same recipe but with flour of rice added. Sometimes this, on a fish day, was made with lobster.

Vyaunde de cyprys in lente was again the same recipe made with ground almonds, rice flour, ground crabs and salmon and sweet wine.

Compare these to eighteenth-century *Blancmanger*, which has lost its meat and is recognizable as the dish we know. Mix cream, ground almonds, lemon peel and cinnamon. Sweeten and add isinglass. Set and garnish with currant jelly, jam, marmalade, stewed pears or quinces.

The seventeenth-century *Soup à la reine* or *Soup Lorraine* is purely a delicious liquid version of the mediaeval *Blamanger*. Simmer a fowl in good stock with herbs, 12 peppercorns and salt. Reduce the flesh of the chicken to a fine paste, stir in 2 oz of ground almonds together with fine breadcrumbs. Gradually stir into the cooled stock (some cooks added hard-boiled eggs mashed to a paste). Let broth simmer for another hour, adding lump of sugar, salt, pepper, ground nutmeg. Stir in a quarter pint of thick cream and serve immediately.

Compare this too with *Mrs. Glasse's Chestnut soup* made from beef broth, puréed chestnuts, ground pigeon and veal meat, ham or bacon, herbs, onions, pepper, mace and carrot.

Ryschewys in lente (lenten rissoles) Stuffling or salt cod (fresh will do) with a fruit and nut stuffing made from chopped figs, dates, pears and almonds, coat them with a batter to which you add a little ale, and fry.

Mediaeval people loved fragrant comforting dishes to punctuate the heavy meats. *Vyande Ryalle* is a spiced sweet gruel which is an ancestor of the famous *Plum Porridge* (page 132) the Puritans derided.

Vyande Ryalle Mix flour of rice into a good consistency with milk, Greek wine, or wine and honey, flavour with cinnamon, cloves, saffron, sugar, fried nuts and a little salt and serve. Some editors suggest mulberries and not nuts were included.

Payn purdeuz

Soak slices of fine white bread in egg yolk, fry them in fresh fat, strew them with sugar and serve.

Prymerose

Mix half a pound of flour of rice, with three pounds of chopped fried almonds, half an ounce of honey and saffron. Add ground primrose flowers, flavour them with milk of almonds, simmer it all together, strew on powdered ginger and serve.

Vyolette (Violet-cakes, Mrs. Gaskell tells us, were eaten in Passion-week)

Boil up with a very little water some violet flowers, strain them, chop them small, flavour them with almond milk, thicken with cornflour, sweeten with honey or sugar and serve garnished with flowers.

Compare the two flower recipes with William Gelleroy's eighteenth-century *Cowslip Pudding*.

Take flowers of a peck of cowslips, cut them small and grind them in mortar with half a pound of grated Naples biscuits and three pints cream. Beat up 16 eggs with rosewater and a little cream. Put all together and stir to thicken carefully over the fire. Sweeten with sugar and serve.

Pety Pernauntes

Heat together gently over the fire to make a custard, dates, raisins, eggs yolks, ginger and sugar. Pour them into a pastry crust and bake.

Leche lumbarde

Simmer dates in sweet wine, mix into a stiff paste with sugar, ginger and cinnamon, cut into slices and serve in a sauce of clarified honey.

Custarde lumbarde

Beat together cream and eggs. Line a dish with pastry. Place in it some chopped marrow, dates and prunes. Pour over them the egg custard seasoned with a little salt and sugar. Bake in a moderate oven until they are set.

Probably the fourteenth-century pie mixtures are the most familiar to us today; the spiced ingredients can be seen to relate directly to Christmas mince-pies and puddings.

Grete Pyes

Make a forcemeat by pounding beef or mutton into a fine paste. Season with pepper and salt. Lay this inside a pastry case. Parboil capons, hens, rabbits, mallards, woodcocks, teal and any other birds. Place inside each of these salt and pepper and lay them inside the pie. Cover them with the remainder of the forcemeat, over which is strewn chopped marrow, hard yolks of eggs, mace, cinnamon, currants, prunes, dates, cloves and saffron. The case is tightly closed and baked in the oven.

Tartes de chare

Grind pork to a paste in a mortar (a fine mince will do) add beaten eggs, and line the pastry case with this forcemeat, add fried *pignolia* or almonds, raisins, pepper, ginger, cinnamon, sugar, saffron and salt, lay in either small birds which have been gently fried in dripping, or hard-boiled eggs, and chopped dates and more raisins, gild with saffron and egg yolks, bake and serve.

Compare these two with Lady Portland's seventeenth-century mince pies. Mince 4 lb veal, beef, or ox's tongues with 8 lb suet. Add 6 lb currants, the peel of 2 lemons, 10 chopped apples, 1 ounce of nutmegs, ⅛ ounce of mace, cloves and cinnamon. Sweeten with rosewater and sugar. Slice candied lemon and orange peel very thin, lay on meats, sprinkle dates on top.

Victorian mincemeat (Also note the two following recipes.)

Stone and cut two pounds of raisins, mix with two pounds of currants, one pound of minced lean beef, two pounds of chopped beef suet, two pounds of moist brown sugar, six ounces of mixed candied peel, one pound of apples, a small grated nutmeg, the rind of two lemons, the juice of one, a teaspoonful allspice, a pinch of salt. Pour over a large wineglassful of brandy, press tightly into an earthen jar and exclude the air. Keep for at least a fortnight before use, and start from bottom of jar.

Cumberland Sweet Pie

Chop finely and mix together half pound currants, half pound raisins, half pound mutton, two large apples, half ounce lemon peel, quarter pound butter, salt, half pound sugar, half a nutmeg, half teaspoon cinnamon, half glass rum, half gill ale. Roll thickly a pastry made from two pounds of flour and one pound of lard and cover dish. The filling must boil during cooking. Bake for approximately two hours.

Herbelade

Mince cooked pork with a good quantity of hyssop, sage and parsley, dates, raisins and fried nuts. Mix with egg yolks, sharpen with ginger and salt, strew with a little sugar and saffron, pour into pastry case and bake.

Herbolace

Chop three leaves each of marjoram, dittany, smallage, tansy, mint, sage, parsley and fennel with two large handfuls of violet, spinach, lettuce and clary. Add a little ginger and enough beaten eggs to make two omelettes, which are fried on both sides like large cakes, strewn with grated cheese and served.

Lombardy Green Tart

Mix two pounds of soft cheese with parsley, marjoram and other good herbs chopped very small. Add beaten eggs, saffron, pepper, a little butter and bake in a pastry crust.

Compare to John Evelyn's seventeenth-century *Herb Tart*.

Simmer fresh cream or milk with a little grated bread, add a pretty quantity of chervil, spinach, beet (or what other herbs you please) being first parboiled and chopped. Then add almonds beaten to a paste, a little sweet butter, the yolk of five eggs, two of the whites. Some add sugar, and spice at discretion. Bake in oven.

Tansy
Chop tansy very fine, add its juice to beaten eggs, fry the mixture until set, sprinkle on the chopped tansy, fold over and serve.

Compare this to Victorian *Tansy Pudding* (especially eaten on Easter Sunday)
Pound a handful of green tansy with three or four young spinach leaves and squeeze out the juice. Pour a pint of boiling milk over a quarter pound of breadcrumbs and let it stand until cool. Add two ounces butter, a glassful brandy, two tablespoons of sugar, the juice of half a lemon and two tablespoons of the tansy juice. Mix these ingredients thoroughly, then add four well-beaten eggs. Pour the pudding into a dish and bake in a well-heated oven. Serve very hot and sift sugar thickly over the top of the pudding. A superior tansy pudding may be made by mixing the milk with pounded almonds and lining the edges of the dishes with puff paste before putting in the mixture.

And to *Sir Theodore Mayerne's Pippin Tansy*
Fry as many sliced apples as will cover the pan bottom gently in butter. Beat eight eggs with grated white breadcrumbs, half pint cream, nutmeg and sugar, pour over apples. When thick serve with melted butter and sugar.

Again, to seventeenth-century *Apple Omelette*
Pare three or four apples cut in slices, fry in frying pan with butter and sugar. When tender add beaten eggs, seasoned with a little salt. Cook gently until set. Robert May recommends that currants, candied lemon peel, rosewater, and fried nuts also be added.

The seventeenth century is a transitional one in English cookery. The Puritans forbade spices and all rich dishes. During the Restoration one finds instructions for extremely elaborate and highly seasoned dishes. These come mainly from books which are written by members of the nobility, who were affected by the Puritan movement only in their reaction against it. But gradually with the rising of an increasingly literate middle class the Puritan disapproval becomes evident, and a peasant economy and local tradition emerges. The recipes are written for unskilled people that inexperienced cooks might follow them. In France, under the patronage of the *grands seigneurs*, cookery techniques advanced, and reached their peak at the end of the eighteenth century with Carême's complicated concoctions. The improvements passed over the Channel, especially during the Napoleonic Wars, and influenced English tables. With the development of the great trading companies foods now so familiar to us were introduced: tea, coffee, oranges, lemons and tomatoes. So that as the nineteenth century opened the cooking that we now understand as English was well under way, with its pies, puddings, pickles and conserves, its creams and its blancmanges, its collared and potted meats.

Sir Theodore Mayerne's London Pye

40 chestnuts, quarter pound eringo roots, one pound sweet potatoes, 2 sliced lemons, 12 hard-boiled egg yolks, 2 or 3 artichokes, handful of pickled barberries, a peck of oysters, 2 ounces lettuce stalks, 18 larks or sparrows, ¼ ounce peppercorns, ⅛ ounce cinnamon, ¼ ounce whole cloves, ½ ounce mace, ¼ pound currants are all baked in butter in a pastry case.

Paris Pye

Chickens, cockles, 9 or 10 yolks of eggs, pine kernels, marrow, mushrooms, ginger, nutmeg, mace, a little pepper, a good quantity of butter all baked in a pastry case.

Robert May's Olio Podrida

Take a Pipkin or Pot of some three Gallons, fill it with fair water, and set it over a Fire of Charcoals, and put in first your hardest meats, a rump of beef, *Bolonia* sausages, neats tongues, two dry, and two green, boiled and larded, about two hours after the Pot is boiled and scummed: but put in more presently after your Beef is scummed, Mutton, Venison, Pork, Bacon, all the foresaid in Gubbins, as big as a Duck's Egg in equal pieces; put in also Carrots, Turnips, Onions, Cabbidge in good big pieces, as big as your meat, a faggot of sweet herbs well bound up, and some whole Spinage, Sorrel, Burrage, Endive, Marigolds and other good Pot hearbs a little chopped; and sometimes *French* Barley, or lupins green or dry. Then a little before you dish out your Olio, put in your pot, Cloves, Mace, Saffron etc. Then next have divers Fowls; as first a *Goose*, or *Turkey*, two *Capons*, two *Ducks*, two *Pheasants*, two *Widgeons*, four *Partridges*, four *Stock-doves*, four *Teals*, eight *Snites*, twenty-four *Quails*, forty-eight *Larks*. Boil these foresaid Fowls in water and salt in a pan, pipkin or pot. Then have Bread, Marrow, Bottoms of Artichokes, *Yolks of hard Eggs, Large Mace, Chestnuts* boil'd and blanch'd, two *colliflowers, Saffron.* And stew these in a pipkin together being ready clensed with some good sweet butter, a little white-wine and strong broth. Some other times for variety you may use Beets, Potatoes, Skirrets, Pistaches, Pine Apple-seed or Pomegranates, Almonds, Lemons. Now to dish your Olio, dish first your Beef, Veal or Pork; then your Venison, and Mutton, Tongues, Sausages and Roots over all. Then next your largest Fowl, Land-Fowl, or Sea-Fowl, as first, a Goose, or Turkey, two Capons, two Pheasants, four Ducks, four Widgeons, four Stock-doves, four Partridges, eight Teals, twelve Snites, twenty-four Quails, forty-eight Larks etc. Then broth it, and put on your pipkin of Collyflowers, Artichokes, Chestnuts, some Sweet-breads fried, Yolks of hard Eggs, then Marrow boil'd in strong broth or water, large Mace, Saffron, Pistaches, and all the foresaid things being finely stewed up, and some red Beets over all, slice't Lemons, and Lemon-peels, whole and run it over with beaten butter.

Compare this to Meryell Williams of Ystumcolwyn's recipe for *Turine La Savoy*: Cut up 2 chickens, 2 partridges, 6 squabs, 2 rumps of mutton, a fillet of beef,

2 pounds of pork, 2 pounds of veal, 2 young rabbits. Lard all but the rumps and pork. Season with pepper, salt, cloves, mace, thyme and parsley mixed with celery, cardoons, savoys, blanch some chestnuts and some pistachoes. Roast meat and fowl until a quarter done. Put in bottom of pot some sheets of bacon. Lay over a dozen slices of veal, some forcemeat, some savoys, some celery, chestnuts, cockscombs, morels, truffles, sweetbreads, seasoning, pour over a strong stock, and a purée of asparagus, spinach and peas, pour over the top a ragout of onions and lay over the whole some sliced artichoke bottoms. Bake in the oven and serve with the juice of a lemon squeezed over.

Hung beef
Rub meat with a pickle of baysalt, brown sugar, saltpetre, a clove of garlic, pepper and allspice. Let it stand in the pickle for a fortnight, basting it with brine every day and turning it. It will be ready for smoking in a fortnight. A handful of hay in the water when boiling improves the flavour.

Pudding to boil with beef. (This is delicious eaten with salt beef.)
Mix the crumbs from a white loaf with one pound of beef suet, half a pound ground, or chopped and fried almonds, one quart of cream, six egg yolks, two whites, nutmeg, ginger, and sugar. Dip napkin in melted butter, scatter raisins over it, lay on pudding, tie and boil with beef, both fresh and salted.

Giles Rose's Boiled Cream
Stir cream and ground almonds together, and heat with egg yolks and castor sugar.

William Rabisha's (Master Cook) Leach
Pour a custard made with milk, cream, ground almonds, egg yolks and isinglass, sweetened with sugar and rosewater and flavoured with musk, ambergris, cinnamon, mace, nutmeg and salt over slices of bread.

Sweet Potato in Orange Cups (delicious with roast pork)
Mash potatoes, add sugar, salt and butter. Beat well. Add orange juice (probably the juice of one orange to two pounds sweet potatoes), stuff mixture into emptied halved oranges, and bake in moderate oven.

John Farley's Tea Cream
Boil a quarter of an ounce of fine China tea with ½ pint cream. Strain the leaves, either thicken and set the cream, or separate it into junket with two tablespoons of rennet and set over a slow fire in the dish in which it is to be served.

Elizabeth Raffald's Syllabub made under a cow
Put a bottle of strong beer and a pint of cider into a punch bowl. Grate in a small nutmeg, and sweeten it to your taste. Then milk as much from the cow as will make a strong froth, and the ale look clear. Let it stand an hour and strew over it a few currants well washed, picked, and plumped before the fire, then send it to the table.

Plum Porridge (Kidder's recipe)

Simmer two gallons of strong broth, 2 pounds currants, 2 pounds raisins, half ounce sweet spice, a pound sugar, a quart of claret, a pint of sack, the juice of three oranges and lemons, thicken with grated biscuits or rice flour and add a pound of prunes. (Mrs. Glasse thickened hers with breadcrumbs.)

Kidder's Quaking Pudding

Mix flour of rice, breadcrumbs, eggs, cream, orange flower water and sugar together. Boil in a cloth and serve with melted butter.

Kidder's Battalion Pye

Line a pastry crust with forcemeat, lay in it chickens, pigeons, sucking rabbits, oysters (tinned ones are good), sweetbreads, cockscombs, tongues and plenty of butter and bake under a pastry crust.

Swan Pye

Skin and bone swan, lard with bacon, season with savoury spice, bay leaves, cloves. Lay on butter. Close pie. Bake.

Venison pasties

Mince venison, parsley, and suet, add salt and pepper. Enclose in paste and bake.

Cumberland Mutton Ham

Pound together 2 ounces bay salt, half ounce salt-petre, 4 ounces coarse brown sugar, 2 ounces common salt, 2 ounces Jamaica and black pepper. Rub them well into ham which is laid in a bowl, or pickling trough. Keep ham carefully covered and baste with brine every day. Turn occasionally and make more brine if necessary. After a fortnight drain and dry it, hang it in the smoke for a week or more. Dried juniper wood gives the best flavour.

Collared beef

Bone and skin twelve pounds of flank beef. Rub it well with mixture of salt, salt-petre and sugar. Stand for five days, wash off pickle, drain and dry. Lard beef with bacon, strew on the inside of the meat a mixture of chopped parsley, sweet herbs, cloves, cayenne, mace and nutmeg. Roll up tightly, tie, put in cloth and simmer slowly in a saucepan of water for six hours. When ready take off and cloth and put in a mould. Set weight on top and stand till cold.

Mrs. Glasse's Chicken Pye

Make a Puff-Paste Crust, take two young Chickens, cut them to Pieces, season them with Pepper and Salt, a little beaten Mace, lay a Forcemeat made thus round the Side of the Dish. Take Half a Pound of Veal, Half a Pound of Sewet, beat them quite fine in a Marble Mortar, with as many Crumbs of Bread, season it with a very little Pepper and Salt, an Anchovy with the Liquor, cut the Anchovy to Pieces, a little Lemon-peel, cut very fine and shred small, a very little Thyme, mix all together with the Yolk of an Egg, make some into round Balls about twelve, the rest lay round the Dish. Lay in one Chicken over the Bottom of the Dish, take two Sweetbreads, cut them into five or six Pieces, lay them all over season them with Pepper and Salt. Strew over the Half an Ounce of Truffles and Morels, two or three Artichoke-bottoms cut to Pieces, a few Cocks Combs, if you have them, a Palate boiled tender and cut to Pieces; then lay on the other Part of the Chicken, put Half a Pint of Water in, and cover the Pye. Bake it well, and when it comes out of the Oven, fill it with good Gravy, lay on the Crust, and send it to table.

Kentish Chicken Pudding
Line a basin with a good pastry crust. Fill three quarters of the basin with chicken joints, half a pound flat cubed pork belly, chopped onion, parsley, salt and pepper. Put on pastry lid. Boil for 2½-3 hours.

Kentish Apple and Cheese Pie
Make an apple pie in the usual way, but cover the apples with a layer of sliced cheese underneath the pastry lid.

Cheshire Pork Pie
Bake steaks of pork, seasoned with pepper, salt and nutmeg, and apples in white wine under a pastry crust.

Devonshire Squab Pie
Bake layers of sliced apple and mutton chops, seasoned with allspice, sugar, onion and salt and pepper under a pastry crust.

Exeter Stew
Place two pounds lean sliced meat in a stewing jar in a cool oven with 2 tablespoons vinegar, leave for at least half an hour. Fry two or three onions in dripping, and enough flour and water to make one and a half pints of brown sauce, pour over meat and cook slowly for three hours. Make savoury balls from flour, suet, parsley, chopped herbs, salt and pepper. Drop them in and simmer until cooked. Approximately thirty minutes.

Cornish Cinnamon Rhubarb for Cold meats
Put half cup of vinegar and half a cup of water to simmer for twenty-five minutes with two pounds of sugar, ¼ teaspoon cinnamon, ½ teaspoon mixed spices, ¼ teaspoon nutmeg, ½ teaspoon ground cloves ties up in a muslin bag. Remove spices. Add rhubarb cut into one-inch lengths and raisins. Simmer till thick. Put in jars and seal.

Cornish Saffron Cake
Warm one and a half pounds flour. Put half teaspoon dried and powdered saffron into jug of three quarters pint of water. Stand jug in saucepan of boiling water until lukewarm. Mix two ounces yeast with one teaspoon sugar, when liquid pour into saffron water. Mix with flour. Cover batter with cloth and leave to rise for twenty minutes, melt one pound of butter, add to batter by degrees and beat till smooth. Stir in one pound currants, half a pound chopped peel and salt. Cover and

leave to rise for an hour. Turn out on floured board and knead a little. Put into tins and prove for twenty minutes. Bake in a moderate oven for one and a quarter hours.

William Gelleroy's polite way to dress a turkey

With a sharp knife cut the turkey down the back, then bone it, and make your forcemeat the following manner: take a pound of veal, half a pound of sewet cut and beat fine, a pound of grated bread, two cloves, some beaten mace, some lemon peel, the yolks of two eggs, half a nutmeg grated, and some pepper and salt: mix all together, and fill up the places where the bones came out, and fill the body, that it may appear just as it did before, and sew up the back and roast it. You may have oyster sauce, or what you please.

John Farley's Lobster Sauce

Boil a little mace and pepper in water to take flavour of spice. Strain. Melt three pounds of butter smooth in the water. Cut lobster very small, stir it in the butter and water with an anchovy until tender. Season if necessary with a little more mace, pepper and salt.

Potted lobster

Beat cooked lobster flesh very fine in mortar or if preferred it may be left in pieces, season with mace, nutmeg, pepper and salt. As you beat add a piece of butter the size of a walnut. Pack it in potting-pot as tight as possible. Seal with clear butter.

Lobster loaves

Remove the centres of french rolls, reserving the tops for lids. Make a thick white sauce, add onion, parsley, anchovy, three beaten egg yolks, lobster. Fill rolls with mixture, tie with tape, dip roll in milk, fry in deep boiling hot dripping until crisp.

Oyster loaves are made in the same way. Kidder recommends that the hollowed rolls should be fried in deep dripping before being lined with a tender forcemeat of oysters and eel, then the cavity should be filled with a white sauce containing white wine, anchovies, oysters, spice and mushrooms.

Shoulder of mutton with oysters, or cockles

Mix oysters or cockles with parsley, thyme, savory, six hard-boiled yolks, bread and three soft yolks. Stuff shoulder, or any other joint, with the mixture. Let the sauce be oyster liquor, red wine, anchovy, some oysters, a little onion and nutmeg. Serve with horse radish.

William Gelleroy's Chestnut Pudding

Take a dozen and half of chestnuts, put them in a saucepan of water, boil them a quarter of an hour, blanch them and peel them, and when cold, put them in cold water; then beat them in a mortar, with orange flower and sack (sweet sherry), till they are a paste; mix them in two quarts of cream, or milk, and twelve yolks of eggs, the whites of three or four; beat the eggs with the sack, rose water and sugar;

put it in a dish with puff paste; stick in some lumps of marrow or fresh butter and bake it.

Mary Kettilby's Orange Cheese Cake

Blanch half a pound of sweet almonds (or use ground almonds), beat with two spoonfuls of orange flower water, a little salt, half a pound of sugar, three quarters of a pound of melted butter. When nearly cold add eight egg yolks, put in a very light pastry crust and bake.

Floating Island

Sweeten thick cream with sack, add a squeeze of lemon. Pour into a bowl. Lay in the middle a thin slice of french roll which is spread with a layer of current jelly. Continue building alternate layers of roll and currant jelly until it rises out of the cream sea like an island. Cover the whole with whipped cream and decorate with sweetmeats, nuts or flowers.

Eggs in Moonshine

Beat cream and ground almonds together with rosewater, fold in stiffly beaten egg whites and gelatine. This is set in various moulds, one should be in the shape of the crescent moon, one like a large star, and two or three lesser ones. They should be appropriately stationed round the table.

Ginger Pudding

Mix a half a pound of flour, four ounces moist brown sugar, a pinch of salt, a quarter pound of beef suet and a dessertspoonful of powdered ginger. Put them dry into a well buttered mould into which they will fit exactly. Boil for three hours. Turn out and serve with cream of madeira sauce.

Wiggs

Rub half a pound of butter into a quarter pound of flour, add half a pound of butter to a little milk, four eggs, one ounce of carraway seeds and some yeast. Mix all the ingredients together so that they make a stiff paste, let it stand in a warm place to rise. Work in one pound of sugar. Butter tins, lay in the mixture. Bake.

Dorothy Hartley's Treacle Roly Poly

Make a good firm suet crust and roll it into a long, smooth strip. Cover it, to within two inches of the edge, with fine breadcrumbs; over these sprinkle lemon juice in summer and ginger in winter. Cover the crumbs with syrup, wet the edges of the paste, and roll it up, damping and pinching the edges together so that the juice cannot escape. Roll up in a greased paper and finally in a pudding cloth. Boil steadily for an hour at least.

Meat Roly Poly

Make the suet crust as before, cover it with a mixture of minced meat and kidneys, a little liver if liked, onions and herbs and a few oysters. Roll up and boil. Serve with a good brown gravy.

Cumberland Herb Pudding

Wash any available herbs—cabbage, brussel sprout tops, curly cale, young nettles, cauliflower, or broccoli sprigs, a few dandelion leaves, watercress, dock, onions or leeks, blackcurrant and gooseberry leaves. Chop them finely, mix with boiled barley and salt and pepper, or oatmeal, tie either in a pudding cloth or steam in a basin for two hours. Turn out, season and eat with a beaten egg and butter.

Yorkshire Dock Leaf Pudding

Wash, destalk and chop, two pounds young dock leaves, 2 large onions, half pound nettles. Boil in a very little water until tender. Add a handful of oatmeal and boil for twenty minutes, stirring carefully to prevent sticking. Store in jar, fry in bacon fat and eat with fried potatoes and bacon.

Mrs. Beeton's Shepherd's Pie

Cut half a pound cold mutton into thin slices, line a dish with some good buttered mashed potato. Put in meat, onion, salt and pepper. Pour in gravy. Cover with potato, brush with egg and bake in oven.

Pupton of Pigeon

Make a rich forcemeat from veal or chicken, fat bacon, suet, mushrooms, spinage, parsley, thyme, marjoram, savory and onions. Roll this into a paste and line a dish. Over this lay thin strips of bacon, pigeons, asparagus tops, mushrooms, hard egg yolks, cocks combs, pallets, cover with another layer of forcemeat, bake in the oven and serve covered with gravy.

Mrs. Glasse's Ragoo of Leg of Mutton

Take all the skin and Fat off, cut it very thin the right Way of the Grain, then butter your Stewpan, and shake some Flour into it. Slice Half a Lemon and Half an Onion, cut them very small, a little Bundle of sweet Herbs, a Blade of Mace: Put all together with your Meat into the Pan, stir it a Minute or two, then put in six Spoonfuls of Gravy, and have ready an Anchovy minc'd small; mix it with some Butter and Flour, stir it all together for six Minutes, and then dish it up.

Cutlets à la Maintenon

Roll chops in melted butter, coat in breadcrumbs, parsley, marjoram, thyme, savory, nutmeg, a few mushrooms, bake in sheets of oiled paper and serve.

Beef à la Tremblade

Put a rump of beef in a pot with madeira, an onion stuck with cloves, lemon peel, sweet herbs, pepper and simmer gently for a long time. Serve with a sauce made with its own stock, small minced onions, chopped parsley, tarragon and a little lemon juice.

Oysters à la Daube

Open oysters and insert a little seasoning of parsley, basil, chives, pepper and white wine. Set under the grill. When cooked remove the top shell.

Carp au Court Bouillon
Souse a brace of carp in a quart of boiling vinegar and salt and leave to cool.
Simmer gently in the vinegar, 3 bay leaves, onion, cloves and white pepper. When
cooked, remove and serve with a sauce of anchovy, a little strong gravy, a few pickled
mushrooms, thickened with butter and flour.

Soup de Santé
Simmer twelve pounds gravy beef, pepper, salt, spices and herbs over night. In
the morning the meat is removed, and a knuckle of veal, a chicken, nutmeg, mace,
bacon and cloves are added, together with butter, carrots, turnips, onions, parsley,
thyme, mushrooms, lettuce, chervil and celery. Finally the soup is served, thickened
with breadcrumbs and poured over a plump young chicken.

Soup au Bourgeoise
A soup of beef stock simmered with celery and endive and thickened with breadcrumbs.

Francatelli's Timbale of Macaroni, à la Mazarin
Boil one pound of macaroni in two quarts of water, with a pat of butter, eight
peppercorns and a little salt; when cooked and cold butter the inside of a mould,
cut the macaroni into half-inch lengths and cover the bottom of the mould with these,
placing them on end; cover this with a thick layer of chicken quenelle forcemeat;
then line the sides of the mould in the same way, and as soon as this is completed
smooth the inside with the back of a spoon dipped in hot water; fill this cavity
with a *blanquette* of fowl, the sauce of which must be thick, and cover the whole with
a layer of forcemeat. Steam gently, turn out of the mould, garnish with *Suprême*
sauce and cocks combs and serve. *Suprême* sauce is made with a good chicken
stock which is thickened with egg yolks and emulsified with cream.

Larousse Gastronomique's Quenelles of Foie Gras
Pound a raw foie gras (or you can make do with ordinary liver) and rub it through
a fine seive. As a separate operation pound half as much raw chicken meat as
there is foie gras, mixing in with it, little by little, half its weight in bread panada.
Rub this forcemeat through sieve. Put it back in the mortar and pound again,
adding it little by little to the purée of foie gras, and two or three egg yolks. Season
with salt and pepper and spices. Mould into round balls. Poach the quenelles in
salted water.

Pâté chaud de Lamproie à la Bordelaise
Line a tin with pastry, lay lamprey fillets (these can be bought in tins) over the
bottom and stud with truffles, or de-salted anchovy fillets. Cover with a layer of
fish forcemeat mixed with chopped parsley and chives, and a layer of the white
part of leeks slightly cooked in butter, then a layer of lamprey fillets. Fill the dish
in alternate layers of leeks and lamprey fillets, cover with another layer of forcemeat,
sprinkle with melted butter and put on pastry lid. Make a hole in the middle to

allow steam to escape. Bake in a moderate oven. At the last moment pour through the hole in the top a Velouté sauce (white sauce made with fish stock).

Carême's pâté chaud de foie gras aux truffes

For this two forcemeats should be prepared. For the first, purée some foie gras with blanched fat bacon, blanched chopped shallots, mushrooms, truffles, parsley, seasoning and spices; second, purée some scallops and foie gras together, add egg yolks and some diced truffle. Line a dish with pastry. Build the pie up with a layer of liver forcemeat, a layer of foie gras studded with truffles and a layer of scallop forcemeat. Continue with these layers until the dish is full. Throw on the top a dozen truffles. Close lid and bake for four hours. When done, open and pour in half a pint of sherry, close lid again, bake for a little more, and serve.

Francatelli's Croquante of Oranges

Let the peel and all the white pith be carefully removed with the fingers from about a dozen sound, but not over-ripe, oranges; then divide them by pulling them into small sections with the fingers, taking care not to break the thin skin which envelops the juicy pulp, then place them on an earthen dish. Next, put about one pound of the finest lump-sugar into a sugar-boiler with sufficient spring water to just cover it, and boil it down until it snaps or becomes brittle, which may be easily ascertained thus: take up a little of the sugar, when it begins to boil up in large purling bubbles, on the point of a knife, and instantly dip it into some cold water: if the sugar becomes set, it is sufficiently boiled and will easily snap in breaking. The sugar should now be withdrawn from the fire. The pieces of orange stuck on the points of wooden skewers must be slightly dipped in the sugar, and arranged at the bottom and round the sides of a plain circular mould, according to the foregoing design. When the whole is complete, and the sugar has become firm by cooling, just before sending to table, fill the inside of the *croquante* with whipped cream seasoned with sugar, a glass of maraschino and some whole strawberries, and then turn it out on a napkin, and serve.

Acknowledgements

I would like to acknowledge and record my thanks to Mr. John Bolt of *The Meat Trades Journal*, Mrs. Renée Tickell, Mr. Loftur Johannson, Mr. John Garrett, Mr. Robert Graves, Mr. George Kay, Mr. John Lewington, Mr. John O'Connor, Mr. Arthur Moss, Mr. Peter Mumford of Simpson's, Mrs. S. Reid-Holgate of Van den Berghs Ltd, the Horticultural Society, Mr. K. J. Tyler, Doctor McClean Baird, Doctor Crawford, Mrs. Mary Saaler, The Federation of Women's Institutes, in particular Mrs. Mary Cottam of the Cumberland Federation, the library staff of the British Museum, the Horniman Museum, the Wellcome Foundation and the National Library of Wales.

I am indebted to Mrs. Rosalind Heywood for permission to reproduce the front page and a medical recipe from Ann Coote's book and Tristan de Vere Cole for permission to print part of a poem of Horace de Vere Cole's; to Michael Foss and Simon Raven for translating Latin texts, Miranda von Kirchberg-Hohenheim for helpful suggestions, Arthur of Dewhurst, West Kensington, Mr. Frank Stevens and Mr. Whaley of Stevens butcher, Deal, who gave me their time for talk, Penelope Jardine for running scholarly errands in Rome, my mother and Mr. Willison of Lloyds Bank for supporting me while this book was being written, Christopher Sinclair-Stevenson who endured my appalling typing and to my friend Michael Holroyd who for years has encouraged me, corrected my grammar and tasted my recipes.

Thanks are also due to the following for permission to quote passages from published books: W. H. Allen & Co. for *My Life and Loves* by Frank Harris; Hawthorn Books Inc. for 'Aphrodisiacs and Anaphrodisiacs' by James Leslie McCary, in *The Encyclopaedia of Human Sexual Behaviour*; and the estate of E. F. Benson and Longmans, Green & Co. for *As We Were* by E. F. Benson. The version of 'The Roast Beef of Old England' on page 152 appears in the *Oxford Book of Eighteenth-Century Verse*, under Richard Leveridge's name, and in *The Greedy Book* by Brian Hill.

Select Bibliography

CHAPTER ONE

Apicius, C.: *De re coquinaria (passim)*
Apuleius: *The Golden Ass*
Athenaeus: *The Deipnosophists*
Balsdon, J. P. V. D.: *Life and Leisure in Ancient Rome*
Carcopino, J.: *Daily Life in Ancient Rome*
Cato and Varro: *The treatises of Cato and Varro: De agricultura rerum rusticarum libri tres*
Dill, S.: *Roman Society from Nero to Marcus Aurelius*
Flower, B. and Rosenbaum, E.: *The Roman Cook Book (passim)*
Frazer, J. G.: *The Golden Bough (passim)*
Gerhardie, William: 'Climate and Character' (from *The English Genius,* ed. Hugh Kingsmill)
Gibbon, E.: *The Decline and Fall of the Roman Empire (passim)*
Grant, M.: *The Climax of Rome*
Grant, M.: *The Ancient Mediterranean*
Horace: *Carmina*
Humelbergius Secundus (Dick): *Apician Morsels (passim)*
Ignotus (A. Hunter): *Culina famulatrix medicinae (passim)*
Jeaffreson, John: *A Book about the Table (passim)*
Juvenal: *The Sixteen Satires (passim)*
Kiefer, Otto: *Sexual life in ancient Rome*
Milne, Lorus and Margery: *The Senses of Animals and Men*
Ovid: *Amores*
Partridge, Burgo: *A History of Orgies (passim)*
Petronius: *The Satyricon*
Pliny the Elder: *The History of the World*
Pliny the Younger: *Epistolae*
Ryley-Scott, G.: *Phallic Worship*
Soyer, Alexis: *The Pantropheon*
Suetonius, T.: *The Twelve Caesars*
Warner, R.: *Antiquitates Culinaries (passim)*

CHAPTER TWO

Allegro, J.: *The Sacred Mushroom and the Cross*
Ausonius, D.: *The Mosella*

Dill, S.: *Roman Society in the last century of the Western Empire*
Dion Cassius: *Roman History*
Herodian History
Jerome: *The Principal Works of St. Jerome*
Marcellinus, Ammianus: *The Roman History*
Nicolson, Harold: *Good Behaviour*
The *Scriptores Historiae Augustae*
Waddell, Helen: *Desert Fathers*
Wasson, Gordon: *Soma: Divine Mushroom of Immortality*
Wasson, Gordon: *Mushrooms, Russia and History*

CHAPTER THREE

Caesar, Julius.: *Conquest of Gaul*
Cambrensis, Giraldus: *The historical works of Giraldus Cambrensis*
Diodorus Siculus: *History*
Ghillany, F. W.: *Les Sacrifices humains chez les Hébreux de l'antiquité*
Graves, Robert: *The White Goddess*
Kendrick, Thomas: *The Druids*
Liversedge, Joan: *Britain in the Roman Empire*
Michell, John: *The View over Atlantis*
Piggott, Stuart: *The Progress of Early Man*
Piggott, Stuart: *British Prehistory*
Richmond, I.: *Roman Britain*
Rivet, A. L. F.: *Town and Country in Roman Britain*
Ross, Anne: *Pagan Celtic Britain*
Tacitus: *Life of Agricola*
Strabo: *The Geography of Strabo*
Wheeler, Sir Mortimer: *The Excavation of Maiden Castle, Dorset*
Wright, T.: *Guide to the Ruins of the Roman city of Uriconium at Wroxeter, near Shrewsbury*

CHAPTER FOUR

Aelfric's Colloquy
Anglo-Saxon Poetry
Anglo-Saxon Chronicle, The
Bede: *Ecclesiastical History of England and English People*
Beowulf
Bruce-Mitford, R. L. S.: *The Sutton Hoo Ship Burial*
Cockayne, O.: *Leechdoms, Wortcunning and Starcraft*
Volta, Ornella: *The Vampire*
Whitelock, Dorothy: *The Beginnings of English Society*

CHAPTER FIVE

Austin, Thomas: *Two fifteenth-century cookery-books*

Bartholomaeus, Anglicus: *Medieval Lore*

Baskerville, G.: *English Monks and Suppression of the Monasteries*

Bellot, Jacques: *The Booke of Thrift*

Boorde, Andrew: *A Compendyous Regyment or a Dyetary of healthe*

Boorde, Andrew: *The Breviary of Healthe*

Cambrensis, Giraldus: *Autobiography*

Chaucer, G.: *The Canterbury Tales*

Chronicle of Jocelin Brakelond, The, ed. Sir Ernest Clarke

Clair, Colin: *Kitchen and Table (passim)*

Coulton, George: *Mediaeval Panorama*

Crisp, Sir Frank: *Mediaeval Gardens*

Culpeper, Nicholas: *The Complete Herbal*

Drummond, J. C. and Wilbraham, Anne: *The Englishman's Food (passim)*

Epulario: *The Italian Banquet*

Estate Book of Henry de Bray, ed. Dorothy Willis

Fitz-Stephen: *Description of the City of London*

Froissart, J.: *Chronicles*

Furnivall, F. G.: *Early English Meals and Manners*

Gerard, J.: *Herball*

Googe, Barnaby: *Foure Bookes of Husbandry*

Hare, Kenneth: 'Food and Drink' *(passim)* (from *The English Genius*, ed. Hugh Kingsmill)

Hartley, Dorothy: *Food in England (passim)*

Household Roll of Richard Swinfield, ed. John Webb

Inglis, Brian: *Fringe Medicine*

Jusserand, Jean: *English Wayfaring Life in the Middle Ages*

Labarge, Margaret Wade: *A Baronial Household of the Thirteenth Century*

Langland, William: *Vision of Piers Plowman*

Legrand d'Aussy: *Histoire de la vie privée des François*

Mead, William Edward: *The English Medieval Feast*

Morris, R.: *Liber cure cocorum*

Napier, Mrs. Alexander: *A noble boke of cookery*

Neckham, Alexander: *Alexandri Neckham de naturis rerum libri duo. De utensilium nominibus*

Nelson, William: *A Fifteenth Century School Book*

Origo, Iris: *The Merchant of Prato*

Paris, Matthew: *Matthew Paris's English History*

Pegge, Samuel: *The Forme of Cury*

Physicians of Myddvai, The

Power, Eileen: *Medieval English Nunneries*

Power, Eileen: *The Goodman of Paris* (translation)

Riley, H. T.: *Memorials of London and London Life*

Runciman, Steven: *A History of the Crusades*

Singer, C. and Underwood, E. A.: *A Short History of Medicine (passim)*

Tirel (Taillevent): *Le Viandier*

Trevelyan, G. M.: *Illustrated English Social History (passim)*

Tusser, Thomas: *Five hundred points of Good Husbandrie etc.*

Visitations of Religious Houses in the Diocese of Lincoln, ed. A. Hamilton
   Thompson

Walter of Henley: *Husbandry*

Wardrobe and Household of Henry, The, ed. H. Johnstone

William of Malmesbury: *Chronicle*

Wilson, Francesca: *Strange Island (passim)*

Wright, T.: *A History of Domestic Manners and Sentiments in England during the
   Middle Ages*

Wright, T.: *A Volume of Vocabularies*

Wright, T.: *Narratives of Sorcery and Magic, from the most authentic sources*

CHAPTER SIX

Aubrey, John: *Brief Lives*

Bowles, John: *Henry VIII*

Burton, Robert: *The Anatomy of Melancholy*

Buttes, Henry: *Dyets Dry Dinner*

Cogan, T.: *A Hauen of Health*

Coke, John: *The Debate betweene the Heraldes of Englande and Fraunce*

Digby, Sir Kenelm: *The Closet of the Eminently Learned Sir Kenelme Digbie
   Kt opened . . .*

Earle: *Microcosmography*

Elyot, Sir Thomas: *The Castell of Health*

Ernle, Lord: *English Farming Past and Present (passim)*

Evelyn, John: *Diary*

Evelyn, John: *Acetaria*

Evelyn, John: *Fumifugium; or the inconvenience of the aer and smoake of London
   dissipated, etc.*

Harrison, W.: *An historicall description of the Island of Britayne etc.*

Hentzner, Paul: *A journey into England in the year 1598*

Hill, Brian: *The Greedy Book (passim)*

Holinshed: *Chronicles*

Jesse, J. H.: *Memoirs of the Court of England during the Stuarts, including the
   Protectorate*

La Varenne: *The French Cook*

Markham, Gervase: *The English Huswife*

Mascall, Leonard: *The first booke of Catell*

May, Robert: *The Accomplisht Cook*

Misson, H.: *M. Misson's memoirs and observations in his travels over England*
Moryson, Fynes: *An Itinerary etc.*
Mountain, Didymus (Thomas Hill): *The Gardner's Labyrinth*
Muffet, Thomas: *Health's Improvement (passim)*
Murell, John: *A delightfull daily exercise for Ladies and Gentlemen*
Papin, D.: *A New Digester*
Partridge, John: *The treasuries of Commodious Conceites and hidden secrets*
Pepys, Samuel: *Diaries*
Platt, Sir Hugh: *The Jewell House of Art and Nature*
Platt, Sir Hugh: *Delightes for Ladies, to adorne their Persons, Tables, closets and distillatories*
Rabisha, William: *The Whole Body of Cookery dissected, taught and fully manifested . . .*
Root, Waverley: *The Food of France*
Rose, Giles: *A perfect School of Instructions for the Officers of the Mouth*
Rumsey, Walter: *Organon Salutis*
Salmon, William: *The Family-Dictionary*
Scott Thomson, Gladys: *Life in a Noble Household*
Speed, Adolphus: *Adam out of Eden*
Starkey, Thomas: *England in the reign of Henry VIII*
Starkey, Thomas: *A Dialogue between Reginald Pole and Thomas Lupset*
Stow, John: *Annales*
Stow, John: *A summarie of the Chronicles of England*
Stow, John: *The survey of London*
The Progresses and Public Processions of Queen Elizabeth, ed. J. Nichols
Turquet de Mayerne: *Archimagirus Anglo-Gallicus*
Walton, Izaak: *The Compleat Angler*
Whitehead, C.: *Lives and Exploits of English Highwaymen, Pirates and Robbers*
Wolley, Hannah: *The Cook's Guide*
Wolley, Hannah: *The Gentlewoman's Companion*
Wriothesley: *A Chronicle of England during the reigns of the Tudors*

CHAPTER SEVEN

Addison, Joseph and Steele, Richard: *The Spectator*
Bloch, Ivan: *Sexual Life in England past and present*
Boswell, James: *London Journal*
Boswell, James: *Samuel Johnson*
Brillat Savarin: *Psychologie du goût*
Bryant, Arthur: *The Man in the Making*
Burton, Robert: *The Anatomy of Melancholy*
Carême: *French Cookery*
Clare, John: *The Shepherd's Calender*
Clare, John.: *Selected Poems and Prose*, ed. Robinson and Summerfield

Creevey, Thomas: *The Creevey Papers*, ed. Sir Herbert Maxwell
Croker, J. W.: *The Croker Papers*, ed. L. J. Jennings
Defoe, Daniel: *Tour through the Island of Great Britain*
Eales, Mary: *The Compleat Confectioner*
Ernle, Lord: *English Farming Past and Present*
Farley, John: *The London Art of Cookery*
Fuller, Ronald: *Hell-Fire Francis*
Gaskell, Mrs.: *Cranford*
Gelleroy, William: *The London Cook*
Glasse, Hannah: *The Art of Cookery*
Hickey, William: *Memoirs of William Hickey*, ed. Peter Quennell
Jackson, Sarah: *The Director's Book*
Kidder, Edward: *Receipts of Pastry*
Kitchiner, William: *The Cook's Oracle (passim)*
Lamb, Patrick: *Royal Cookery*
Macaulay, Lord: 'Samuel Johnson'
Mannix, Daniel: *The Hell-Fire Club*
Mason, Charlotte: *The Ladies Assistant*
Moritz, Carl: *Travels through various parts of England, in 1782*
Nichols, R. H.: *The History of the Foundling Hospital*
Palmer, Arnold: *Moveable Feasts (passim)*
Peckham, Ann: *The Complete English Cook*
Raffald, Elizabeth: *The Experienced English Housekeeper*
Trusler, John: *The London Adviser and Guide*
Trusler, John: *The Honours of the Table*
Turner, E. S.: *All Heaven in a Rage (passim)*

CHAPTER EIGHT

Burnett, John: *Plenty and Want*
Cassell's *Dictionary of Cookery*
Cobbett, William: *Rural Rides*
Evans, Joan: *The Victorians*
Francatelli: *The Modern Cook*
Hare, Augustus: *The Years with Mother*
Harris, Frank: *My Life and Loves*
Hayward, A.: *The Art of Dining*
Kingsmill, Hugh: *After Puritanism*
Kirwan, A. V.: *Host and Guest*
Kitchiner, William: *The Art of Invigorating Life*
Lamb, Charles: *Dissertation on Roast Pig*
Malthus, Thomas: *An Essay on the Principle of Population etc.*
Marcus, Steven: *The Other Victorians*
Mayhew, Henry: *Selections from London Labour and London Poor*

Pearson, Hesketh: *The Smith of Smiths*
Rundall, Maria: *A New System of Domestic Cookery*
Smith, Albert: *The Natural History of Evening Parties*
Soyer, Alexis: *The Gastronomic Regenerator*
Soyer, Alexis: *A Shilling Cookery for the People*
Tschumi, Gabriel: *Royal Chef*
Walker, Thomas: *The Original*
'Walter': *My Secret Life*
Whiting, S.: *Memoirs of a Stomach*

CHAPTER NINE

Annual Abstract of Statistics, 1968
Asquith, Lady Cynthia: *Diaries 1915–1918*
Carson, Rachel: *Silent Spring*
Cooper, Derek: *The Bad Food Guide*
Goldring, Patrick: *The Broilerhouse Society*
Harrison, Ruth: *Animal Machines*
Holroyd, Michael: *Lytton Strachey*, Vols. 1 and 2
Maclean Baird, I. and Howard, Alan: *Obesity, Medical and Scientific Aspects*
Massingham, H. J.: *The English Countryman*
Morrell, Ottoline: *The Early Memoirs of Lady Ottoline Morrell*, ed. Robert
   Gathorne Hardy
Moss, Arthur: *Memoirs* (unpublished)
Overseas Trade Accounts of the United Kingdom, May 1969
Priestley, J. B.: *The Edwardians*
Renner, H. D.: *The Origin of Food Habits*
Stuart Collis, John: *Drift of My Life*
Woolf, Leonard: *Sowing*
Woolf, Leonard: *Beginning Again*
Wyden Peter: *The Overweight Society*
Yudkin, J. and McKenzie, J. C.: *Changing Food Habits*

the populace had come to rely on unlimited supplies of ample
varieties of cheap foreign food. In the First World War short-
ages and consequent food price rises caused industrial unrest,
and the governments between 1939 and 1945 were determined
to prevent a recurrence of this disaffection. So from January
1940 they introduced food rationing, the principle of which was
fair shares for all. The obvious rightness of rationing kept up
morale and, surprisingly, improved the nation's health, because
it enforced good nutritional practices that were not widely
recognized until the 1980s. In fact, rationing really bit just after
the war. Bread rationing was only introduced in 1946, and lasted
until 1948; potatoes hadn't been on ration during the war either,
but controls on them were introduced from 1947 to 1948.

Though it was a great leap forward from bread rationing to
the world's best-known baker, Lionel Poilâne of Paris, opening
a bakery and shop in London in 2000, there are some constant,
and negative features of British food behaviour. Above all, the
country is still used to and still demands cheap food. Post-war
farming subsidies kept down the retail costs of home-produced
cereals, dairy products and even meat, and then, despite the
European Union's agricultural policies that have contributed to
the sorry state of British farming at present, Britons nevertheless
continued to spend a much smaller proportion of their disposable income on food than did our European colleagues. Even
now, when we're as food-conscious as the next country and you
can buy three or four sorts of crème fraîche in a big British
supermarket, most of us still prefer cheap food to better food.
There is a minority who expect to pay for quality in their food,
as they do, say, for their car or their entertainment, but in our
still class-divided society these are the better educated and
higher earning. Despite the demise of traditional working-class
culture, there is still a working-class attitude to food; or perhaps
it would be more accurate to say a lumpen proletariat attitude.
The old working class, both urban and rural, had shopping and
cooking skills, traditional dishes and recipes, and used fresh
ingredients. Today's underclass do not know how to cook, get
bad value from their shopping by paying the 'added-value' com-

ponent of convenience food, instead of paying less for the cheaper fresh ingredients they don't know what to do with. No politician dares suggest that single mothers, or families on the dole, could profit financially and nutritionally (and culturally— but nobody even dares *think* this) by learning to prepare their own food in the traditional way, rather than zapping the contents of a packet in a microwave oven. Instead, domestic science and home economics courses have been dropped from the curriculum, thus ensuring that underclass children remain, foodwise, in the social stratum to which they were born.

And there's worse. No government of either party since the war has dared to challenge the appetite for cheap food. The hunger for cheap food is, however, the cause of all the food scares, scandals and plagues of our age. Why did virtually all hens' eggs have *salmonella entereditis*? (Edwina Currie was speaking no less than the truth, though she lost her nerve—and her job for saying it.) Because we didn't care that battery-laid eggs had thin shells and watery whites (or that the conditions under which they were produced were barbarous). All that mattered was their price. What other reason, except the production of cheap meat, could there be for grinding up the corpses of dead ruminants and feeding them to other ruminants? Who would ever even have thought of doing this if it didn't lower the cost of animal feed? The real cause of BSE was the policy of cheap food—as France and Germany began to learn at the end of the year 2000, when BSE was discovered in *their* national herds.

One result of Britain's closer integration into Europe will be the gradual erosion of this policy—though we'll always have some aspect of it so long as there is an underclass to feed; and better food will not itself make the underclass upwardly mobile. Gastronomically, at least for the foreseeable future, Britain will be two nations. The nation of the better off will be ever better fed; that at least is cause for satisfaction amidst the more general gloom.

I can mark the beginning of the foodie phase of British history with some precision. That is because in 1972 Philippa Pullar took me to a restaurant in Lower Sloane Street in London. It was run by two brothers called Roux, who were French and had both been in private service as cooks. The name of the modest restaurant came from Victor Hugo; it was Le Gavroche, the original of the Mayfair eatery that, at its acme, with the older Roux brother, Albert, at the stove, had three Michelin stars. The food was different from the imitation French food you could get all over London, simply because it was authentic, like the food we were used to eating in ambitious provincial restaurants in France, with the sauces carefully made and the ingredients carefully chosen. it was old-fashioned, classic French cooking, nothing like what we were then hearing about some new culinary movement that was stirring in the kitchens of restaurants near Lyons.

Philippa gave me my first taste of that the same year, in the unlikely surroundings of the Capital Hotel on Basil Street. She had discovered a young cook called Richard Sheppard, who was up to something new. Against all my inclinations, she insisted I order a starter of scallop mousse with two sauces. It wasn't that I disliked scallops, but her description of one of the sauces made it sound like raspberry jam. My memory of the dish, a slice of a loaf-shaped terrine with two circles of white scallop in a coral-pink surround, is that it was like one of those mad *nouvelle cuisine* excesses of the 1980s, when every lobster had to have its flavouring of vanilla; but probably it was merely a then-daring pairing of the fruity and the fishy. Richard Sheppard went on to fortune and a certain amount of fame at Langan's Brasserie, with his partners, the notorious lovable drunk Peter Langan and film star Michael Caine; but I am pretty certain that the credit for introducing *nouvelle cuisine* to Britain belongs to him and the Capital Hotel. At the time, few of us understood that the movement involved anything more than pairing shellfish and raspberry jam. Indeed, because Michael Guérard's *Cuisine Minceur* was the first of the series of cookery titles translated and adapted by Caroline Conran for Caroline Hobhouse at Macmillan, it was many years before most of us stopped confusing that slimming diet with the whole of *nouvelle cuisine*. Some writers have never got it straight, and persist to this day in writing *cuisine minceur* when the food they mean to refer to can be as full of calories as any cream cake.

At first the chefs of Britain didn't understand any better than their customers what Guérard, the brothers Troisgros, Alain Chapel, Georges Blanc, Alain Senderens, Marc Meneau, Bernard Loiseau, Roger Vergé and the others were up to. (I omit Paul Bocuse from this list, because he made it more apparent than the others early on, both in his menus and in his published books, that he was the Sydney Webb of the stove, not the Lenin of Lyons—merely reforming, not revolutionizing the traditional and *haute cuisine* of his region. When the kitchen dust finally settled in the 1990s, we could see that Reformism was the culinary ideology of most of the three-star French chefs.)

As London diners-out we were still happy enough to eat at Parke's on Beauchamp Place, where a *prix-fixe* meal was still a fiver and every plate came garnished with a flower. The full force of plate service hit London like a hurricane. Assembling the plate in the kitchen, not at the table, was an essential part of the food revolution, because it gave the chef the final control over what appeared in front of the customer. But what a blow to the waiters. The waiter's sole task was now to ferry a plate from the 'pass', where the head chef approved its appearance, to the diner's table. Overnight waiting went from being a 'profession', a lifelong job from which you retired an elderly man, to being a way for young 'resting' actors to support themselves. Some waiters saw that the new trend spelled the end of silver and *guéridon* service and, with that, any interest the job might hold for them, and became militant. I'll never forget a lunch in the early 1980s for a few food writers in a private room at the Ritz Hotel, the management of which was very proud of its new British chef. My seat at the table allowed me to see into the doorway through which the waiters passed with the plates the chef had lovingly prepared in the kitchen. At the entrance to the dining room stood the head waiter, salt cellar in hand, sabotaging the chef's efforts, plate by plate.

Though almost every self-respecting chef adopted plate service sometime in the 1980s, the less superficial culinary developments in France were ill-digested here. The Roux brothers, like Michel Bourdin of the Connaught Hotel and a few others, though they may have lightened a sauce or two, to their credit never ceased to prepare and dish up traditional French food. They appeared old-fashioned to some commentators, but they were never guilty of faddism or the search for novelty that still mars plates in restaurants today. Some professional cooks had an instinctive understanding of the virtues of *nouvelle cuisine*, simplifying dishes and making flavours cleaner, emphasizing ingredients rather than techniques, and making the whole meal lighter. Chief among these in the older generation were Anton Mosimann and Raymond Blanc, who were the avant-gardist chefs of the 1970s and 80s.

Not everybody was in sympathy. Their dining rooms were booked up and it could take weeks to get a table at the Dorchester, where the Swiss-born Mosimann was Maître Chef des Cuisines or at Blanc's tiny restaurant in North Oxford. Among those slow on the uptake were the inspectors of the British *Michelin Guide*, who never came to terms with the changes in French food. (Michelin was terribly important to the ambitious chef's sense of self-esteem. This is sad because, as we'll see below, its inspectors were never really competent to assess the British food scene. Mosimann eventually dropped out of the Michelin stars-rat-race by opening a members-only private club, and Blanc, who has yet to score more than two of the maximum three Michelin stars for cooking, has managed to achieve recognition as one of the world's great restaurants without the ultimate Michelin accolade.) Part of the difficulty was structural: the red *Michelin Guide* used (and still uses) symbols alone to classify and rank restaurants and hotels, without any explanatory prose. As they never adopted a symbol to indicate *nouvelle cuisine* as opposed to traditional cooking, readers of the guide could never know whether an unfamiliar eatery dished up Japanese-ly pretty titbits on a plate or what American writer Calvin Trillin calls 'heavy heavy stuff stuff'. This is the reason *Michelin France* lost its pre-eminence in the 1980s to the *Gault Millau Guide*. There was, however, no competition to Michelin in Britain, for the *Egon Ronay Guide* never quite got the hang of *nouvelle cuisine* either, though it was quick enough to recognize the merits of Mosimann, Blanc and those who followed the trail those two had blazed. The *Good Food Guide* had a better record, though it lost its way after Christopher Driver ceased to be its editor in 1982.

Most British food journalists also failed to be shocked by the new, resulting in a dramatic change in the treatment of food and eating, first in magazines and newspapers and then on television. Editors no longer wanted recipes alone—they wanted food news and features. This in turn created a whole new, male readership of food columns, and some of these were actually written by men. When Philippa was writing *Consuming Passions* the great food writers were Elizabeth David and Jane Grigson, and they were principally writers of recipes. Now the most important book in the library of anyone interested in food is Alan Davidson's *Oxford Companion to Food*, which contains over a million words and no recipes at all. With the single exception of Fay Maschler, all the good restaurant critics in Britain are men, as are many of the food columnists (and even the best recipe writers) on national newspapers.

Our appetites have changed as well. When Philippa was finishing her book, it was still difficult to travel abroad because of the £50 currency limitation. Nobody would have believed you if you'd predicted cheap package holidays to India; and if you'd said that in less than thirty years Australia and New Zealand would be exporting their style of cooking you'd have been thought lunatic, and if you'd said that British supermarkets would stock lemon grass nobody would have known what you were talking about. But food trends are now led by restaurants, and foreign travel has given us the taste for pesto and Thai green curry and yardsticks by which to measure their authenticity.

Some foreign cuisines are universally represented in Britain (it has become usual to refer to foreign cuisines as 'ethnic', but English cooking, if there is any such thing any more, is ethnic too). Every market town now has an Indian and Chinese take-away, and probably a Thai restaurant as well. Manchester and

Leeds boast a great many good restaurants, and so does Edinburgh. Oxford no longer numbers gastronomy among its lost causes. The little town of Ludlow in Shropshire has three ambitious eateries at the time of writing. Food is serious business, an important sector of the service economy.

What is still surprising, however, is the diversity of cuisines that can be found in London, with at least sixty different cuisines represented by restaurants within the circle of the M25. Virtually all the cuisines of Southeast Asia are dished up in the capital—Thai, Vietnamese, Singaporean, Malaysian, Indonesian, Philippine, even Burmese. The only gaps I can think of are Cambodia and Laos, and I expect dishes from these countries can be found in the outlying postal districts, along with tucker from the Pacific Rim. There are Mexican and other Central American restaurants, Brazilian, Argentine and other South American restaurants, Austrian, German, Czech, Hungarian, Polish, Russian, Korean, Afghan and Nepalese eateries. Lebanese eating places occupy a good stretch of the Edgware Road, and there are Moroccan, Algerian, Tunisian, Syrian, Persian and Israeli cooks plying their trade somewhere in London. The best-known cuisines, French, Italian, Chinese, Japanese and Indian, are further diversified by region or style— Breton crêperies vie with Italian pizzerias, while entire menus are devoted to dishes from the Loire, Provence, Alsace, Piedmont, Tuscany, Szechuan, Hong Kong, Peking, Bengal, the Punjab, Bombay or Lahore, and there are dining rooms specializing in Thai court cuisine and Japanese country cooking. There are halal and kosher places to eat, and vegetarian bean-eries galore. You can see why the Michelin men just aren't competent to deal with London, and pretty well have to restrict their inspections to the French cooking they understand.

There is even a style of cooking calling itself 'Modern British'. This does not mean roast beef and Yorkshire pudding made without flour. It means eclectic. While the over-exposed-on-television Gary Rhodes found new things to do with faggots, he was almost alone in seeking to reinvigorate traditional British dishes (though Anton Mosimann has almost reinvented bread-

and-butter pudding). While Mr Rhodes was renovating roast potatoes, most of his mates were experimenting with basil sorbet.

Of the top chefs who came to prominence in the 1980s and 1990s, only Nico Ladenis and his one-time pupil, Marco Pierre White, were faithful to classic French *haute cuisine*, and both of them were quick to adapt it for British ingredients. Each achieved three Michelin stars and each, seeing the handwriting on the wall and realizing that it was definitely not a classic menu, handed back their stars—all of them, not just the third star, to the Michelin men in 2000. They both cut their prices in their flagship restaurants by a third and did what they could to make their dining rooms less stuffy.

Simon Hopkinson, whose last stint in the kitchen was at Bibendum, learned his skills on the job, and had a basic French bias. So did Gordon Ramsay, for whom the Paris kitchens of Joël Robuchon and Guy Savoy were a sort of finishing school. Most of the chefs of their generation, however, while acknowledging the primacy of the techniques of French cooking, were more interested in the flavours of other countries and regions. Alastair Little began cooking with a little chilli here and a little ginger there, but eventually became so interested in Italian food that he gave residential cookery courses in Italy. Rowley Leigh, who learned his craft in one of the Roux brothers' kitchens, has a deep interest in Italian food, but has taken Modern British cuisine a step in the direction of California. Sally Clarke's restaurant is almost opposite his Kensington Place on Kensington Church Street. She is an alumna of Alice Waters's Chez Panisse, where, by common consent, California cuisine began, and has adapted what she learned there to British ingredients. She is one of the few chefs to serve a Chez Panisse-style no-choice menu (in the evening; there is a limited choice at lunch).

Another important development is the growth of the restaurant group. These have obvious advantages, such as centralized buying of food and wine, and therefore bigger discounts; a pool of labour for both the kitchen and front-of-house staff; and a single accounts department. The biggest restaurant group is the one that bears Sir Terence Conran's name. He started with Bibendum, but that, though partly owned by him, is not part of the Conran Group. Quaglino's was the first of this lot, followed by the Blueprint Café, Pont de la Tour, Cantina del Ponte and the Chop House, all at Butler's Wharf, Mezzo, Zinc, Orrery, Sartoria, Coq d'Argent and the restaurants in the Great Eastern Hotel in London, plus places in Paris and New York. Marco Pierre White has given up cooking to be an art-collecting businessman. He is evidently a superb delegator, for the quality of his restaurants remains high. They start with his flagship, the Oak Room, and include the Criterion, Quo Vadis, Titanic, Belvedere, MPW in Belsize Park and Drones.

Claudio Pulze's *A–Z Restaurants* included Zafferano, Spiga and, in a departure from his Italian bias, the Indian Zaika. This is representative of a long-standing trend to luxury and careful cooking in Indian restaurants, which began in the 1980s when Camellia Panjabi, a high-ranking executive of the Taj Hotel chain in India, set up the Bombay Brasserie in London. Since then, her sister, Namita Panjabi, has started Chutney Mary, one of the few restaurants anywhere in the world to offer authentic Anglo-Indian dishes, and revamped Veeraswamy, one of London's oldest restaurants. There are quite a few posh Indian restaurants now, including Tamarind and Chor Bizarre. Oliver Peyton began with Mash and Air in Manchester, before moving the operations of his group to London, with another Mash microbrewery, the Atlantic Bar and Grill, Isola and the Admiralty restaurant in the gloriously restored Somerset House. Luke Johnson's Belgo Group not only owns the two Belgian moules-frites places that bear that name, but has swallowed up the Caprice, the Ivy and J. Sheekey's.

You would guess that all this can't just be about food, and you'd be right. The restaurant is an essential part of the London social scene, as much as it is in Manhattan. When it was managed by Chris Corbin and Jeremy King, who left when their contracts were up in 2000, the Ivy was restored as the place for the theatre crowd; but with its serious art by Howard Hodgkin,

Alan Jones, Peter Blake, Barry Flanagan, Bill Jacklin and many others, it became an artist's hang-out, and was also loved by several successful writers. Film stars were often seen dining there, and even the presence of pop stars did not wreck the ambience of the place. Despite its location in Hammersmith, miles from central London, the River Café is also a centre of social activity, owing to the personalities of its co-owners and chefs, Lady (Ruth) Rogers and Rose Grey. It was something of a favourite place for Tony Blair's New Labour. Restaurants figured greatly in the New Labour social scene, ever since the pre-1997 general election succession to the deceased leader, John Smith, was settled between Tony Blair and Gordon Brown over a meal at Granita in Islington.

Restaurants have become not just temples of gastronomy, but destinations, aspirational goals in today's Britain, with the weirdest example being when Tony and Cherie Blair gave a private dinner to Bill and Hillary Clinton at Conran's Pont de la Tour, where, presumably, the Clintons had been longing to eat. But sometimes the wrong group aspires to eat in a place. In one swanky, designer-led West End venue, the owner's friends would no longer be seen dead in the place, which filled up with what Manhattanites call bridge-and-tunnel-people, in this case, customers of whom many appeared to be used-car dealers from Essex who paid for their meals in cash. By the same token, some eateries have been saved by being colonized by a single crowd: I can think of a place or two that would have gone under if they had not become the beneficiaries of pink-pound spending.

Social class is more interesting and more crucial for the story of food than is sexual orientation. Chefs have been upwardly mobile, while their clients have climbed down the social ladder a rung or two. Once all professional restaurant cooks were working class. They normally left school at sixteen, and either did a vocational course at a catering college, or went straight into a kitchen as an apprentice. The influence of the *nouvelle cuisine* changed this, for chefs who made flourless sauces based upon reductions of cooking liquids, who tended to undercook rather than overcook fish, meat, poultry and vegetables and who plated up their food in the kitchen, found that kids who had done these vocational courses had simply acquired a lot of mis-information and bad habits that needed to be unlearned. There was the additional problem that catering used to be regarded as the industry of last resort, and careers officers regarded it as a sort of dustbin for the dimmest, most slow-learning school-leavers.

This could never be ameliorated until the social status of the chef improved. Oddly enough, this had been one of the goals of the greatest chef of history, Auguste Escoffier. In the late nine-teenth and early twentieth centuries he introduced improved conditions, such as gas-fired ranges replacing dirty coal-fired ones, and practices, such as insisting that chefs not be seen by customers unless wearing clean 'whites' and never wearing working clothes in the street. His failure to raise the profession's social profile may have had something to do with his failure to raise the profession's ethical standards. He himself was guilty of accepting the chef's traditional perks of kickbacks from suppliers, for which he was fired from the Savoy Hotel in 1898, along with his accomplice, César Ritz. The foodie culture of the 1980s was able to achieve what Escoffier could not, and make the working-class trade closer to being a middle-class profession.

Socio-culinary upward mobility began in California with the student political unrest at Berkeley in the late 1960s. Alice Waters and Jeremiah Tower were the first university-educated chefs to come to international attention, but soon such exotic creatures were to be found all over the US, at Stars in San Francisco, at the Quilted Giraffe in New York, culmi-nating in one of the most influential chefs of the new millen-nium, Charlie Trotter in Chicago, who studied philosophy as an undergraduate. Young people who, only fifteen years ago, would have become lawyers, dentists, accountants, business-men, teachers and even university lecturers are choosing to be cooks. In Britain, we still have some top chefs of working-class origin, such as Mr White and Mr Ramsay, but their very success (and its attendant celebrity) has pushed them into another stratum, where they join grammar-school kids, ex-public-school boys and university graduates such as Nico Ladenis,

Alastair Little, Rowley Leigh, Sally Clarke, Simon Hopkinson, Rose Grey, Ruth Rogers and Fergus Henderson of St John's.

In the 1950s, and well into the time when Philippa was researching and writing this book, restaurants were for the middle classes. That's not to say that there weren't places for working people to eat outside the home—there were canteens at work and caffs in urban centres—and by the late 1970s it had become the fashion for working-class youths to drink too much lager at the pub on Saturday night and absorb some of it by eating a hellishly hot vindaloo at the local Indian restaurant and take-away. Better-off working-class families often celebrated wedding anniversaries and important birthdays by going out for a meal. But one indication of how different things are in the year 2001 is that today most restaurant customers drink wine—which would have been unthinkable in the 1950s, 60s and 70s. Of course, the fact that restaurant customers are drawn from further down the social scale has a great deal to do with changes in the social scale itself—the disappearance of the traditional working class. But it has also to do with the evolution of different socio-economic groupings, such as the Yuppies, first spotted in the 1980s, young professionals, especially found in the financial sector, whose parents probably were traditional working class.

Yuppies, with their high incomes achieved at an early age, rapidly acquired the tastes and habits of the upper-middle class—smart cars, loft-living and especially wine-drinking and restaurant-going. The wine bars of the City were full of young people speaking what was (in the 1990s) identified as Estuary English (as opposed to the Mockney adopted by public-school kids from the late 1960s on)—and drinking Champagne, real Champagne, and lots of it. The reason for the restaurant explosion is that the size of its customer base has increased hugely. Eating out is a hobby for the young, and one they continue even after marriage and children, of all affluent people. In effect, this now means that only the urban underclass and the rural poor, who suffer from an impoverished diet at home, to add injury to insult, are excluded from restaurant-going (as they are from the enjoyment of most marginal goods except, seemingly, television sets, designer clothes and recreational drugs).

The really extraordinary thing about this expansion of the market for restaurants is that it has been achieved without a levelling of the quality of the commodity. Never in human history has the best food been so good, and never has good food been so widely available and eaten. The fact that most diners may not have been brought up with food of the style and quality on offer in Britain's restaurants (as they would have been when restaurants were the preserve of the middle classes) does not affect their taste, discernment or gastronomic aspirations. They do not want a continuation of the diet of home or school, they want posh nosh and they prize novelty, not familiarity, on the plate. Regardless of educational level or class origin, they crave exactly the same food as the upper-middle class, university-educated, professional man or woman wants. And, whatever they drink at the pub or in bars, when they eat out they are wine-drinkers.

They may well be the new middle classes—eating out in restaurants in leisure time may indeed be a defining character-istic of what it is to be middle class in early twenty-first-century Britain (and America and Australia). But they want pad thai, pho, pata negra, sushi, bulgogi, boutarga and foie gras, and they know what these exotic foods are. How they got that way and came by their knowledge is a story of working-class families having holidays abroad, of television programmes and cookery books and magazines.

How they can afford it is a question for economic historians and sociologists; the first to explain why restaurant-goers seem to have so much disposable income and the second to explain why they spend it on food and drink. The question of money is especially acute in Britain. Though it is very difficult to get accurate statistics, it is obvious that of all the people in the affluent Western world, Britons spend the lowest proportion of household income on food. At the beginning of 2001, I heard it suggested that the figures were 45 per cent of disposable income for the French, 15 per cent for Americans and 11 per cent for

Britons. (My efforts to verify these figures were thwarted by the fact that for some countries the official figures include alcohol and tobacco consumption along with food, that others exclude housing from household expenditure statistics, and that the French and British gather their statistics in such different ways that I found a study for France that gave its 1997 food, alcohol and tobacco expenditure at 18 per cent and one that gave the British expenditure on the 'same' items as 24 per cent. If you believe that, you'll believe the moon is made of green cheese.)

Why is it, then, so much more expensive to eat out at the same level in Britain than in France? At the beginning of 2001, a three-course meal at Raymond Blanc's Le Manoir aux Quat' Saisons, for all that it was probably the best restaurant in the country, with a single, modest bottle of French country wine shared between three, came to £100 each. I was not shocked by the bill, although a similar meal at the same period at almost any of the seven Michelin three-star restaurants of Paris would have been no more expensive, and probably a little less dear. At a less starry level, Paris is a great deal cheaper than London (so are New York and Sydney, but for different reasons). Food costs for good restaurants the world over run at about 30 per cent—not astronomic.

The problem is rent. London commercial rents (and presumably interest on Le Manoir's mortgage and other borrowings) are very high. Most French restaurateurs own the freehold of their premises, for they are businesses that have been in the family for more than a generation. Though in France the restaurant trade would appear—on paper—to be burdened with paying the 'social wage' (of benefits and entitlements) for every employee, and punitive overtime rates for any time worked over thirty-five hours, many smaller establishments are family concerns. When family members benefit from the profits of the restaurant they do not need to be waged employees. Constant food and wine prices, no rent, plus small or no wage bills equals a lower bottom line for the French customer. (Those three-star French chefs who have acted as consultants in London must have found us and our ways headache-making. Jean-Michel

Lorain of La Côte St Jacques at Joigny and Jean-André Charial of Baumanière at Les Baux-en-Provence each worked with large London hotels in the 1980s, and achieved some wonderful results. But how they must have marvelled at British employment practices; and how puzzled Alain Ducasse must have been by the reluctance of people to join the not-quite-U Knightsbridge private club that used him as a consultant, before he opened his weird and wonderful Philippe Starck-designed Spoon+ at Ian Schrager's Sanderson hotel in London.)

The phenomenon that would have most perplexed the first readers of *Consuming Passions* is the torrent of cookery books and television programmes. Most of both of these are the products of chefs, but often of 'chefs' who do not work in restaurants. (There is a big difference between real chefs and plain old cooks, the most salient being that chefs, like ladies of the night, do it for money. The idea is abroad, particularly in America, that chefs are on the verge of ceasing to be a trade and becoming a profession, like doctors, lawyers and accountants. A few things are lacking, such as a chefs' professional accrediting body—and a code of practice. Nobody has ever worried much about chefs' ethics. Imagine the chaos if it were an offence to steal recipes, or sous chefs.) Sometimes, as in the case of Sophie Grigson and Nigella Lawson, TV 'chefs' have the good sense not to pose as professional cooks, but Ken Hom, Madhur Jaffrey, Ainsley Harriot, Michael Barry and a clutch of others whose names I admit I do not know, were not originally celebrated or even identified as restaurant cooks. Obviously these television cooks were not all as good as the superb Mr Hom and Mrs Jaffrey, but the television executives who commissioned their programmes were not interested in the quality of the food they were capable of producing. The books of the series vary in quality as well, though that doesn't much interest their publishers.

Cookery books have changed radically. Some classic books were produced in the second half of the twentieth century, particularly those of Elizabeth David, Jane Grigson and Claudia Roden—by home cooks writing for other domestic cooks. However, in the late 1970s, we began to get chef's books like, but mostly inferior to, those Caroline, Lady Conran, was translating and adapting from the French. The Roux brothers published books of recipes undo-able in the ordinary domestic kitchen; Raymond Blanc and Anton Mosimann wrote books that varied from the just possible to the quite practical. Soon no chef could be happy until he had published his 'own' recipes, preferably with lots of arty colour photographs of the food and black-and-white ones of him looking moody and sexy. Hundreds of these books were published. Most had a short shelf-life and, *sub speciae aeternitatis*, for all that they cost to produce, most are ephemeral, completely worthless except to the social historian. It was not sufficient for the chef to become rich and middle class—he had to become a celebrity as well, and the television programme and cookery book were an essential part of his raised profile. TV appearances can sell almost anything. Delia Smith, a non-chef who has no obvious talents as cook, television presenter, or writer, and who has been slow to appreciate the changing food trends and tastes of her compatriots, has enjoyed sales of her cookery books that Elizabeth David and Jane Grigson could never have imagined. Jamie Oliver, whose chief attraction is that he is amusing on television, has sold over one million cookbooks.

The happier part of this story of wretched excess is that, with the same exceptions as above, we all eat better at home, for the food revolution, which began with food journalists and writers, then became restaurant-led. And we insisted on eating at home the same ingredients we ate in restaurants and saw on television cookery programmes. So supermarkets began to carry rocket, 'wild' mushrooms, Parmigiana-Reggiano, crème fraîche, filo pastry, dry-cured bacon, pancetta, six named-variety potatoes, a dozen kinds of rice, of pasta and of olive oil. An ancillary revolution happened in cheesemaking, with English, Welsh, Scottish and Irish cheesemakers catching up with artisanal French producers. Specialist cheese shops flourished, and at least one supermarket chain, Waitrose, began to offer a huge selection of cheese *affiné*, as ripe and ready to eat as any you could buy in Boulogne. Bread has improved out of all recognition and, not only can you buy in London the best bread made in France, Pain Poîlane, but it is baked daily on premises in Belgravia; while superlative bakers such as Dan Schickentanz and Dan Lepard make bread that is supplied widely in the southeast. It remains to be seen whether BSE has given the British shopper a salutary enough fright, so that she will be more particular about the meat she buys, and be willing to pay more for a higher quality.

However, the organic food movement, with the explicit blessing and, indeed, participation as a producer, of the future king, has wrought miracles in almost every department of the supermarket, and smallscale producers are banding together to hold farmers' markets and food fairs such as those organized by Henrietta Green. Animal welfare and conservationist concerns join with a desire for better food to see that genuinely free-range eggs and poultry are available; and the movement is spreading to other livestock farmers. An EU directive means that even foie gras will have to be produced by artisanal methods, resulting in a ban on unpleasant industrial practices. Niche-marketing means that soon it will be routine to buy beef or pork of a particular breed. Game has never been so cheap or so widely available. Though there are still strawberries and asparagus on the supermarket shelves all year around, the concept of minimizing food miles—the distance the produce has to travel from farm to plate—is catching on. By contrast, good wine is made in many, many countries, and finds its way to our tables. Our main problem is fish—we've over-farmed salmon and over-fished cod. The sturgeon that produces caviar is endangered.

Those who are interested in their food are beginning to be curious about how it is produced. Environmental matters are joining animal welfare concerns on the food-lover's menu, and it looks as though the twenty-first century will have kinder, safer and better food than ever in human history.

Index

INSPECTION COPY REQUESTS

Lecturers in the United Kingdom and Ireland wishing to apply for inspection copies of Classic Penguin titles for student group adoptions are invited to apply to:

Inspection Copy Department
Penguin Press Marketing
27 Wrights Lane
LONDON
W8 5TZ

Fax: 020 7416 3274

E-mail: academic@penguin.co.uk

Inspection copies may also be requested via our website at:
www.penguinclassics.com

Please include in your request the author, title and the ISBN of the book(s) in which you are interested, the name of the course on which the books will be used and the expected student numbers.

It is essential that you include with your request your title, first name, surname, position, department name, college or university address, telephone and fax numbers and your e-mail address.

Lecturers outside the United Kingdom and Ireland should address their applications to their local Penguin office.

Inspection copies are supplied at the discretion of Penguin Books

READ MORE IN PENGUIN

In every corner of the world, on every subject under the sun, Penguin represents quality and variety – the very best in publishing today.

For complete information about books available from Penguin – including Puffins, Penguin Classics and Arkana – and how to order them, write to us at the appropriate address below. Please note that for copyright reasons the selection of books varies from country to country.

In the United Kingdom: Please write to *Dept. EP, Penguin Books Ltd, Bath Road, Harmondsworth, West Drayton, Middlesex UB7 0DA*

In the United States: Please write to *Consumer Services, Penguin Putnam Inc., 405 Murray Hill Parkway, East Rutherford, New Jersey 07073-2136.* VISA and MasterCard holders call 1-800-631-8571 to order Penguin titles

In Canada: Please write to *Penguin Books Canada Ltd, 10 Alcorn Avenue, Suite 300, Toronto, Ontario M4V 3B2*

In Australia: Please write to *Penguin Books Australia Ltd, 487 Maroondah Highway, Ringwood, Victoria 3134*

In New Zealand: Please write to *Penguin Books (NZ) Ltd, Private Bag 102902, North Shore Mail Centre, Auckland 10*

In India: Please write to *Penguin Books India Pvt Ltd, 11 Community Centre, Panchsheel Park, New Delhi 110017*

In the Netherlands: Please write to *Penguin Books Netherlands bv, Postbus 3507, NL-1001 AH Amsterdam*

In Germany: Please write to *Penguin Books Deutschland GmbH, Metzlerstrasse 26, 60594 Frankfurt am Main*

In Spain: Please write to *Penguin Books S. A., Bravo Murillo 19, 1°B, 28015 Madrid*

In Italy: Please write to *Penguin Italia s.r.l., Via Vittorio Emanuele 45/a, 20094 Corsico, Milano*

In France: Please write to *Penguin France, 12, Rue Prosper Ferradou, 31700 Blagnac*

In Japan: Please write to *Penguin Books Japan Ltd, Iidabashi KM-Bldg, 2-23-9 Koraku, Bunkyo-Ku, Tokyo 112-0004*

In South Africa: Please write to *Penguin Books South Africa (Pty) Ltd, P.O. Box 751093, Gardenview, 2047 Johannesburg*

READ MORE IN PENGUIN

PENGUIN CLASSIC BIOGRAPHY

Highly readable and enjoyable biographies and autobiographies from leading biographers and autobiographers. The series provides a vital background to the increasing interest in history, historical subjects and people who mattered. The periods and subjects covered include the Roman Empire, Tudor England, the English Civil Wars, the Victorian Era, and characters as diverse Joan of Arc, Jane Austen, Robert Burns and George Melly. Essential reading for everyone interested in the great figures of the past.

Published or forthcoming:

E. F. Benson	**As We Were**
Ernle Bradford	**Cleopatra**
David Cecil	**A Portrait of Jane Austen**
Roger Fulford	**Royal Dukes**
Christopher Hibbert	**Charles I**
	The Making of Charles Dickens
Christopher Hill	**God's Englishman: Oliver Cromwell**
Marion Johnson	**The Borgias**
James Lees-Milne	**Earls of Creation**
Edward Lucie-Smith	**Joan of Arc**
Philip Magnus	**Gladstone**
John Masters	**Casanova**
Elizabeth Mavor	**The Ladies of Llangollen**
Ian McIntyre	**Robert Burns**
George Melly	**Owning Up: The Trilogy**
Raymond Postgate	**That Devil Wilkes**
Peter Quennell	**Byron: The Years of Fame**
Lytton Strachey	**Queen Victoria**
	Elizabeth and Essex
Gaius Suetonius	**Lives of the Twelve Caesars**
	translated by Robert Graves
Alan Villiers	**Captain Cook**

READ MORE IN PENGUIN

PENGUIN CLASSIC HISTORY

Well written narrative history from leading historians such as Paul Kennedy, Alan Moorehead, J. B. Priestley, A. L. Rowse and G. M. Trevelyan. From the Ancient World to the decline of British naval mastery, from twelfth-century France to the Victorian Underworld, the series captures the great turning points in history and chronicles the lives of ordinary people at different times. Penguin Classic History will be enjoyed and valued by everyone who loves the past.

Published or forthcoming:

Leslie Alcock	**Arthur's Britain**
John Belchem/Richard Price	**A Dictionary of 19th-Century History**
Jeremy Black/Roy Porter	**A Dictionary of 18th-Century History**
Ernle Bradford	**The Mediterranean**
Anthony Burton	**Remains of a Revolution**
Robert Darnton	**The Great Cat Massacre**
Jean Froissart	**Froissart's Chronicles**
Johan Huizinga	**The Waning of the Middle Ages**
Aldous Huxley	**The Devils of Loudun**
Paul M. Kennedy	**The Rise and Fall of British Naval Mastery**
Margaret Wade Labarge	**Women in Medieval Life**
Alan Moorehead	**Fatal Impact**
Samuel Pepys	**Illustrated Pepys**
J. H. Plumb	**The First Four Georges**
J. B. Priestley	**The Edwardians**
Philippa Pullar	**Consuming Passions**
A. L. Rowse	**The Elizabethan Renaissance**
John Ruskin	**The Stones of Venice**
G. M. Trevelyan	**English Social History**
Philip Warner	**The Medieval Castle**
T. H. White	**The Age of Scandal**
Lawrence Wright	**Clean and Decent**
Hans Zinsser	**Rats, Lice and History**

READ MORE IN PENGUIN

PENGUIN CLASSIC MILITARY HISTORY

This series acknowledges the profound and enduring interest in military history, and the causes and consequences of human conflict. Penguin Classic Military History covers warfare from the earliest times to the age of electronics and encompasses subjects as diverse as classic examples of grand strategy and the precision tactics of Britain's crack SAS Regiment. The series will be enjoyed and valued by students of military history and all who hope to learn from the often disturbing lessons of the past.

Published or forthcoming:

Correlli Barnett	**Engage the Enemy More Closely**
	The Great War
David G. Chandler	**The Art of Warfare on Land**
	Marlborough as Military Commander
William Craig	**Enemy at the Gates**
Carlo D'Este	**Decision in Normandy**
Michael Glover	**The Peninsular War**
	Wellington as Military Commander
Winston Graham	**The Spanish Armadas**
Heinz Guderian	**Panzer Leader**
Christopher Hibbert	**Redcoats and Rebels**
Heinz Höhne	**The Order of the Death's Head**
Anthony Kemp	**The SAS at War**
Ronald Lewin	**Ultra Goes to War**
Martin Middlebrook	**The Falklands War**
	The First Day on the Somme
	The Kaiser's Battle
Desmond Seward	**Henry V**
John Toland	**Infamy**
Philip Warner	**Sieges of the Middle Ages**
Leon Wolff	**In Flanders Fields**
Cecil Woodham-Smith	**The Reason Why**